TABLE OF CONTENTS

SPRING 2025
VOLUME 5 / NUMBER 3

EDITOR
LEON WIESELTIER

MANAGING EDITOR
CELESTE MARCUS

PUBLISHER
BILL REICHBLUM

ASSOCIATE PUBLISHER
CHRISTOPHER McCAFFERY

JOURNAL DESIGN
WILLIAM VAN RODEN

WEB DESIGN
BRICK FACTORY

EDITORIAL ASSISTANTS
PHILIP MOUSAVIZADEH
DYLAN PARTNER

Liberties is a publication of the Liberties Journal Foundation, a nonpartisan 501(c)(3) organization based in Washington, D.C., devoted to educating the general public about the history, current trends, and possibilities of culture and politics. The Foundation seeks to inform today's cultural and political leaders, deepen the understanding of citizens, and inspire the next generation to participate in the democratic process and public service.

Engage
To learn more please go to libertiesjournal.com

Subscribe
To subscribe or with any questions about your subscription, please go to libertiesjournal.com

ISBN 979-8-9854302-8-8
ISSN 2692-3904

EDITORIAL OFFICES
1101 30th Street NW, Suite 310
Washington, DC 20007

DIGITAL
@READLIBERTIES
LIBERTIESJOURNAL.COM

Liberties

YAROSLAV HRYTSAK

The Canary, the Historian, and the Ukrainian War

I have a friend who takes other people's suffering as her own, and almost physically. When she visited Babyn Yar — the place where Kyiv's Jews, thirty-three thousand men, women, and children, were shot in the fall of 1941 — she described being torn by excruciating pain. Her experience reminds me of Simone Weil, who died in London in 1943, a year after she left Nazi-occupied France, refusing to eat because of her compassion for prisoners of the Nazi camps. Like Weil, my colleague has mystical experiences. Her health is frail, and she has experienced clinical death. From that time on she has claimed she could see the future. I am a rational person, and normally the last to believe such claims, but there was one episode in August 2021, when we were drinking coffee on a summer terrace in our native city of Lviv, in western Ukraine, when she told me that this was "the last peaceful summer." She predicted the date when Russia would launch its invasion, erring only by a day. After the war started, she moved to Krakow. I have since met her there, and she told me when and how this war would end. I keep her words to myself, because I do not wish to expose her to derision. I can only say that with the development of events at the front, and after Trump's victory, her forecast looks very plausible.

My friend is a poet. In our part of the world, poets are believed to have a gift for prophecy. The greatest of them are even called national prophets. This is in contrast to us, the historians: we can barely deal with the past, so what could we possibly say about the future? Still, historians do have one advantage. They can look at daily events from a historical perspective and reveal long-term tendencies of the past that may be working both for the present and the future. In the 1960s, a group of historians and political scientists at the University of Michigan started a project entitled Correlates of War, or COW. Since then, they have compiled a rich dataset on military conflicts of the past two hundred years. The most significant finding of the project is a general constancy in warfare. There have only been twelve years during this period when a new war did not start — but there has never been a year with no war ongoing. These findings pose a challenge to the literature of "democratic peace," and its projections of a declining trend in warfare.

Ironically, one of the most bellicose periods was the end of the Cold War, at precisely the time when Francis Fukuyama published his infamous essay on the end of history. Its last paragraph reads:

> The end of history will be a very sad time. The struggle for recognition, the willingness to risk one's life for a purely abstract goal, the worldwide ideological struggle that called forth daring, courage, imagination and idealism, will be replaced by economic calculation, the endless solving of technical problems, environmental concerns, and the satisfaction of sophisticated consumer demands. In the post-historical period there will be neither art nor philosophy, just the perpetual caretaking of the museum of human history.

Would he have retracted his article if he had been familiar with the statistics of the COW project? In any case, for historians a "return of history" is not a surprise. History neither ended nor returned. It has been always with us, as have its darker themes of mass violence, wars, and genocides. The Russo-Ukrainian war is another proof of this historical tendency.

This war can be compared with many military conflicts of the past. As a war between a smaller democratic state and a large authoritarian neighbor, it can be compared to the Greco-Persian wars, in which a smaller and more free-spirited tribe of Greeks gained an empire. If we remove democracy from the comparison, then this war is similar to the Finnish-Soviet war of 1939–1940. If we add a colonial dimension, then it looks like the French-Algerian war, or any other war of decolonization.

When Putin started his full-scale invasion of Ukraine, he was counting on a victorious *Blitzkrieg* — just as Hitler had expected of his *Blitzkrieg* against Poland in 1939, against France in 1940, and against the Soviet Union in 1941. The facts show that those who start a war tend to lose it. The rate of victory for initiators of inter-state hostilities has been on a constant decline, and now comprises thirty-three percent. The reason for this is that decisions to go to war are often emotional rather then rational, with no real goals and no real appreciation of the war's ultimate costs.

After his *Blitzkrieg* plans for Ukraine failed, Putin resorted to a war of attrition. And here a comparison with the First World War — a classic case of this kind — comes to mind. In this type of war, the outcome depends not so much on what happens on the battlefield, but on who is able to bear the brunt of war longest. Such a war ends not in a military victory but in a collapse. The latter occurs, to borrow Hemingway's famous remark about bankruptcy, gradually and then suddenly. Collapse can happen not only to one of the parties in the conflict but to all of them. World War I ended with the collapse of the Russian empire in 1917 and of the Austro-Hungarian and German empires in 1918. It may be said that the Russo-Ukrainian war is a competition between two countries for who will collapse first.

Ultimately, in a war of attrition, the outcome depends on resources. If Ukraine is left on its own, its prospects — no matter how bravely the Ukrainians fight — look bleak, even doomed: Russia has a three-to-four times advantage economically and demographically. But if Ukraine has access to the West's resources, then Russia's chances are slim. Russia's GDP is slightly larger than that of Italy, and comprises only about ten percent of that of the European Union and nine percent of that of the United States. It is not surprising that both countries are looking for allies. Ukraine counts on the West; Russia counts on China, Iran, India, and most recently North Korea. This is not a world war, but a war that is distinctly global.

Comparisons can also be treacherous. In the summer of 2024, the Center for Applied History at Harvard's Kennedy School prepared an analytical report on the possible outcomes of the Russo-Ukrainian war. The experts looked for the best possible solutions that could satisfy the national interests of all the belligerents and their primary patron states, i.e. Ukraine, Russia, the United States, and China. Their choice fell on the outcome of the Finnish-Soviet war. Although Finland lost a part of its territory and remained neutral during the Cold War, in the long run it aligned strongly with the West, joining the European Union in 1995 and NATO in 2023. Such a scenario offers a hope for Ukraine's long-term democracy and self-determination under a similar outcome.

The authors of the Harvard report, however, ignored an important detail. I refer to Putin's attitude toward Ukraine. It has the character of an obsession. More than once, he and his spin doctors have stated that Ukraine is a nation artificially created by the West in order to undermine Russia. For this reason, comparisons with the Soviet-Finnish war, or the two similar cases of the Korean War and the division of Germany after World War II, do not quite work. Even Stalin, in his wars with Finland, Germany, and Korea, did not aim to destroy their national identity. Not so with Putin. In this sense, he can be compared with Cato the Elder, who ended his every speech with the words "Carthage must be destroyed." Or with the current Muslim leaders who set themselves the obsessive goal of destroying Israel.

In some ways this is an uprecedented war, and the longer it goes on, the less history has anything to say about it. Pavlo Kazarin, a Ukrainian journalist who volunteered for the war in its first days, wrote that he could not watch Hollywood war movies anymore: they did not reflect the realities of war as he experienced them.

> The protagonists of *Apocalypse Now* were not attacked
> by guided bombs. The de-miner from *The Hurt Locker*

> doesn't know what tank combat looks like. John Rambo's position was never hit by a 152-caliber shell. . . . We are the only ones who have ever shot down hypersonic missiles. The only ones who have destroyed long-range radar detection aircraft. No such experience exists in any army in the world — including the US Army.

Before Russia's full-scale aggression of 2022, there were futuristic speculations that wars would come to resemble scenes from the *Terminator* movies. Warfare, it was said, would undergo a transition from industrial war, with the clash of tanks, to war of the information age, when military equipment is controlled by computers via the Internet, with minimal involvement of manpower. The first phase of the Russo-Ukrainian war was nothing of the kind. It looked exactly like conventional modern warfare, with extended front lines, infantry, tanks, and planes. But soon drones brought a change. They now control large strips of territory on both sides of the front line, making close combat virtually impossible and snipers largely redundant. Drones helped Ukrainians to neutralize the Russian fleet in the Black Sea and to compensate for manpower shortages on the ground. The end of last year saw another breakthrough: in a location north of Kharkiv, Ukrainians conducted a ground attack using exclusively unmanned ground vehicles and drones for the first time.

The war may move to other zones that were previously unaffected. The First and Second World Wars brought warfare underwater and into the sky. Now the sky is no longer the limit. The British philosopher A. C. Grayling warns that as the new space race intensifies, conflict over resources on the moon is all but inevitable. The moon, the New Frontier, may become a new Wild West. And I have not mentioned AI, which is being frantically integrated into the militaries of many countries. It was used in the war in Gaza.

As the Russo-Ukrainian war drags on and acquires unprecedented features, it seems that history has less and less to say about it. Yet it is important to point out that many things are not new. We used to talk of the Soviet Union as the last empire and believed that with its demise the age of empires was finally over. Now the Russian Empire is attempting to return and reclaim its status as a superpower. The same can also be said about China, its ally. So we may indeed be facing a new age of empires. We also believed that "the short twentieth century," 1914 to 1989, the era of war and revolution, is over. Ukraine may undermine this conclusion, too. Since the country's independence in 1991, it has experienced two revolutions and two wars. You might say that Ukraine is stuck in the twentieth century.

Moreover, the Ukrainian case may not be so exceptional. Since the end of the Cold War, the world has experienced two great revolutionary waves — the "Color Revolutions" of the 2000s and the short-lived Arab Spring in the next decade — as well as the wars in Iraq, Afghanistan, Sudan, and Gaza. From this perspective, the period between 1991 and 2001 looks like a short respite between two major periods of wars and revolutions, just as the period between 1919 and 1939 was a respite between two major wars. The twentieth century is proving to not be all that short. In significant ways we are still living in it.

Two paradoxes characterize the current situation on the Russo-Ukrainian front lines. First, since the fall of 2023, the Russian army has overcome a positional stalemate and made a steady advance — but despite tremendous efforts and tremendous losses, it has made no strategic breakthrough. After three years of fighting, the front line is largely where it was at the beginning of the war, and no large Ukrainian city has been captured. Second, the war has entered a stage in which soldiers are becoming harder to send into a battle. An overwhelming majority of the Ukrainian population (88 percent in November 2024) believes in Ukrainian victory — but many if not most of them are not willing to go to the front. The same may be said about the Russians: they support Putin, but they want this war to stop.

For historians, these paradoxes are not really surprising. They may easily recognize a familiar pattern from the First World War, when after three years of fighting the initial patriotism faded away and military advances had little effect. During the next two years, the front line collapsed, as did the whole European geopolitical order. The latter had been established in 1815 at the Congress of Vienna after the defeat of Napoleon. With all its imperfections, the Viennese system set a historical record. For almost a hundred years, the European continent did not have a major war, and the nineteenth century went into the annals of European history as the longest peaceful century.

With the end of the Second World War, an opportunity arose to beat this record. Putin, with his aggression against Ukraine, destroyed it. In this war, another geopolitical order is at stake. That order emerged in postwar Europe. In the past, Europe was an exceedingly warlike continent: the two world wars originated there, and it was the Europeans who brought about major advances in military technology. Nowadays, it is hard even to imagine a war between England and France, France and Germany, or Germany and Poland — even though in the past these countries fought each other ferociously. After the Second World War, military conflicts were replaced with the politics of reconciliation. These improvements began with the Franco-German reconciliation of the 1950s and ultimately led to the creation of the European Union, which was defined as a "no war zone." That was an unprecedented achievement. There had been nothing like it in the past.

Since the fall of Communism, there was a chance that this "no war zone" could be extended further east. Polish-Ukrainian relations were a test case. In the past, Poles and Ukrainians fought frequently, and in the twentieth century their conflicts over the disputed Polish-Ukrainian borderlands took the form of mutual ethnic cleansings. There were fears that, with the collapse of communism, the Polish-Ukrainian war would resume with a renewed force. In 1969, the Polish poet Czesław Miłosz wrote to Jerzy Giedroyc, the editor of the Paris-based Polish émigré journal *Kultura*:

> For several years now and especially recently, I have been obsessed with the thought of a coming catastrophe . . . Politically we are facing the growth of nationalisms of the Nazi type. It takes place in Russia, it also takes place in Ukraine and other republics, and it is the same in Poland . . . If that outburst occurs, it will be completely blind, with people slaughtering each other, and the problems of Lviv, the Treaty of Riga etc. will be revived, and this time we are prepared to ultimately perish under the heaviness of that cataclysm.

Fortunately, this did not come to pass. A solution to the conflict was proposed by Giedroyc. In the early 1950s he suggested that, for the good of Poland, Poles should agree that Lviv is a Ukrainian city. This proposal was so radical that a majority of Poles refused to accept it — for them, it was tantamount to treason. The situation changed when the anti-communist Solidarity came to power in Poland in 1989: Giedroyc's doctrine served as the basis of its foreign policy. Since then, whoever comes to power in Warsaw or Kyiv — and regardless of any "ups and downs" in their relations — treat each other as allies.

The "Giedroyc doctrine," as well as the entire system of postwar European reconciliation, was built on the premise that while there are no just historical borders, the existing borders are best left alone, lest interference with them provoke a domino effect. History should be bigger than applied politics. Hence the "Never Again" slogan of the postwar European system. Nowadays, with the annexation of Crimea and other Ukrainian territories, this humane and pragmatic system is in jeopardy.

In Putin's mind, his war of attrition against Ukraine is just another episode in the millennial confrontation between Russia and the West. According to his worldview, the past dominates the present and there is no room for a future other than permanent war. After the start of the Russo-Ukrainian war, we witnessed how this precedent was used by Azerbaijan to reclaim Nagorno-Karabakh from Armenia; and Xi is brooding about Taiwan; and Trump is running his mouth about annexing or buying or conquering Canada, Greenland, Gaza, and Panama.

Still, there is a basic difference between the language of Trump and the language of Putin. Trump talks about interests, however wildly, but Putin talks about values. On many occasions, Putin and his satraps have claimed that they stand for traditional values against a corrupted liberal West — that theirs is a holy war. In this rhetoric they sound similar to Muslim terrorists. No wonder they treat each other as allies.

And so this war is not about Ukraine alone. Nor is it even about the global order. It is at its heart a war of values. This gives it a completely different dimension. It is easier to reach a truce when it comes to interests, but it is much harder to strike a compromise when it comes to values. For values, people are ready to go at each other's throats.

Values are like air: we cannot see them but they affect all our lives. This is one of the main findings of the *World Values Survey*, the largest academic social survey project, which has collected data from one hundred and twenty countries over the last hundred years. Societies with secular values that prize self-expression tend to be richer and democratic. Societies with traditional values and an overriding concern about survival tend to be poorer and autocratic. There are many differences between the two types, but the most distinctive difference concerns gender, particularly the status and rights of women.

When we talk about values and living standards, it is impossible to determine what is the cause and what is the effect — they are forever locked in a "chicken-and-egg" relationship. What matters, however, is that the choices that societies make are to a large extent determined by their past. There are three major historical factors: traditional religious denomination — Protestant or Catholic, Christian or Islamic, and so forth; an imperial legacy; and the presence or absence of communism in the past. All factors combined, as Ronald Inglehart and Christian Welzel have shown, Western countries have fared better.

With the fall of communism, Russia and Ukraine started from a similar position. They were somewhere between the

West and the Rest. In the 2000s, however, their historical trajectories began to diverge. Ukraine tilted to the West and democracy, while Russia sank into isolationism and authoritarianism. In both countries, there emerged a large and educated middle class that stood for political freedom against predatory and corrupted elites, but the outcomes diverged. In Russia, the opposition was either suppressed or forced to emigrate; in Ukraine it came to power in the two Maidan revolutions. The last one, the Euromaidan of 2013–2014, was called the Revolution of Values or the Revolution of Dignity. Those were not empty words. The Ukrainian revolutionaries were risking their well-being, their health, and even their lives for what they saw as the European values of dignity and liberty.

As a former KGB officer, Putin does not believe in spontaneous mass protests. He managed to suppress them at home, but he failed in Ukraine, despite his persistent interference since 2004. To explain his failure, he came up with the myth that the two Ukrainian revolutions were the result of a Western conspiracy against him and Russia. Putin believes — or wants us to believe — that he is waging a war not with Ukraine, but with the West on Ukrainian territory, in the name of traditional family values against the permissive Western liberal order.

The values-based character of the war was evident from its first weeks. Back then, groups of Russian mercenaries were reported to have been in Kyiv with a mission to assassinate Volodomyr Zelensky and to destabilize the government. There was a debate among military experts regarding how this plan would affect the war if it succeeded. The consensus was: not very much. Ukrainian army commanders and city mayors acted independently and were not looking to Kyiv for guidance. These were the values of individual autonomy and self-expression in action.

The Russo-Ukrainian war may be considered a military conflict between a vertical establishment and a horizontally organized society. Among other things, this is reflected in the fact that Ukraine has demonstrated the cutting edge in military technology. Very often these innovations come from private IT companies and other non-state organizations. Owing to their ingenuity, Ukrainians have managed to hold back a stronger and more numerous enemy. It is not surprising that the Pentagon and NATO are watching the Ukrainian experience closely — they are attempting to learn how to conduct a new type of war from Ukranians.

But the enemy learns, too. Russians, using their advantage in resources, adopt and scale up many Ukrainian innovations. It takes months for this to happen, given the usual slowness of the administrative vertical. And the time lag is important: during those months the Ukrainians invent something new, and the race continues.

All these stories may arouse skepticism. If Ukrainians are so resourceful, then why do they retreat all the time? Historical studies may provide an answer here, too. They reveal that free societies tend to fight better, but their advantage diminishes as the war drags on. The greater the losses and the suffering, the more survival values come to the fore.

Values not only distinguish one society from the other; the dividing line also runs within every society. And since the army is a snapshot of the society, this division affects military forces, too. It has been said that there are actually not one but two Ukrainian armies, with two contesting military cultures. One army is trained according to NATO standards and is made up of units that are allowed to fight the way they want to fight.

They are able to figure out the best way to use their people and resources and they have the authority, the duty, to improvise according to circumstances. The other one is very similar to the Russian or the old Soviet army, where commanders lack flexibility, strictly follow commands from above and demand that their subordinates follow them as well, without particular regard for rationality or changing conditions or consequences.

The first army is made up largely of volunteers, often the same people who stood on the Euromaidan. They were at the front from the very first days. Many of them have perished or been promoted to senior officers' positions; some are burned out after three years on the battlefield and the latest escalations in fighting. In short, their role has decreased, and the second army, the rigid army, has come to the fore. In the end, the conflict looks like a large Soviet army fighting a small Soviet army — and the situation is often saved by an even smaller NATO-like army. This affects the general mood. As a recent survey on Ukrainian concerns about military service shows, initial enthusiasm is being tempered by the reality of a protracted war. Apart from the fear of death or disability, there is the fear of unprofessional commanders, the fear that military equipment would be inadequate or not arrive in a timely manner.

New realities have forced Ukrainians to redefine their understanding of victory. At the beginning of the war, they regarded victory as a return to the 1991 borders. Now many see it as the preservation of Ukraine as an independent state with international guarantees for its security. This would not be a complete victory. Still, it would be a strategic gain against the backdrop of

Putin's plan to erase Ukraine from the political map altogether.

To be sure, a large part of the responsibility for Ukrainian failures falls on the Ukrainian leadership, its inefficiency, its corruption, its chaos, and its populism, which does not allow unpopular but necessary decisions to be made. At the beginning of the war, the Ukrainian state enjoyed enormous social trust. Now there is a rift between state and society, and the rift is growing.

Yet the West also carries its share of the blame for the Ukrainian situation. It does not want Ukraine to lose, but neither does it want Ukraine to win. It fears the repercussions of a Russian defeat, just as in 1991 it feared the collapse of the Soviet Union. Experts say that if the Ukrainians had sufficient weapons and support from the West, they could have won the war as early as 2022. The same goes for the failure of the Ukrainian counteroffensive in 2023 and the fact that Ukrainians were slowly losing ground in 2024. The Russian army was able to go on the offensive because the package of military aid to Ukraine was blocked in the U.S. Congress for seven months — from October 2023 to April 2024. According to American officials, by the end of 2024 only about half of the total dollar amount that the United States had promised from American stockpiles had been delivered, and only about thirty percent of the promised armored vehicles had arrived.

To better understand the importance of this factor, imagine what would happen to the young state of Israel if it were supplied with American aid at the same pace and level as Ukraine. One of the factors in the victory of the *entente* in the First World War and the Allies in the Second World War was American aid. This was recognized even by Stalin: he admitted that if the United States had not helped the Soviet Union, the latter would not have won its war against Hitler.

They say that old generals fight wars in the old ways. President Biden was formed as a politician during the years of the Cold War. He believed in the containment strategy that had been central to keeping the peace for nearly seventy years. This strategy was carried over and applied to the current Russian "hot" war — so as not to turn it into World War Three and not to provoke a nuclear attack by Russia. His support of Ukraine was genuine but it lacked alacrity. Yet what worked during the Cold War does not necessarily work in the conditions of a hot war. The strategy of "helping Ukraine for as long as it takes" does not work, because for Ukraine, given its smaller resources, "as long as it takes" can be, certainly by impatient American standards, too long. It is true that Russia is exhausting its resources, and its economic prospects beyond 2025 look bleak. But it would be naive to think that the collapse of Russia is imminent, whereas Ukraine most certainly may collapse. As the Ukrainian proverb says, the dew will burn your eyes before the sun rises. The West, in sum, must move to more decisive action. Otherwise the Western leaders are themselves condemning Ukraine to protracted agony. The signs are not auspicious.

It is not hard to imagine what would happen to Ukraine if Russia wins. Even before the Russian invasion, there was information about Russian "kill lists." Their existence has been confirmed since the war started. The people on these lists included teachers of Ukrainian language, literature, and history; journalists, scientists, and writers; priests of the Orthodox Church of Ukraine and other denominations that support Ukraine; and public and political figures, chiefs of regional authorities and self-government. What may appear to the West as an exaggerated fear is for Ukrainians a harsh wartime reality, reinforced by the memory of the Holodomor, the Stalinist repressions, Chernobyl, and, most recently, in 2022, the massacres in Bucha, Irpin, and Izium.

At demonstrations abroad in support of Ukraine, Ukrainians have adapted Golda Meir's words — "If the Arabs put down their weapons today, there would be no more violence. If the Jews put down their weapons today, there would be no more Israel." — but they replaced "Arabs" with Russia and "Jews" and "Israel" with Ukraine. It is abundantly clear that many in the West do not care about the fate of the Ukrainians, just as before they did not care about the fate of the Syrians. But unlike the savagery in Syria and elsewhere, the war in Ukraine has a stronger impact on the West and its people.

For Putin's war will not end with Ukraine. The degree of his contempt, if not outright hatred, for the West should not be underestimated. Oleksandr Lytvynenko, the head of the Foreign Intelligence Service of Ukraine, predicted that "having failed to defeat Ukraine in three days in a large-scale war, the Kremlin has passed the point of no return in relations with the West," and left for itself only the options to "triumphantly win or lose crushingly." Putin's has geostrategic plans for the next ten to fifteen years; their implementation is to be accompanied by conflicts of various scales and intensity, possibly with the use of nuclear weapons. (I take this analysis from "A Few Theses on Putin's Policy: How The Kremlin Thinks and Wages The War," Foreign Intelligence Service of Ukraine, November 11, 2023.)

Western intelligence confirms these assessments. The Kremlin could be in a position to attack a NATO member within the span of three to five years. The next most probable targets will be the Baltic States and Poland. This prognosis has been recently reiterated by the EU's chief diplomat Kaja Kallas. She warned that "We are running out of time. The Ukrainians are fighting for their freedom and ours. They are buying us time." And Valery Zaluzny, the former commander-in-chief of the Ukrainian army, went so far as to say that with North Korean forces fighting with the Russians on the front line and Iranian and Chinese weapons flying into Ukraine, a Third World War has already begun.

To many skeptics in the West, the Ukrainians are crying wolf. But people who are under an existential threat must be believed over those who are not. People who are fighting for their lives generally do not lie. Ukrainians warned about Putin's plans long before the war. He developed them back in 2008, right after the Georgian-Russian war. According to this plan, Ukraine was to be "punished" by a full-scale invasion if it continued to move out of Russia's orbit. Most of the territory was to be either directly annexed by Russia or turned into a puppet state. The exception was the western part of the country, which historically is least Russified and Sovietized — it was to be divided between its "former owners," Poland and Hungary. This plan leaked to the West and was published first in an Italian geopolitics journal, and then reprinted in one of the main Ukrainian newspapers. Putin spoke about this partition plan in 2008 during his meeting with then-Polish Prime Minister Donald Tusk and then- (and now-) Polish Foreign Minister Radek Sikorski. He offered them Lviv.

Sikorski revealed this offer several years later, when he was out of office. His revelation created a scandal. In Poland, he was asked why he remained silent for so long, and in the West his words were taken as a provocation. Finally Sikorski had to disown his report. But it is worth noting that the British journalist and security writer Edward Lucas insisted that Sikorski was right and that the plan did exist, since he had himself heard of it at numerous off-the-record sessions at security conferences and think-tank meetings. The problem was that Western leaders did not grasp their significance. "Now the West is taking a belated class in practical geopolitics," Lucas wrote in 2014. "It is an education paid for by hundreds of thousands of innocent Ukrainians, in blood and misery. But the full fee for the course will, I fear, be far greater."

Those decade-old words might have been written yesterday. In the very first week of the current war, the German Chancellor Olaf Scholz defined it as a "historic turning point." Now, three years later, it looks like the turning of this point is proceeding according to the same formula as the Western aid to Ukraine — too little, too late. We are witnessing a situation that is reminiscent of the "springtime of nations" in 1848. Back then, the liberal revolutions that broke out in Europe ended in spectacular failure. As G. M. Trevelyan wrote, it was "the turning point at which modern history failed to turn." We may face a similar scenario.

Ukraine is not crying wolf. It is, rather, like the canary in the mine. Outside of Ukraine, many ignore its warnings or are even annoyed by their persistence. Life would be much nicer if the canary would stop chirping. And so they look through a microscope at all of Ukraine's faults, at its corruption and its past sins, to prove that it is not worth helping. In the eyes of some, Ukrainians are the main culprits behind the protracted hostilities: if Zelensky were only more accommodating, the war would have ended a long time ago! All together, they are ready to sacrifice Ukraine to Putin for their own mental peace.

They do not believe that what is happening in Ukraine today may happen to them tomorrow. They forget that attempts to appease aggressors do not work. Must one really remind Westerners of the Munich agreement of 1938? That surrender of Czechoslovakia to Hitler did not prevent the Second World War; it accelerated its beginning. This history lesson seems so banal that it feels embarrassing to bring it up. But as skeptics like to joke, humans do not make the same mistake twice, they usually make it three or more times.

We are living in an era of enormous historical importance in which our politicians usually do not think historically. Their horizons are generally limited to the projected duration of their own political careers. This is especially the case if they, like Donald Trump or Elon Musk, come from fields that are a far cry from a knowledge of history. In their cases, indeed, they evince a contempt for the past and prefer to believe that they are completely without precedent. So they may put the Russo-Ukrainian war on pause, as a discrete matter of policy, but they can hardly stop the looming war crisis. If history has any lessons, one of them should be this: if you see war coming and you are not sure if there is a serious possibility of preserving peace, you would be wise to bet on war as the most probable scenario, and be ready for it. As the Latin adage says, *si vis pacem, para bellum* — if you want peace, prepare for war. Those words should be translated into every known language.

The knowledge of history helps us to sort out what is new and what is old in the current Russo-Ukrainian war. This knowledge does not make us feel better. Still, it leaves room for cautious optimism. The revolution of 1848 was defeated, but seventy years later most of the revolutionaries' demands had become political realities. It took the First World War to make the impossible possible. For war brings not only carnage, but also opportunities. To take constructive advantage of postwar opportunities, you must have a historical imagination.

It was seventy years after the revolution of 1848 when the first volume of Oswald Spengler's *The Decline of the West* appeared. Since then, the decline of the West has been predicted many times. And still the West is still vigorously with us. Over the last two centuries, it has survived several deep crises, including major wars. Some of those wars ended with solutions that provided an impetus for further social and political development. The Napoleonic Wars ended with the Congress of Vienna, which established the "long peace" of the nineteenth century. Without this peace, the quantum leap of the Industrial Revolution would have been impossible. The First World War brought the final collapse of the old regime, and the Second World War led to the emergence of a large "no war zone."

None of these solutions lasted forever, and the time always came for a new crisis and a new solution. The war in Ukraine may be the crisis that the contemporary West needed. Whether the West will take advantage of this opportunity, whether it will recognize the moral and historical lessons of this awful war, is an open question. But Ukraine should be for the West not only a source of anxiety but also a source of hope. Ukrainians are interested in a strong and free West and are ready to work on its renewal. For them, this is not a whim. It is an ultimate need: finally to escape the shadow of Russia, which has a centuries-long historical record of mass repressions and wars. Like the West, Russia also proceeds from crisis to crisis. There is an essential difference, though. Unlike in the West, short-lived attempts to democratize Russia after her defeats in the Russo-Japanese War, the First World War, and the Cold War failed, and ended with protracted periods of reaction by Stolypin, Stalin, and Putin.

In principle, the Russians, too, should be interested in overcoming their harsh past. But for various reasons they are not capable of doing it on their own. The memorable words spoken by German President Richard von Weizsäcker on the fortieth anniversary of the end of World War II could be applied to Russia as well: "May 8, 1945 was not a day of defeat for Germany — it was a day of liberation." The best thing that can happen to Russia is that it loses this war; if not right now, then in the foreseeable future. This will open up a chance for a new democratic Russia that no longer poses a threat to its own people or to neighboring peoples and will no longer constitute a threat to global stability. The "no war zone" could be extended further east of the Polish-Ukrainian borderlands of the West.

According to the custom of the genre, an essay such as this one should end with a ringing conclusion. I will not do this. The text ends but history does not. As the war drags on, it is too early to close the book. Suffice it to say that the canary is still singing.

DAVID A. BELL

The Enlightenment, Then and Now

What is the Enlightenment, for us? Are we its heirs, its continuers, its defenders? Or should we acknowledge our distance from it, and try to imagine a different sort of connection to this now-distant past?

At the present moment, the temptation to identify with the Enlightenment is almost overwhelming. In dark times, after all, few historical subjects exert more allure than one with such a promise of illumination. How inspiring, how reassuring, to think that there was once a moment when reason challenged superstition, when justice promised to overcome power, when the spirit of toleration seemed to prevail over dogmatism and persecution! How tempting it is to think that if only we could reawaken the spirit of the Enlightenment, and rekindle the torches of the *philosophes*, we might yet dissipate the shadows now gathering around us.

If those shadows seem especially menacing, it is partly because the Enlightenment itself is currently under explicit attack, and from many different directions. On the left, progressive scholars and activists denounce it as the birthplace of modern racism and the handmaiden of "settler colonialism." On the right, "post-liberals" and Catholic integralists call it destructive of family, community, and religion. Populists of all varieties decry the faith it promoted in education and science as elitist and evil. If these groups agree on nothing else, it is that the Western world took a disastrous wrong turn sometime in the eighteenth century. They draw a straight line from "Enlightenment" to "liberalism" to "neoliberalism," as if thinkers who failed even to predict the Industrial Revolution somehow bear responsibility for post-industrial decay.

But is some sort of "return" to the Enlightenment the answer? In recent years, many prominent intellectuals have made this case, albeit in contradictory ways. In *Enlightenment Now*, the psychologist Steven Pinker credited the Enlightenment with virtually all human progress since the eighteenth century, equated it with his own brand of technocratic neoliberalism, and argued that everyone would agree if only they overcame some regrettable cognitive biases. The philosopher Susan Neiman, by contrast, in *Left Is Not Woke*, eloquently identified the Enlightenment with the promise of progressive politics and warned about the hijacking of that politics by "woke" activists hostile to Enlightenment values. The historian and legal scholar Samuel Moyn took an oddly similar position in *Liberalism Against Itself*, except that for him the nefarious force that has dragged the left away from its optimistic Enlightenment roots is not wokeness but a fearful "Cold War liberalism."

Historians, too, have been pressing the case for the Enlightenment's living relevance, at sometimes inordinate length. A 984-page survey of the Enlightenment from 1680 to 1790 by Ritchie Robertson associates it with the broad cause of "human betterment." Anthony Pagden's monumental book on the subject describes the Enlightenment as the birthplace of tolerant cosmopolitanism. And then there is Jonathan Israel, the Stakhanovite hero of Enlightenment scholarship, who, since 2001, has produced nine books on or closely related to the subject totaling 7,886 pages. According to Israel, all the political and social values dear to liberal modernity, including human rights, social equality, sexual equality, and racial equality, were already present in a "radical Enlightenment" that emerged in the seventeenth century in the Dutch circles around Baruch Spinoza.

But did the Enlightenment even exist? And is this a serious question? In a provocative new book called *The Enlightenment: An Idea and its History*, the British conservative historian J. C. D. Clark claims that there was no such thing. The various intellectual currents that today go by that name had no real unity or coherence, he argues. Historians and philosophers only started to claim they did long after the eighteenth century, in order to invent historical legitimation for their own progressive reform programs. He notes that the very phrase "the Enlightenment," with the definite article, did not come into common usage in English until the twentieth century, as a Google Ngram search strikingly confirms. (The German "*die Aufklärung*" appeared earlier, but also had limited resonance.)

It is true that mid-twentieth century liberal scholars had strong incentives to find a long and inspiring pedigree for their own beleaguered beliefs. Clark underlines, a little too insistently, the fact that Enlightenment scholarship owes a particularly strong debt to liberal Jews born in pre-war continental Europe (Ernst Cassirer, Peter Gay, Theodore Besterman, Jacob Talmon, Robert Wokler, George Mosse, and others). It is hardly surprising that these men, many of whom fled Nazism, would turn for inspiration to this earlier moment of light, and revere it for helping to emancipate their ancestors from ghettoes. Jonathan Israel, who has continued in this tradition (despite faulting his predecessors for getting almost everything wrong) has stated the core idea clearly: "Jewish emancipation became a realistic proposition from the moment Europe's former predominantly theological view of the world began to crumble under the impact of Enlightenment ideas." Still, the Enlightenment was not a Jewish invention, and claims like this can too easily feed the worst sort of conspiracy theories.

Meanwhile, the idea of the Enlightenment as a coherent movement also owes a considerable amount to two Jewish refugees of a more critical and contrarian bent: Max Horkheimer and Theodor Adorno. But in place of the Enlightenment as salvation, they gave us the Enlightenment as perdition. Their *Dialectic of Enlightenment*, from 1944, speculated that the horrors of the twentieth century ultimately stemmed from a deadly Western "instrumental reason" that had come to maturity in the eighteenth century. "Enlightenment," they wrote provocatively, "is totalitarian." Their book had enormous influence on progressive thought, and it is in part thanks to them that so many scholars today condemn the Enlightenment as a sinister-sounding "project" that bears responsibility for modern racism, imperialism, misogyny, and intolerance of all sorts. The trend has become so popular that currently the best-known adage of Immanuel Kant's — who famously offered his own definition of Enlightenment in an essay in 1784 — is probably, "Humanity has achieved its greatest perfection in the white race," which he later abjured, and which in any case had little connection to the main lines of his thought.

Clark is right to a certain extent. It is absurd to cast the Enlightenment as a single "project," whether redemptive or malevolent. The canonical writers associated with it agreed about relatively little, and liked few things more than attacking each other, often quite viciously. Their number included atheists, deists, and orthodox religious believers; radical democrats and propagandists for absolute monarchy; proto-socialists and proto-libertarians. Intellectually, their works can be best represented as a Venn diagram with many areas of intersection but no union of all the sets. The Enlightenment was also geographically dispersed, with significant differences between the French, English, Scottish, German, and other national varieties. It is hardly surprising, then, that the Enlightenment's contemporary defenders can see it in such different ways.

But historical labels are, by their nature, nebulous and messy. There are always exceptions. There are always contradictions. The crooked timber of humanity — another adage of Kant's — never fits into neat geometrical boxes, and virtually every commonly accepted label used by historians would fail Clark's overly strict coherence test. Eighteenth-century writers may not have used the label "the Enlightenment," but they often described their century as one marked by the triumph of reason and progress. D'Alembert spoke of a revolution "not only in the history of the human mind . . . but also in the history of states and empires." Diderot praised "philosophy" for "advanc[ing] with great strides" and forcing "authority and precedent . . . to yield to the laws of reason." Kant declared, "this age is the age of enlightenment." Edmund Burke, meanwhile, set himself in opposition to what he dubbed, with exquisite sarcasm, "this new conquering empire of light and reason."

The fact that the Enlightenment existed, however, hardly means we should place it on a pedestal and worship it idolatrously. Yes, despite the differences between Enlightenment thinkers, we can identify a set of genuinely noble and admirable beliefs to which most of them (though not all) subscribed: the need for freedom of thought and expression, especially in religious matters; the need to judge matters of general interest according to standards of reason, objectivity, and utility; the possibility of historical progress; the illegitimacy of violence in the pursuit of political objectives. But at the same time very few of them had kind words for democracy, which they tended to equate with mob rule. Freedom of speech did not imply freedom of political action. Kant even wrote that the mark of a good enlightened ruler was to say: "Argue as much as you will and about whatever you will — but obey!" And while some denounced imperialism and advocated toleration of cultural difference, in most cases "Enlightenment universalism" meant defining Western Europe as the high point of human historical evolution and judging all other cultures by that standard. Racism and anti-Semitism disfigured the thought of many *Aufklärer*. Liberal modernity (whatever that means) did not burst forth fully and perfectly formed from the heads of philosophers.

Nor is it even possible to find a coherent subset of Enlightenment authors who might deserve idolization — a "happy few" who fully professed modern liberal principles.

Jonathan Israel has employed this strategy, attempting to distinguish a forward-looking "radical Enlightenment" that inspired everything progressive in the modern world from a "moderate" one that cravenly kowtowed to the European *ancien régime*. But for all his gargantuan energy and erudition, his ultimately unconvincing thesis has met with one of the most hostile critical receptions of any major recent historical enterprise. According to his numerous and persuasive reviewers, his "radical Enlightenment" is his own invention, not a historical reality. Yes, there were intellectual radicals in the seventeenth and eighteenth centuries: materialists who denied the existence of God and denounced Moses, Jesus, and Mohammed as the "three imposters"; republicans who opposed monarchy; egalitarians who wanted to overturn the social order. But some egalitarians were fervent Christians, some materialists had no problem with monarchy or privilege, and so forth. There was no single and coherent "radical" party.

But we do not need to worship the Enlightenment as if it were a god we have failed. Most of the *philosophes*, despite their often immense self-regard, would have been horrified at the idea. Condorcet, one of the last great Enlightenment writers, asserted that "it is easy to see how imperfect the analysis of men's intellectual and moral faculties still is," and predicted that his successors would move far beyond him. Thomas Jefferson memorably asked whether "one generation of men has a right to bind another?" The question has implications for intellectual life as well as politics. We should be free to take from the Enlightenment what we find valuable and disregard the rest — to construct our own twenty-first-century Enlightenment rather than placing ourselves in thrall to an imagined eighteenth-century one.

As we do so, we should remember that what made the Enlightenment so extraordinary was not just a set of ideas but also a set of practices — not just what was said but also how it was said, and how it was understood in its various social contexts. Far too much of the contemporary discussion of the Enlightenment ignores this point, reducing it to a set of disembodied abstractions. The result is to distort the history and impoverish the analysis. If we wish to construct our own twenty-first-century Enlightenment, and we should, the practices are just as important.

Start with the basic issue of audience, and how it was appealed to. Before the eighteenth century, key Western works of thought often still appeared in Latin, and even when they were published in the vernacular they tended to employ recondite and difficult language which appealed principally to fellow scholars and patrons. After the eighteenth century, meanwhile, thanks to the development of modern research universities, intellectual life increasingly retreated into the ivory towers. Enlightenment authors, by contrast, wrote principally in the vernacular for a general educated public, and strove to make their works as accessible, as engaging, even as entertaining, as possible. To be sure, they, too, could sometimes produce arcane philosophical and scientific texts; but more often they presented their ideas in the form of stories, novels, plays, dialogues, reference books, essays, and travelogues. Think of Voltaire's *Candide*, Montesquieu's *Persian Letters*, Lessing's *Nathan the Wise*, Hume's *Essays Moral and Political*. Even didactic treatises tended to employ a clear and accessible prose style. Baron d'Holbach's provocative materialist treatise *The System of Nature* became one of eighteenth-century France's biggest bestsellers, although it had to be sold illegally, "under the cloak," because of government censorship. Enlightenment writers wanted to be widely read.

Audiences, meanwhile, did not just read but became infatuated. They tried to model their lives according to their favorite authors' instructions, wrote those authors worshipful letters, hunted for every scrap of information they could about them. The historian Robert Darnton gives the example of a French merchant named Jean Ranson who for years bombarded publishers with letters asking for news about Rousseau, whom he, like many others, called "friend Jean-Jacques." When Ranson married, he wrote that everything Rousseau had set down about conjugal life "has had a profound effect on me, and . . . will serve me as a rule" (perhaps not the best idea, given that Rousseau admitted to having abandoned five children of his own to orphanages). After Rousseau died, Ranson promised to visit his grave and shed tender tears on it. Many other readers reacted in similar ways, with some claiming that after reading the heroine's death scene in Rousseau's melodramatic novel The *New Eloise* they had to take to their beds for days out of grief. One of the first modern literary celebrities, Rousseau himself felt increasingly oppressed by the insistent public attention.

Readers found it all the easier to get drawn in because they had so much more information available than just the books themselves. In the eighteenth century, for the first time, what we would now call an entire media infrastructure had come into being around authorship and book publishing. Literary periodicals reported on new works and printed stories about writers. They published reviews summarizing and evaluating new books. Printers made cheap engravings of authors available for display in homes. Venues for literary discussion, from officially chartered learned academies to lending libraries to informal societies and café gatherings, all expanded at a furious rate.

This same infrastructure also made it easier than ever for readers to become writers themselves. Periodicals needed contributors (they also published extensive letters to the editor). Diderot and d'Alembert enlisted hundreds of collaborators for their *Encyclopedia*, whose length eventually ran to seventeen million words. Darnton has highlighted the plight of the poor but ambitious young men who flocked to Paris in the hope of becoming the next Voltaire, only to end up as "poor devil" hack writers, desperately churning out crude pornography or political libel, or even spying on fellow writers for the police, to earn money. Meanwhile, learned academies throughout Europe sponsored essay competitions whose winners could leap in a moment from obscurity to glory. The most famous case involved an eccentric thirty-eight-year-old failed music teacher who had spent years fruitlessly promoting a new and unwieldy system of musical notation. After seeing an advertisement for an essay competition on whether the progress of the arts and sciences had proven beneficial to society, he boldly answered in the negative, won the prize, and gained immediate fame. This, of course, was Rousseau.

All these developments were inseparable from rapid and ongoing social and economic change. A warming climate, the end of destructive religious warfare, and furiously expanding global trade — much of it powered by chattel slavery in the Americas — was bringing unprecedented prosperity to Western Europe. The first consumer revolution was underway. Asian spices, porcelain, and tea; American sugar, coffee, tobacco, and textiles, all flooded into European cities. Even modest artisans and shopkeepers could now purchase a wide new range of household implements and decorations, musical instruments, foodstuffs, medicines, religious paraphernalia, clothing — and books. Printed advertising developed, and a new daily practice became part of urban life: shopping. In short, a new sort of public was coming into being that could exercise a new range of choice on a daily basis: choice about what to eat and drink, what to wear, how to furnish homes, how to entertain oneself — and what to read.

This new range of choice seems so familiar today that it is easy to forget how novel it was at the time, and what it meant to ordinary people to exercise such banal but important forms of personal autonomy. Consumerism, in what the historian William Sewell has called (without irony) "capitalism's rosy dawn," was not yet an insidious and exploitative system manipulated by large corporations, but — at least in part — an opportunity for unprecedented forms of self-expression and self-cultivation. Yes, the opportunity was available only to a limited population: urban and relatively well-off. But it was still a much larger population than had previously enjoyed anything similar, and it included women as well as men.

This was the world into which the Enlightenment was born, and its practices shaped the way writers appealed to their expanding new audiences. These audiences wanted help navigating the brave new world of consumer choice, and they found it in the criticism, advice, and information offered by the new periodicals and reference works. Beyond this, they also wanted entertainment and edification, and the Enlightenment provided it. They did not, however, want preaching or indoctrination, and despite what is often thought, very few of the great works of the Enlightenment offered anything of the sort. Indeed, especially in France, many authors deliberately refrained from advancing any sort of clear didactic thesis at all, opting instead for playful ambiguity. In *Candide*, Voltaire offers a savage satire of intolerance but concludes with the deliberately elliptical line "we must cultivate our garden." Montesquieu's *Spirit of the Laws* pivots between endorsing the English constitution and taking the relativist position that countries should choose the government that best fits their climate. Diderot adored the dialogue form, which prompted his readers to evaluate apparently opposing viewpoints. The *Encyclopedia* allowed readers to follow a trail from volume to volume through the editors' provocative series of cross-references (most famously in the article "Cannibals": "See also Eucharist, Holy Communion, Altar"). Voltaire perfectly summed up the spirit of this Enlightenment in the preface to his *Philosophical Dictionary*: "The most useful books are the ones that are half written by their readers."

Even in places such as Scotland, where eighteenth-century intellectual life was less playful (because it was more centered on universities), Enlightenment thinkers mostly took care to write in an accessible manner. Adam Smith, famously, did not simply expound his theory of the division of labor in abstract terms, but led readers to follow his reasoning by offering the example of a pin factory. His fellow Scotsman, David Hume, an admirer of the French salons, wrote that "learning has been . . . a loser by being shut up in colleges and cells, and secluded from the world and good company. . . . Even philosophy went to wrack by this moping recluse method of study, and became as chimerical in her conclusions as she was unintelligible in her style and manner of delivery." Hume's own philosophical works, while intellectually demanding, remained clear and engaging.

Hume insisted that liberating serious intellectual life from "colleges and cells" would have beneficial effects on the public as well. "Must our whole discourse be a continuing series of gossiping stories and idle remarks?" he wrote. "Must the mind never rise higher . . . ?" But for people to benefit, they would have to put in their own intellectual labor, using what they read for the purposes of self-cultivation, and drawing their own conclusions — writing half of the books themselves. In this sense, the Enlightenment was part and parcel of the enterprise of self-cultivation that social and economic change was making possible in the eighteenth century. Kant would describe it as humanity's emancipation from its "self-imposed tutelage."

Not all Enlightenment writing fit this pattern, and as time passed less and less of it did. The idea of letting readers make up their own minds, especially on questions of religion and political authority, did not sit well with established eighteenth-century authorities, especially in Catholic Europe, in parts of which the Inquisition remained a going proposition. (It was not abolished until 1834.) As Enlightenment writing gained popularity, these authorities increasingly perceived it as a threat — indeed, as a unified conspiracy against throne and altar — and moved to repress it. In response, Enlightenment writers themselves turned increasingly rigid and militant and intolerant. "O my *philosophes*!" wrote Voltaire to his followers in the 1760s. "You need to march in close order like a Macedonian phalanx." And he scolded them for a lack of zeal: "You bury your talents and are content with despising a monster you should be struggling to abhor and destroy." When the cranky French cleric Augustin Barruel tried to prove that the *philosophes* had deliberately plotted to overthrow France's Old Regime, he found much to quote from in Voltaire's published correspondence. Later works of the French Enlightenment, such as d'Holbach's popular but turgid treatises, increasingly told readers what to think rather than prompting them to think for themselves.

Moreover, absolutist rulers found that they could make use of Enlightenment works that insisted on applying standards of reason and utility to matters of general interest. Frederick II of Prussia, Joseph II of Austria, and Catherine II of Russia all invited *philosophes* to their courts, flattered them, debated with them, and sought their cooperation. They did so above all because Enlightenment ideas justified their campaigns to exert greater control over established churches and social elites, and not for the purposes of promoting toleration and equality. The point was to weaken domestic opposition, and to make autocratic regimes more powerful and efficient. In the end, these sovereigns mostly treated their visiting *philosophes* as hired help. "I shall have need of him for another year at most, no longer," Frederick wrote about Voltaire. "One squeezes the orange and throws away the peel."

And we should remember that even when the Enlightenment did prompt readers to reflection and self-cultivation, the results still could be pernicious. One infamous French academic essay competition invited participants to explain why Africans had dark skin. Some of the entries veered off into the far extremes of racist speculation. Enlightenment natural science emphasized that humans did not represent a separate creation, but in many respects belonged to the animal kingdom. Although the idea represented a fierce challenge to Christian beliefs, it also encouraged speculation about the differences between human races, which slaveowners in the Americas jumped upon to justify holding people of African descent in bondage or civic subordination. One of the French revolutionaries most influenced by Enlightenment writing,

Emmanuel Sieyès, speculated about breeding humans with monkeys to create a race of natural slaves.

In sum, putting the Enlightenment back in its social and cultural contexts, looking at practices as well as ideas, makes it much harder to celebrate it simply as the birthplace of an admirable liberal modernity. The Enlightenment contained multiple tendencies, both laudable and deplorable, both constructive and pernicious. As already noted, it was not a single thing. Horkheimer and Adorno's intellectual heirs are not wrong to see some danger in the Enlightenment, although they mistakenly conflate this danger with the Enlightenment as a whole. The abuse of reason, instrumentally and otherwise, should not be mistaken with reason itself.

If we decide to draw as we please from the eighteenth-century Enlightenment to construct our own Enlightenment, we should not neglect what we can learn from these contexts — what we can learn from its practices. In our own world, increasingly dominated by social media and video and podcasts, it is as important as ever not to keep serious learning "shut up in colleges and cells" — cordoned off in university echo chambers where the faculty only hear each other talk. It is all the more important to find ways of engaging a larger public in a serious manner, and using every available genre and medium to do so. And all the more important to do so in a way that encourages people to seek the answers for themselves and to undertake the work of their own cultivation. This is not asking too much, even now. A liberal society cannot flourish without the confidence that its members can do the work of Enlightenment themselves, as best they can.

DURS GRÜNBEIN

Ominous Pieces

A.D.

My unchristian ancestors: for a lifetime
they got along without God.
Though something always happened
that they had not foreseen. Two world wars,
the downfall of their city, diseases, or

what it is like to lose everything — freedom
stripped from them, twice in a row.
When unchristian beings (Hitler, Stalin)
took this only world they had and turned
it into a trap for millions, into hell.

They survived, with a good deal of luck,
though without religious persuasion. No word
about the hurried prayers in the air-raid
shelter, when under the sign of revenge, of justice,
the one with the latest technology
brought the empty skies crashing down.

They (the ones who existed) never
mentioned those fleeting moments
in which fear dissolved and everyday life
broke open like a fruit, a brittle fruit,
that contained more than just seeds, tears, grief,
and the ecstasies of the little people.

NAZI PARTY RALLY GROUNDS

It was a grey February day in Nuremberg. I was due to give a reading that evening, and I could think of nothing better to do with the time until then than to take the tram out to the site where they used to hold Nazi Party rallies. At the reception desk of the *Deutscher Kaiser* hotel, the young woman who requested that I speak English with her was so put out when I asked how to get there that I withdrew and sheepishly looked for a map of the city so as not to have to consult my cell phone. Not only was I a stranger in this place, but my interest in a location that was rarely sought out by tourists to this medieval city, the city of Albrecht Dürer, seemed strange to her. She looked me up and down, as if I might turn out to be a troublesome guest. In terms of age, I was not unlike one of those Germans who, for obscure reasons, make pilgrimages to places that are taboo for most. And yes, I must admit, it was film images, scenes from the notorious propaganda film *Triumph of the Will* directed by Leni Riefenstahl, that brought me here. And also curiosity about what remained of this central forum of the Third Reich and its real historical dimensions: the Zeppelin Field, the Congress Hall, the Luitpold Hall, the Märzfeld, the Silbersee (Silver Lake, a name that evoked associations of the fantasy world of Karl May and his Winnetou novels that I grew up with). I wanted to see it all for myself, this massive site built around the Dutzendteich Lake, which still lay on the outskirts of the city at that time.

How reassuring it was to arrive there at last and find a formula that absorbed everything and steered the inconceivable insanity of National Socialist projection and construction into the reassuring channels of a democratic culture of remembrance. After several stops, the tram halted at the Nazi Party Rally Documentation Center. First impression: you could easily get lost there, the signs lead into a vast area, only a drone could give you the desired overview. You pass through a large parking lot, and only then does it become apparent that the building before you is the huge rotunda of the Congress Hall, the back elevation of an arena that remained unfinished at the beginning of the war in 1939, like so many kilometres of the planned Reichsautobahn. Plus, a surprise for any resident or admirer of Rome: the building turns out to be a remake of the Colosseum in the style of a film set. Shades of Cinecittà, remnants of the set for a Nazi blockbuster mixed with those for a historic film about the fall of the Roman Empire. The inner courtyard doesn't make much of an impression with its construction site fences and containers of rubble, a garbage-strewn antiquity of yesteryear that was never realized, a shell that is reminiscent of many things — prison yards, stormed fortresses, ruins forever left wanting. Somewhere in the jumble of mock theater boxes and empty rows, it was designed to give pride of place to the speaker's pulpit for the "Führer." The whole thing was intended as the theater for a pseudo-parliament — a foretaste of the gigantic meeting rooms planned by Albert Speer for Berlin after the final victory in the capital called Germania. Yet the relocation of the Nazi court to the Reich capital of Berlin was already so advanced at the time that the Nazi Party Rally Grounds only ever had a symbolic function. Ruins by design in every direction, a monumental building abandoned midway; and yet everything testified to the ambitions of the regime's leaders, their bid to capture the imagination of a physically trained and mentally aligned population with a kind of National Socialist theme park.

Modern stadium buildings came to mind, arenas of all kinds, from rock concert stages to the Super Bowl fields to be found in major American cities — and one wondered where the mass audience was supposed to go back then. A colosseum in Nuremberg, was this to be the venue for political gladiator fights? On the eve of the war, were the Germans really ready for such grandiose imperial showmanship? The total state remained an irresistible vision until its demise — at least for the Nazis. At the Sixth Reich Party Congress, the one filmed by Riefenstahl, hadn't Hitler admitted that it was not the state that created the German people,but the other way around, that the people created the state for themselves?

Wandering about, lost among the open spaces beyond the Great *Dutzendteich*, or Dozen Pond (*nomen est omen!*), one began to suspect what all this was conceived to do. The state that was so densely concentrated in the relatively small space of Berlin was here to be given a symbolic parade-ground along with the Zeppelin Field, the so-called March Field, a festival site outfitted with various halls and groves, laid out according to the model of Rome in Augustan times. But by then Germany had become a modern industrial nation, so it also needed a substation, a train station, its own small "Strength Through Joy" city kitted out with a stadium and swimming pool to contribute to the general merriment.

Laid low by the absurd scale of the place, exhausted, I gave up my inspection at some point. There was just enough time to take a look at Luitpold Hall, where an interim exhibition with pictures and panels instructed visitors about the temporary use of the whole thing at the time, the construction measures and their background. From the deployment of the German Labor Front, the architects and companies involved, to the forced laborers and Russian prisoners of war who were made to toil and die until the futile plan came to an end, everything here was pre-meditated. As is so often the case, history had fragmented, and was presented through individual stories and small erratic objects, the significance and meaning of which a good schoolteacher could unravel if the curriculum allowed. The city of Nuremberg and its museum directors tried to distract the accidental onlooker for the time being with the promise of an eventual and final reappraisal of the whole thing. Meanwhile, next door in the documentary hub, the good folks of Nuremberg courted the audience with evening concerts. Unfortunately, there was no time for Shostakovich and Schulhoff. I had to get back for my reading and was glad that a tram was there to restore me to the main station. At the reading in the Literary House that evening, I did not breathe a word about my excursion into the past.

SPOILS OF WAR

And they almost kidnapped the child,
the girl with the black braids
the broad cheekbones, my mother,
who looked like one of their own,
a child of the Siberian steppes.
They would have just taken her with them
on that dusty suburban street in Dresden
on their march back to the East,
just as they took anything with them
that was not nailed down.
She was already up on the small horse-drawn cart,
a princess perched on top of the spoils,
said the neighbour who ran after her
screaming and snatched the child
back from the Russians still screaming
and cursing. From the victors of the World War,
lads fond of children and a song.
They didn't like screaming women.

WHAT WE KNEW ABOUT DICTATORSHIP

I do research into dictatorship, said the young woman at the table that evening at her friend's birthday celebration. That was the invitation to the dance: finally a conversation partner for a serious topic that interested no one else in the group. We establishedthat dictatorships can be divided according to the degree of severity — tryannies and autocracies. It comes down to the cooking time: how long it takes to prepare the dish. We know little about the recipes of cannibals. The longer people stew in a form of rule in which unlimited power deprives them of all natural rights, the easier it is to prepare them socially; particularly coveted is the brain. And it doesn't take much for neighbors to turn each other into sausage meat, I recalled. At some point, having themselves fallen into the meat grinder of the murderous system, they dig into the frozen soil with their bare hands for edible roots (as in the Gulag). They rummage through the legacies of those who have fallen under the wheel, ensuring that they are utilized to the full (as in Auschwitz). They are ready to cull their fellow citizens, to send them to the gas chamber, into the cold, the fire, even to betray their own relatives, parents, the sick, people on a dying branch.

Depending on the degree of bedevilment, a distinction is made between three forms of dictatorship: terrorist, trivial mythical (tinnitus-like), and totalitarian. There is not a single dictatorship that has not been based on law, rules of exclusion, even on a constitution, an implicit intergenerational contract. The young bring down the old, the old sacrifice the young to maintain their power until they themselves must be sacrificed before their time — for example, in war. The dictatorship records everyone according to their live weight, every gram of fat is counted in the food allocation. Without ever really asking themselves what happened to them, everyone is silently wondering how they can survive the centrifuge of mass mobilization, of mass management. The failure to speak, the silence of each individual is unmistakable even in the midst of the greatest jubilation — on the wide boulevards, in the lion's den where they are whipped up by propaganda, in the fascist forums or even simply in the sports stadiums where they cheer on the victory of their own athletes. Dictatorships radiate out from a center of emptiness: a stable source of radiation, permanently sending out negative energies in the form of physical violence. This is, at the same time, also psychological violence, because all the morality consumed by a dictatorship emanates from the totalitarian state; the individual soul weighs next to nothing.

Dictatorship grows imperceptibly. It is often confused with a medium that is considered the embodiment of all its fears and desires, a leader, a generalissimo, or a chairman, who appears on the scene one day out of the blue and can no longer be voted out of office. Dictatorship does not come from nowhere (whatever the Greeks say about it, and the Romans, and the annals of the Renaissance); for us, the moderns, it comes from democratic elections. A savior is elected, a redeemer in the guise of a party that hovers above all the other parties, "other parties" which the leader then forbids as soon as the *populus* has elected him. He starts straight in on culture, on the icons, the cooking recipes, the religion. He collects campaign money from those who have the funds and also the hope that the money is better invested with him than in the culture of a thousand opinions, which leads to nothing and only confuses the people. Once he has neutralized all his opponents, he is soon regarded in popular superstition as a benevolent sovereign, takes to stroking children, and is ubiquitous overnight in millions of images, with the help of newspapers and other media, in every size from postage stamps to monumental sculptures.

What else? I asked her. Dictatorships, she said, have their own way of reckoning time, they can last for a shorter or a longer time, in which the lifetime of the leader plays a certain role. In any case that role is gradually absorbed under the daily overcast skies. False expectations are the binding agent of every dictatorship, barely visible to the naked eye (except under a sociologist's microscope), interchangeable just like ideology, religion, or policies. It is like in the opera: the song of the chorus swells to fill the stage, but there are moments when the high C of a mortal voice emerges from the wall of sound. In an emergency (martial law, trouble among the cooks, betrayal in the innermost circle), the Iron Curtain is lowered, while the audience sinks into a collective trance. Until the prompter rises from the pit and signals that she has forgotten the text. Then, and only then, it may come to pass that a child appears, suddenly, in the emergency exit. It is looking for its father (shot long ago) or its mother, who has been dreaming of a better future all along, hidden behind a fan.

ONE-WAY STREET TO JERUSALEM

Can anything be learned from anecdotes? This question arises when the experience on which they turn is so striking that it leads to far-reaching conclusions. In exile in America, the director and producer Erik Charell, one of the most successful in his field in the Weimar years, liked to describe a Berlin street scene from the time shortly before Hitler's accession to power. He was a visitor to an automobile show on Kaiserdamm and got caught up in the crowd in front of one of the halls. Along with the police, uniformed SA men were passing through the crowd with collection boxes. One of the young men was going from person to person with the advertising slogan, "Donations please, donations towards the construction of the one-way street to Jerusalem." The narrator, who could hardly believe his ears, asked for the snappy slogan, to be repeated to him, and approached the little man in the brown shirt and waited to see if the policeman nearby would intervene in the face of this open threat against Jewish fellow citizens. But he turned away embarrassed. The small incident had finally opened his eyes. From that moment on, he knew: "It's over." He left the car show that very moment. Over the next few days he organized his departure from Germany. The image of the one-way street had hit him so hard that there could be no hesitation. There was no question as to the future of road construction in this country.

GRAY MICE

The twentieth century was, among many other things, also the time of collective laboratory experiments. Breeding humans so that they become grey mice, mottled mice, or completely uniform mice was the research goal to which not only the new mass leaders, but also many of the scientists, felt committed. Political views only counted if they could be scientifically substantiated. Entire faculties of racial scientists, behaviorists, and armaments experts were busy whipping the nation into shape. After the apocalypse of a world war that had swept away emperors and kings, many of the liberated subjects longed for a zoological dictatorship. It was the moment for mouse-breeding. A whole nightmare world of order-obsessed mice was released onto the streets, into their future professions: police mice, kapo mice, Gestapo mice, cultural mice, youth and sports mice, stewards and jumpers in all niches of society.

They did what highly trained and meticulously conditioned mice do: monitor their own kind, ensure that the common mouse-life runs smoothly. It did not occur to them that they could have been something else, that each individual mouse could live in its own way and be happy. No, no, and again no: it was about controlling each other, rounding up men, women, and children and keeping them under strict laboratory conditions, in the glare of the anti-aircraft searchlights, keeping them together and reminding them of the misery of their mouse existence every second of their lives. They weren't stupid, these mice. Each one of them knew what position they could hold in this new total mouse-state, or that they could make their way for themselves by maneuvering skillfully through the labyrinth of the laboratory.

Let no one say that freedom did not exist in this system. It was only when the experiments were halted — another world war was necessary to bring that about — that it dawned on some that the conditions under which they were bred had nothing whatsoever to do with the world as such and with the fact of their uniformity. At that moment they were ashamed, as far as grey mice can be ashamed. It appears that their descendants are ashamed to this day. In any case, most have shed their grey and now prefer garish colors and exotic patterns.

GERMAN LISTENERS

Lübeck looked terrible
when it was finished, an etching
by Churchill based on a design
by Adolf Hitler, recognized by
Thomas Mann as a fellow artist.
There was St. Mary's Basilica.
It was still standing there
as if emerging from the smoke
and next to it an empty portal
in the light of the postwar sun.
Lübeck marzipan was what
my father always wanted
for Christmas, he liked
the bitter taste of almonds
in memory of Thomas Mann,
whom he liked to read, aloud
ideally, in the small circle of family.

THE MEAT GRINDER

Were I a painter, my motif of choice to represent entire phases of world history in this century of my birth which has cast its shadows and its conflicts onto the next, would be a meat grinder. The device that was clamped to the table in my grandparents' kitchen and used to twist a lump of meat into blood-red strands of "ground" or "minced" meat, even if there was never any sign of grinding or mincing, but always only twisting, until in the end a steel perforated disc produced portions of minced beef or minced pork, depending on the animal being processed. I would have put my motif through the meat grinder.

Just as the painter Philip Guston finally limited himself to a few recurring forms — hooded figures, shoes, cigarettes, fingers, severed feet, open books — I would have concentrated on this one ugly device, the domestic meat grinder. I would have painted its maw, in an objective or maybe fantastic manner; or, no, as primitively as possible, this mouth-like funnel of cast iron, the belly of the monster torn open and rendered visible with its innards: the screw, the sharp-edged wing-blade. The hand crank with its wooden handle I would have given an especially crude shape: the screw clamp that held the voracious wolf fixed to the kitchen shelf, the desk in the torture chamber, the altar, the butcher's workbench. Do not misunderstand me: none of this would be done in honour of its inventor, Freiherr von Drais, that quick and keen thinker, Citizen Drais, a democrat of the first hour in Germany, who, in addition to this practical monster-machine, also invented the two-wheeled hobby horse and the speed typewriter. Nor is it part of the quest for an equation to capture the acceleration of everything; the crank-accelerated processing of the mountains of meat into each individual household. Nor the urge for a symbol — yes, that is the right word — for the perennial suffering, the cycle of all flesh, in this murderous century, in which eating and being eaten has taken on something mechanical. Why, then? Simply so as to depict a meat grinder on a pink pedestal against a sky-blue background, a thing that in the end stood only for itself — useful and abysmal in equal measure, and in the most progressive way inconceivably primitive.

THE HISTORYLESS

History seldom lands on their doorstep
with burning car tires, chanting crowds,
tanks on the prowl, ready to be deployed,
the turret turned down.
An Iron Curtain falls, a regime
bites the dust, they don't catch on until
the late evening news.
Then it's routine again for a lifetime
and it's business as usual
with the end of school exams, the driver's license,
the beach holidays and
the children's first teeth.
Tears time and again
at every bend of existence,
sometimes accompanied by insight, rarely
bringing any comfort.

In retrospect: often resentment, muffled
by something like nostalgia.
That's not what they wanted, not like that,
just fell into it by chance.

Later the arithmetic, they like to do their sums,
balance sheets of disappointment. The politicians —
none of them any different from the rest, all corrupt.
What can we hold onto, culture perchance?
The annual Christmas party,
a few brands of car, the success
of the local football club,
a few hits belted out
on karaoke night.
And suddenly they say: give us
our history back.

THE BUTTON

One day Franz Kafka sewed on a button. He did it thoroughly, as with everything he did. In his little room in his parents' Prague apartment, the one that he was afraid to call home, he sat with his legs crossed and struggled with the needle and thread, as a bachelor might. But something kept getting in the way. First, a stork jumped out of the cupboard and wandered across the room; then a large black bird crashed against the windowpane flapping its wings wildly. Then a picture fell from the wall, a view of the old Prague synagogue; then there was a knock at the door and his mother came in, bringing him a glass of milk. Despite all this, he remained focused on his needlework. Indeed, he managed this feat better than many an experienced seamstress. In the end the button was fastened so firmly that you could have lifted not only the trousers, but their owner too, by the button, and slung them over your shoulder. A sturdy removal man would have been quite strong enough.

Translated by Karen Leeder

CLIFFORD THOMPSON

On Skin Color and the Individual

In memory of Albert Murray

I am what might be called an integrated black man. Many of my friends are white, and I live in a mostly white neighborhood; my long marriage is an interracial one, my grown children are biracial. I offer these facts neither as a lament nor as a boast. They are simply facts. Born in the 1960s, I am a member of a generation who grew up in the wake of Martin Luther King, Jr.'s assassination and, more importantly for me, in the light of his message of openness, his call to judge one another, if we must judge one another, as individuals. That is how I have tried to live my life. In an era of the greatest divisiveness of my lifetime, what I am saying may sound hopelessly naïve, and, indeed, a few of the public responses to my work have included that word among other critical ones — one reader declared that I was merely "singing kumbaya," another that I was speaking "nonsense." I am not complaining. To write about so-called race is to invite an especially vehement and personal kind of criticism. The criticism has done nothing to change my view, which is that for black people to judge white people on the basis of their whiteness, however understandable that judgment may be, is to fail to grasp the most important lesson of slavery and its continuing aftermath: that the way we treat others must not depend on skin color. I will hold this view as long as I have a head to hold it in.

Yet I am vividly aware that this belief in the importance of the individual is not, by itself, an adequate response to the racial challenges that we face, for two reasons. One is that this belief may seem not to take into account the sheer enormity of what was done to people of color in this country in the past, as well as its implications and ramifications for the present. The other is that this belief may have the effect of entrenching people in comfortable indifference to ongoing problems. But my purpose here is to point to two ways in which this belief in treating people as individuals can serve as a radical tool for understanding history and for addressing the challenges we face today.

Thankfully, when it comes to American slavery, no equivalent of the Holocaust-denier movement appears to have gathered steam (which is not to say that it never will). So far no one is claiming that slavery did not happen — only that its effects on black people were not entirely bad, that the enslaved learned useful skills, to cite one argument of the Ron DeSantis crowd. I want to sidestep that argument, which is ridiculous on its face — roughly comparable to a man's saying that, yes, he beat his wife, thereby teaching her self-defense — and widen the lens to include not just slavery and discrimination themselves but what was done to justify them, which is the true source of the trouble that plagues us to this day. A visitor from outer space, told about American slavery and left to observe the current reality, might ask why so many white people have contempt for black people rather than the reverse (not that the reverse isn't also true — I will come to that in a bit); and the answer to the space alien, ironically enough, is white people's egregious violation of their own sense of morality.

The impetus for slavery was economic. In order to square America's slavery with the Christian beliefs of most of America's citizens, it became necessary for religious figures, scientists, politicians, educators, newspaper editors, editorial cartoonists, and others, like men coming together to push a stalled car, to put all of their energy into advancing the notion that whites were superior to blacks intellectually and (more irony) morally, and that whites were the rightful beneficiaries of the condition that Americans never tire of celebrating, that is, freedom. A measure of the resounding and tragic success of this campaign was that so many white people's sense of identity came to rest on that belief in their superiority.

Whatever disrupted the white sense of supremacy was considered a threat, an attack. That was true during slavery and for a century afterward, and among some whites it is true today. Hence the Tulsa massacre in 1921, in which whites decimated a thriving black business community; hence the white woman depicted in Bliss Broyard's memoir of her father, *One Drop*, who researched her lineage and was reduced to tears by the discovery of her black ancestors (Broyard's father, Anatole Broyard, was a distinguished book critic at *The New York Times* who passed for white); hence, as well, the way some reacted to Barack Obama's election with the feeling of betrayal that a man might have if his wife ran off with his brother. This sense of superiority was enshrined in law, encoded in every detail and nuance of cross-racial interaction. Underneath it all, no doubt, like the pea under twenty mattresses in the fairy tale, was a feeling of guilt, remote but still felt — but one of the paradoxes of human nature is how guilt midwifes the vilest of acts.

The black victims of these acts can easily be thought of as one undifferentiated, and thus not quite human, mass. Focusing on such people as individuals, however, helps us to think about the actual experiences of these victims, each one a real human being with hopes, emotions, and people who loved them, and to consider, at the human level, what these experiences meant. Pain is supremely an individual feeling. No essay, no book, no series of books could capture every instance of blacks' suffering due to racism, so I will cite only one. Think of a woman who was owned by others and forced to breed human beings; think of a woman in your life — your mother, wife, sister, daughter, favorite aunt, friend, lover, yourself — and imagine her having no say in who had sex with her, or how, or when, or whose children she carried and gave birth to. Such a woman was my great-great-great grandmother.

Speaking of individuals, let us consider one individual in the present. As a boy, I was raised in the bosom of a loving family and never once got into trouble with the law. I had the benefit of a college education, and today I live in an area that is as safe as a city neighborhood can be, one that does not provoke an aggressive police presence. I have a driver's license but drive very rarely and thus have never been stopped for Driving While Black. I am polite — to a fault, some would say — and do not make a habit of arousing people's ire, whatever those people look like. While I love my whiskey, I have imbibed no illegal substances to speak of, and I have certainly never sold any, not least because I have never had to do so; I have never had a lot of money, and at some points in my life I have had very little indeed, but even in those moments I was spared the bleak choices facing those for whom the legal economy simply has no place, so that I have not once run afoul of the law for drug-related reasons and been subject to the inequities of the criminal justice system.

Consider, in short, that I am probably as protected against racism as it is possible for a black man in America to be. Now consider that over the course of my life I have been followed out of stores, chased by a police car, told by an officer with his hand on his pistol to put my hands in the air, addressed with a nasty slur on the street, in a bar, and via email, told that I could not rent an apartment, greeted by police who were called after I was spotted at the door of my own residence, prevented from completing a job application, stopped by a cop who told me to quit following a group of women I had not noticed before then, told on the morning a job ad appeared that the job had been "filled," stopped by a security guard on a college campus where I was a visiting writer, and I've forgotten what else — all for one reason, and perhaps I do not have to tell you what it is. My point here is that if these things have happened to me, we should consider what has happened to other black people in contemporary times. Better yet, read about the individual stories of flesh-and-blood individuals such as Trayvon Martin, Eric Garner, Sandra Bland, and the others whose skin color became their lethal fate.

Now here comes the tricky part. It is difficult for black people to go from being immersed in thoughts of anti-black racism to considering the ethics of their attitudes toward whites. For many, the thought would simply never arise, and many others would not see the need or the benefit. It is a lot to ask of a historically oppressed group, one that continues to face discrimination and its attendant psychological burdens in the present, to bring objectivity and fair-mindedness to their encounters with representatives of the group that oppresses them. To be honest, I sometimes wonder why I care about this issue as much as I do, whether it means that I am just a strange person or have suspect motives, and I cannot say with perfect certainty that neither of these factors plays a part. I can say, with equal honesty, that I am not a self-hating black man who is prejudiced against other black people, as I have been accused of being. Do I, though, simply want to justify the life path on which my interests have taken me, in others' eyes if not my own?

That path led from the all-black neighborhood in Washington, D.C., where I grew up, to a mostly white college in the Midwest, the very first college to contact me, one that had what I wanted: a writing program. Certain that so-called race would be unimportant on a college campus in the post-civil rights world of 1981 (yes, I know), I thought nothing of being surrounded by so many whites. I held onto my high school friends, and I made new black friends, but I also made a slew of white friends, and that extended, eventually, to my dating life. I sigh, thinking of those friendships. One of my favorite memories from those years — really, from any years — is of staying up all night with a black friend, my roommate during our semester in London, drinking wine and gin and laughing our damn heads off in an upstairs room in the home of our host family, who were out of town. A white female friend still recalls the time I ran to her dorm room after she phoned me upset over a young man she was dating. Those friends and I still think of one another lovingly, even if, in some cases, we talk only sporadically. Our bond is eternal: we were young together.

One of my black friends from that time, who is gone now, had the experience in high school that I had in college, of having a mostly white group of friends. If I discovered white people in college, he discovered black people — the tightly knit and frankly separatist group who lived for the most part in a dorm called African Heritage House (and who were deeply skeptical of me). "These black people here got their shit *together*," I heard him say once, and for a time — which did not last for the rest of our college years — he put distance between himself and whites. For better or worse, probably some of both, I never went through that kind of rebellion, maybe in part because I grew up around black people who had "their shit together." No, my rebellion, if it can be called that, was of a different sort and, unlike my friend's, seems to be permanent. While I happily celebrate my black heritage, I also rebel, if only in my mind, against the importance that everyone attaches to skin color, and I rebel against those — and they are white as well as black — who feel there is something odd about me because of the way I have lived my life. I am not insensitive to those judgments, and perhaps I have internalized them to some degree, but something deep in me also shouts back, Am I crazy, or are all of you?

The question may or may not be rhetorical.

Perhaps a black person would have to be a little crazy, or at best hopelessly naïve, not to be wary of certain situations.

I have a desire to tour large swaths of the country by car, but I am very leery of some of the people I might encounter on such an adventure. Most black people I know, including me, will look through the window before entering an unfamiliar bar or restaurant, scanning for brown faces, just to make sure we are not unwelcome. This kind of wariness is a tradition for us, a part of survival. These are not examples of what I mean by judging whites on the basis of their whiteness — and, by extension, judging blacks who associate with them. Here, rather, are examples. Another black college friend of mine told me that a black man visited his apartment, saw a picture of my wife and me on the wall, and wanted to know, "What's up with the brother and the white chick?" To my friend's lifelong credit, he replied, "That's my brother and sister-in-law." Then there was the flak that Darius Rucker of Hootie & the Blowfish got for making music with white guys. Such examples, and they are numberless, may be trivial and harmless in themselves, but I am troubled by the narrowness and provincial nature of the attitude they suggest — an orientation that defines blackness not by what it is but by what it must not become, as if blackness were mortally threatened by mere contact with the infamous "Other," like the Wicked Witch of the West doused with water. Are we that fragile?

I have digressed. Perhaps, as I was saying, some part of me simply wants to justify my life. But I also believe, deep in my heart, that the bulk of what I feel is something else.

It is natural, even commendable, to want to protect and support one's own, whether that means one's immediate family or the people who look like oneself and thus have many of the same life experiences. No reasonable person would dispute that. We would think amiss of a father who did not care what happened to his children. Black people, including me, have great respect for a black person who stands up for them. And yet there is a sense in which to stand up for one's own is to stand up for oneself, and while I admire this, there is something else I admire, too.

If we are not careful, society can become one interminable game of Us and Them, and if Team Us is perpetually outnumbered and on the losing end, life for its members can be a never-ending effort to correct this imbalance. But this game is not all there is, because there is, or should be, more to life than self-defense and survival. I have in mind such things as pleasure, love, friendship, a sense of purpose, and another item I would sneak onto the list, which is the desire to be the best versions of ourselves. Many turn to religion for this; others of us do not see the need to enlist God in the effort. For me, being my best self has a very particular meaning. It means not placing my skin color over my own humanity, especially since others, some of whom wear badges, seem only too happy to do that for me. It means not judging others on the basis of superficial characteristics. Does this not sound like something we were all taught early in our lives? And is not skin the most superficial of all our traits, as in the phrase "skin deep?" It also means treating others, all others, as I would like to be treated. How I would like to be treated is with forgiveness, with the understanding that I intend well even when I don't do so well.

This brings us back to white people. I have known many in my life, some casually, some well. To be sure, those I have known might be called — if I am using this term correctly — a skewed sample, since I move in liberal circles. It has been my experience that most of the white people in those circles —

by no means all — have good hearts and mean well, even if their experiences do not necessarily give them the insights that others of us gain just by walking around with brown skin and kinky hair. I have reached this conclusion, which is based on decades of personal experience, by being open to people as individuals. Can appearances of good-heartedness be deceiving? Of course. Is the most open-hearted progressive white person capable, in a bad moment, of saying something most black people would find objectionable, something that may reveal a questionable attitude? Yes, and I have experienced that, too.

I have seen the horror on a white person's face when they realize what they have just said. It is the same horror I feel when I have unthinkingly misgendered a student, the same horror I felt many years ago when I made a joke about the SS to a co-worker who was, as I remembered two seconds too late, Jewish. The horror is often followed by a heartfelt apology. But not always; sometimes there is not even horror. Would I want to keep company with someone who tells racist jokes and can't be convinced that they are not funny? Or with someone who otherwise will not be made to see his own cluelessness? As some black folks say, *Aww, hell naw.* (Or as some whites say, *Hard pass.*) But others respond well to being told that they have crossed a line. I have done this with people whose friendship I value. To the initial unease of one friend, I did it with her father, who responded very graciously. (I had told him I would have a story in an anthology of African-American fiction. He joked, "I didn't know black people wrote." I sent him a lengthy list of black writers.)

Some will say that life is too short to spend trying to teach white folks how to behave. But I want to stress two points here. The first is that life is not only short but also thrillingly unpredictable, and you never know where your words will end up or the impact that they may have. Thanks to a conversation I overheard in a Starbucks, I went the next night to a screening of a film by Bertrand Blier, whose work I now want to explore further — and now you have heard of him too, if you hadn't before. For a brief time as a young man, I, the son of two postal clerks, had the ear of a former First Lady of the United States, and the most famous and glamorous one at that; she was an editor at the publishing company where I worked as an editorial assistant in the years rights after college, and at one point her office was about ten feet from my desk. I remember talking to this woman about my mother, who was still living then, and I like to think, though I cannot recall, that I passed on some of Ma's folksy Virginia-bred wisdom.

The second point is that I would not have been in a position to share my point of view with my friends, to speak words to them that could — you never know — someday end up far from my mouth, had I not been open to those friends as individuals. I lay much of the blame for the divisiveness of our era on our forty-fifth president, whose election (and now re-election) was, to my mind, the worst thing to happen to this country in my lifetime, largely because he has made so many people feel that it's fine not to give a damn about others. I do not know to what extent the treatment of others as individuals, as a tool for both conveying an understanding of the past and emphasizing what needs to happen in the future, can help put an end to this divisiveness. Nor do I know to what extent individual encounters and personal relationships can have an impact on institutional racism. I applaud the efforts of Black Lives Matter and earlier civil rights organizations to address institutional racism through group-based direct action, but I do know that institutions are made up, in the end, of individuals. And I know that while individuals do not necessarily care about groups to which they do not belong and which, for that reason, may live in their minds only as abstract notions, they care about other individuals, who can serve as their entry points for thinking about the concerns of those groups. This is where my hope lies.

It was this hope that led me to a small experiment.

Through social media and email, I asked volunteers to write to me if they had had the following experience: "meeting and talking with someone whose skin color, ethnicity, or sexuality was different from yours led you to consider, in a way you had not before, the experiences of the group to which that person belongs." Sixteen people responded, thoughtfully and at some length, in ways that underscore, for me, the importance of cross-groups encounters; many of these encounters and exchanges would not have been possible without the willingness, on both sides, to treat others as individuals. In the following paragraphs I paraphrase some of the respondents' stories and quote a few lines directly.

A white woman, when she was much younger, asked her late brother-in-law, who was black, if black people use sunscreen. He responded, "Some do, some don't, just like white people." That response, spoken without anger or a lecture, was "a brilliant way of getting me to consider that 'Some do, some don't, just like other people' is the answer to most questions about how any group behaves or any group's preference." The same woman worked, in the pre–George Floyd era, on publications for a college where a black colleague and friend capitalized the word "Black"; the woman told her colleague that the organization did not cap the word, but when the colleague explained her reasons, the woman agreed and relayed the explanation to higher-ups, who did not change their minds. This revealed to the woman "the kneejerk response of all of us gatekeepers to just do the same old thing unthinkingly; and then how quickly it all changed, as if there had never been a rule to begin with and all the old reasons we relied on went out the window."

A man of mixed black and Hispanic heritage noted that he has friends who are Chinese and gay, and that "their world and experience is so different from that of the Hispanic, white, or black gay men whom I know. Based on what they have told me, they have it tougher with little to no support." Another black man came to a similar conclusion, thanks to interactions with Asian friends. A Chinese-American friend, he said, "blew my mind for thirty minutes straight with tales of micro and macro aggressions." The friend told of riding his bike while carrying takeout food and hearing a white man, in the course of "explaining the world" to his toddler, saying, "That's the delivery guy who brings us food" — words that left the friend "literally dizzy with rage." The black man learned that Asians "are on the receiving end of a particular kind of dehumanizing that I've never experienced in white liberal spaces."

Whites who responded also told of realizing from individual encounters what other groups — blacks in particular — experience. One white woman wrote that a friend of hers, a black woman, confided that she is leery of being friends with white women because she doesn't know if those women simply want to have a black friend. Another white woman, accompanying her daughter's fifth-grade class on a trip to Ellis Island, watched the white kids "happily looking up their ancestors on computers" while the black kids "just sat on the steps with their faces in their hands. All they had to look at was a lone and unimpressive map of the slave trade." The kids who got in trouble with the teacher that day were mostly black, and when the woman told the teacher that "maybe the field trip triggered some resentment," the teacher refused to hear it. A third white woman wrote, "A black friend ended up in handcuffs when she went to check her mail because the police didn't expect a black woman to be living in a white neighborhood. I've never had that problem." Still another white woman, who had not been around many blacks while growing up but made black friends as an adult, wrote that "it took some intimacy to progress from the intellectual conviction that human beings are human beings, that racism is a foundational American evil, etc., to losing in my bones a sense of the otherness of Black people. . . . Now that I've written this I'm kind of embarrassed about it." One white man recalled that in high school, he joined a previously all-black music group. His experience of becoming close to the band members "helped me see how being black meant you were less likely to be seen by whites (like me) for who you were. You were simply 'black.'" A couple of other white people wrote of their surprise on hearing black people celebrate the European parts of their heritage — and of what their own surprise revealed to them about their previous assumptions, which one called "totally stupid and narrow-minded."

Several people had their eyes opened by the experiences of spouses or close relatives. A white man wrote of talking to his transgender son and other young trans people and becoming "very conscious that the feeling of being trans is deep-going and genuine, not some fad." A white man observed that seeing his child's transgender male friend appear "so much happier and lighter than throughout the years before" made him realize "how right this seemed." A white immigrant woman who married a biracial/black man in the 1970s was exposed to many instances of racism, such as hearing that the apartments the couple went to see together had already been rented — even though those apartments "had been available when I called 30 minutes earlier." One white woman respondent was raised Catholic, married a Jewish man, and raised their sons as Jews; the woman wrote of "being able to witness [Jews'] collective identity and faith and then . . . witness their collective fear as well. I'm not sure I had connected those before."

All well and good, as Ma used to say. But in one of my books I identified indifference as being at the heart of our troubles surrounding so-called race. The obstacle to equality is not that white people are racist — though of course many are — but that many, perhaps most, simply do not care enough to want to make a change. Indifference is a chillingly powerful force. The testimonies that I have cited above, which come from exposure to the experiences of individuals, are heartfelt, and all of them are stories of personal enlightenment that may lead in some cases to the waning of indifference. But are the feelings that they express of the kind that ever translate into change at the institutional level?

Here are two more testimonies, which I present to suggest the value of cross-racial exchanges and the potential power of a focus on individual experience. One story is from a white man who directed a creative writing program. He was in charge of hiring guest faculty, mostly through his network of personal acquaintances. "I don't remember," he writes, "if I even thought about the fact that most of them were white. At some point a few MFA students talked to me about their frustration with the lack of diversity among the teachers in the program. One Hispanic student told me that in both of the workshops she'd taken so far, her teachers and peers compared her writing to that of Sandra Cisneros, a writer with whom she said she actually had nothing in common — it was just that they seemed to lack a better frame of reference. These conversations really stayed with me and in their wake I completely rethought my hiring practices. This took place before the modern era of DEI bureaucracies, which, whatever their problems, do much to ensure that white 'gatekeepers' no longer rely unthinkingly on their personal networks, as I did at first."

The second story is also from a white man, who in this case was moved by the death of an individual: George Floyd. What happened to Floyd "made me wake up and recognize," he writes, "that I couldn't just let myself rest in my accomplishments and privilege." He went on to build a startup company called Homesy, which "is designed to lower the barriers to home ownership by creating a data-driven, no-commission network of homesellers, buyers, and real estate–curious people who have faced a history of 'real estate racism'" — racism that was "supported by the US government in concert with the National Association of Realtors."

I want to end with the most important thing I have to say, which is that what I am suggesting is not for the benefit of white people. No, I have others in mind.

I am at my desk, writing this by hand, using the pen that Ma gave me, in the room where my children used to sleep. My wife now calls this room my office. I suppose it is. Taped to the wall in front of me are handwritten lists of names, including Jackie Ormes, Sam Milai, Mansa Musa, and Ali Ber; there is a sketched likeness of E. Ethelbert Miller, and to the left of that, a postcard reproduction of a work by William H. Johnson. If some or all of these names are unfamiliar to you, I encourage you to investigate them, should you feel so inspired. They all have one thing in common, and they have it in common with the group of people for whom I am writing.

Near my desk, beneath my hat rack, is my stereo. On days when I am in my office preparing to teach, jazz plays. I hear the mostly wordless eloquence of Louis and Lil Armstrong, Charles Mingus, Eric Dolphy, Booker Little, Joe Pass, Bill Evans, Esperanza Spalding, or Lafayette Harris, and even when I am too absorbed in reading student work to take in every note, I feel sustained by this music, this black creation (whoever is playing it now), this testament to our resourcefulness, grit, imagination, intelligence, and adaptability. I was reared in the black world that created this gift to world culture. I care profoundly about our heritage and our well-being. I want us to be as fine as we can be.

DAVID GROSSMAN

It Takes So Little

Thousands of minutes and hours,
deeds and words,
specifications,
delusions,
mistakes
without end,
longing,
flesh —
it takes so much
to create
a single person —
that he be,
that he survives,
that he feels a hand on his shoulder,
that others say to him "It is you."
And it is so easy for him
not to be,
not to be this person,
to be done,
to be gone.
Or for a place that was a home
to no longer be the home
that it was.
It takes so little
for a home to cease,
to crumble,
to return to dust,

and for a land that was a place
no longer to be the place
that it was,
for a home to fail in it
and for a person to return
to its dust.
So little is required for a place
once again to not be a home.
So little is required
to not be.
The desire must be so strong,
so strong the desire to live,
so as to come back,
so as to come back to being.

December 12, 2024

Translated by Leon Wieseltier

ALFRED BRENDEL

Haydn: Order and Contradiction

It is well known that over the years the evaluation of Haydn underwent a number of changes. Towards the end of the eighteenth century, no one would have hesitated to call him the greatest of all composers. According to the *Allgemeine musikalische Zeitung* in 1802, "The inexhaustible spirit of his masterpieces is admired from Lisbon to St. Petersburg and Moscow, as well as behind the ocean and at the Polar Sea." In the London press he was even called "the Shakespeare of music."

This international fame was triggered by the six string quartets Op. 33, owing to the recent proliferation of newspapers and musical publishing houses. As soon as his works ceased to be the property of Count Esterházy, Haydn offered them to a multitude of publishers at once, even inviting subscriptions to handwritten copies. Ten years earlier, the incredible novelty of the string quartets Op. 20 had created a stir among musicians: Mozart and Beethoven copied them out, and later Brahms ended up being the happy owner of the autograph. Has there been another composer who bestowed us with a musical cosmos comparable to Haydn's quartets? Schubert's lieder may qualify.

In the nineteenth century, a counter-reaction occurred. Schumann, Liszt, Wagner and their spokesmen Adolf Bernhard Marx and Franz Brendel (no relation) voiced criticisms, while Mendelssohn, Weber, and Brahms seemed to have remained faithful admirers. Opinion-makers such as Eduard Hanslick and Theodor Adorno saw in Haydn mainly the precursor of greater masters. A different kind of sympathy and insight came from musical thinkers such as Heinrich Schenker and the composer, pianist, and brilliant writer Donald Francis Tovey, who dared to express the view that "in the history of music, no chapter is more important than that filled by the life-work of Joseph Haydn." Haydn scholars such as H. C. Robbins Landon, Jens Peter Larsen, Anthony van Hoboken (who created the standard catalogue of Haydn's compositions), James Webster, and Georg Feder — to mention only a few — then discovered missing works, eliminated inauthentic ones, and helped to correct mistakes. By 1935, not even one tenth of Haydn's works had been printed. We cannot be grateful enough to the publisher Henle, whose complete Haydn edition is now available.

In comparison to most of the other great composers, it is anything but easy to acquire an overview of Haydn's work. Let us try to assess his life's achievement. His compositions include sixty-seven string quartets, a hundred and four symphonies, fifty-five piano sonatas, forty-five piano trios, fourteen masses, three oratorios, one Stabat Mater, and one Te Deum — not forgetting his seventy-three operas and other music for the stage. We should also mention the approximately two hundred baryton trios that he composed for the pleasure of Esterházy, whose hobby was playing the baryton, a now-defunct string instrument with some added strings to be plucked. There were also approximately four hundred canzonettas and settings of Scottish and English folk songs, and more than forty canons. Haydn liked to sit down at the piano after dinner and sing some of his canzonettas for the pleasure of the English nobility. (As a boy he had been trained as a singer, and he remained particularly fond of cantabile even as an instrumental composer.) In addition, Haydn mounted twelve hundred opera performances for his employers the Esterházys, and was responsible for running their marionette theater. Conducting some of the performances of his oratorio *The Creation*, he seems to have used a baton, which did not become standard practice until a few decades later.

Let us also not forget his numerous piano, voice, and composition students who, in his later years, he taught in the early morning before breakfast. Unlike Mozart or Beethoven, Haydn's constitution seems to have been unshakeable, enabling him to live productively into old age. Only after the composition of his oratorio *The Seasons* did his vitality decline. In this weakened state, he carried visiting cards pronouncing "I am old and frail," and enjoyed playing his "Kaiserlied" three times a day on the clavichord, happy if one of the performances turned out to be particularly emotional. With all these activities, Haydn was no quill-driver. Please note the spectacular increase of achievement in his late symphonies and quartets. Haydn himself resisted being labelled a hasty composer. How all this can be reconciled in a single human life is hard to comprehend.

The Esterházys belonged to the wealthiest of noble families. To spend a large part of his life in their service was, for Haydn, a stroke of luck. No one has expressed this more clearly than Haydn himself: "My sovereign was pleased with all my work, I was able to earn his approval, I could, as the director of an orchestra, experiment, observe what makes an impression and what would diminish it. I could improve, add, subtract, dare; I was separated from the world. No one in my vicinity was able to lead me astray or distress me. Thus, I had to become original." This last sentence gave rise to controversy: is it possible to become original, or is a genius, in Kant's sense, born an original, endowed with an ability that surpasses what can be acquired? To the last question I would cautiously reply in the affirmative — after all, Haydn himself seemed to have been sufficiently aware of it.

Today we see in Haydn not only the foundation of later music but also a phenomenon of originality and inexhaustible vigor. The fact that during his lifetime vocal music ceased to dominate while instrumental composition gradually gained the foreground was in no small measure due to Haydn's activity. It was Haydn who led the string quartet from its rudimentary beginnings into the most concentrated, treasured, and "democratic" way of music-making, the democratic element becoming even more pronounced when a growing public gathered in larger halls to listen to Haydn's "overtures," as the symphonies were called in England.

In the more recent Haydn literature, the image of Haydn has become many-faceted, with some old notions still cropping up. According to these views, Haydn was rustic, and devoid of melancholy (Stendhal's opinion). This is incorrect, but the bright side does dominate. Haydn was a formalist, the composer who put the house of music into order, and at the same time an audacious adventurer, as well as the musical humorist *par excellence*. He was popular and "simple," but he was also complex. He was naively religious but also an exponent of the Enlightenment. He was ironic and sophisticated, but at the same time a revolutionary. He was "the friend of the house who is always welcome without having anything new to offer," but also the master of surprise and amazement. He incorporated both harmony and contradiction, risk and inner confidence.

The formula derived from Friedrich Schlegel that was spelled out by Goethe and Zelter in the journal *Athenaeum* as signifying genius — namely, a fusion of naivete and irony — seems to aptly sum up Haydn's musical persona. Let me quote more extensively from Goethe's and Zelter's text:

> Our Haydn is a son of our region and brings about things without heat: Who would enjoy being hot anyway? Temperament, sense, spirit, humour, flow, sweetness, power, and finally the true ingredients of genius, naivety and irony, should be assigned to him. As the elementary particles that we cannot imagine without warmth and substance can be recognized as Haydnesque peculiarities, we welcome his art as antique in the best sense. On the other hand, no one known to us has disagreed in finding him modern, which would be a difficult task as all modern music rests on him.

Here we have a remarkable early insight, but it should not mislead us into underestimating Haydn as a mere forerunner, only a precursor of greater things to come. Haydn constantly invented music anew. A typical feature of many of his quartets and symphonies is the fast burlesque finale, likened by an English writer to a clown suddenly appearing onstage. Haydn toys with the listener who should be pleased and thrilled as long as he or she enjoys the comical, and relishes the superior appeal of nonsense. Already in his lifetime Haydn was compared to the great humorists among contemporary writers, Laurence Sterne and Jean Paul. With the author of *Tristram Shandy* he shares the sudden stops, the jerkiness, the countering of expectations.

Haydn bestows on his music its formal order but at the same time provides us with its contradiction, the relentless detail that seems to place this order into question. For some of the Romantics, the words humor and irony were interchangeable. When the word "irony" entered the German language, Lessing translated it as *Laune* — mood, frame of mind. In this sense, it has remained a keyword for Haydn's music. Many of his contemporaries — his early biographers Georg August Griesinger and Albert Christoph Dies as well as the music aesthetician Christian Friedrich Michaelis — were well aware of it. Ignatz Ernst Ferdinand Arnold made this acute comment on Haydn's comic style:

> Being in command of all artistic means, this play of easy imagination endows even the smallest flight of genius with a boldness and audacity [*Keckheit und Dreistigkeit*] that expands the area of aesthetic achievement into the infinite without causing damage or anxiety . . . the last allegros or rondos consist frequently of short, nimble

> movements that reach the highest degree of comicality by often being worked out most seriously, diligently and learnedly . . . any pretence at seriousness only serves the purpose of making the playful wantonness of the music appear as unexpected as possible, and of teasing us from every side until we succumb and give up all attempts to predict what will happen next, to ask for what we wish for, or to demand what is reasonable.

I cite this because, on the occasion of the two-hundredth anniversary of Haydn's death in 2009, I came across a number of obituaries that not even in passing mentioned the comic aspect of Haydn's music. In Columbia University's massive *Encyclopedia* of the last century, the only explanation for the word "humor" was that of bodily fluids, while the *Haydn Encyclopedia* of Oxford University Press does not mention humor, irony or wit at all. It appears there are still people who are not prepared to take humor seriously.

Next to the confounding diversity of his production, the other main reason for underestimating Haydn's greatness seems to me an absence of humor. As we know, many thinkers have suffered from it. Among the exceptions were Spinoza and Darwin, who believed in the cheerful and blissful roots of laughter. I am happy to join them. Over long spans of time, religions did their best to stifle laughter. Adversaries of laughter were called agelasts. I side with the anti-agelasts, the advocates of laughter. It depends, however, when you are laughing, and how. In his novel *A Raw Youth*, Dostoyevsky tells us: "Show me how you laugh and I'll tell you who you are."

What happens while we laugh? We shake, emanate strange noises, "lose control." The body seems to be in charge and not the mind. Some philosophers seem to think that this abandonment of self-control represents the worst that could possibly happen. Others, however, may see laughter as a welcome liberation from the constraints of reason. Not for nothing is laughter at the center of Dadaism. One can laugh softly as well; Haydn is said never to have laughed out loud. And even music can laugh. Listen to the beginnings of Haydn's late C Major Sonata or to some of Beethoven's Diabelli Variations! At the end of this C Major Sonata, Haydn seems to be making fun of his listeners.

The means of expression that Haydn applies in order to achieve comic results have been thoroughly scrutinized. For my part, I would mention: seeming absentmindedness, sudden interruptions, repetitions of motifs, marking time, sudden manifestations of power, feigned naivete next to the genuine kind, musical twinkle, the idea to start a piece with its end, unfounded insistences, the relish of the unforeseen. And of course the surprises of instrumentation. Not all that is unexpected is necessarily comical: in the magnificent Military Symphony No. 100, we may prefer to experience the incursion of pandemonium as a frightening *memento mori*. And not every finale is a big joke: the whispered fugues in some of his early quartets convey a different, partly cryptic, partly intellectual message.

Among the surprises that Haydn springs on us is his string quartet Op. 42. It stands all on its own, a wallflower between those larger quartets in series of six or three. It is terse and avoids virtuosity, a work of touching modesty, a starting point for a new mode of expression that Haydn decided not to pursue. On the interaction between Haydn and Mozart, Tovey writes that Haydn's effect on Mozart resulted in an increased concentration of symmetry, while Mozart aided Haydn in liberating himself, making it possible to be no less capricious in his larger pieces than in his minuets and anti-minuets. In his quartet Op. 42, it seems the reverse: Haydn simplifies. Only the finale makes use of counterpoint.

The diversity of Haydn's composing becomes most readily evident in his string quartets. According to Mary Hunter in *The Cambridge Companion to Haydn*, it reaches from the gallant to the learned, from the supremely original and progressive to the universally accessible, and from the popular to the sublime. Let me add: from the capriccio to the fugue, from opera singing to the virtuosity of his violinists Tomasini, Tost, and Salomon, from the idiosyncratic to the refined simplicity of Op. 42.

Haydn was not handsome. Of less than medium height, short-legged but always scrupulously dressed, his features were notable for a prominent nose and a protuberant lower lip. He continued to wear a wig even after it had ceased being fashionable. His marriage was a mistake, but there seemed to have been no dearth of feminine company. For Luigia Polzelli, a singing member of the Esterházy Ensemble, he transcribed, transposed, and facilitated operatic arias. His later piano sonatas and most of the piano trios are dedicated to lady pianists. For good measure, string quartets and orchestras remained in male hands.

Three of his sonatas are particularly forward-looking. The C minor Sonata Hob. XVI: 20, from 1771, as well as the last of his E flat Sonatas, XVI: 52, open up new vistas: important sonatas by Mozart, Beethoven, and Schubert would take up the key and character of C minor, while the big Sonata in E flat was the first one to turn the fortepiano into an orchestra. But not even Schubert, with his predilection for chromatic neighboring keys, would have dared to follow up a first movement in E flat immediately with an E major adagio; in his *Wandererfantasie*, it needed an extensive transition to get from C major to C sharp minor. In Haydn's Sonata XVI: 50, the display of grotesquery ranges from the shortest staccato to mists of pedal.

I shall mention the magnificent achievement of the late symphonies only in passing. A number of recordings of the twelve London Symphonies are available, but in the concert hall we encounter them all too rarely. Let me point to Frans Brüggen's performances of the 1980s, and among contemporary conductors, Simon Rattle, as a most sensitive Haydn exponent who, both in concert and on records, has realized in some of Haydn's most perplexing movements documents of this composer's inclination to surprise.

The fact that Haydn was able to conclude his career with his two great oratorios brought him supreme international fame and the most ardent admiration of his fellow composers. What he didn't achieve with his operas he clearly accomplished with the universal success of *The Creation* and *The Seasons*. I wish there were a sufficient number of listeners to bring about concert performances of his Stabat Mater or the late masses. In his religious music, naivete is more than capable of foregoing irony and standing on his own.

AGNES CALLARD

The Missing Shade of White

Would you rather see the world in black and white or live without music? This is one of my favorite questions. Most people tell me that they would give up color before giving up Bach and the Beatles and so on — except kids, who usually make the opposite choice. I'm with the kids, and I always have been.

In the third grade, we were asked to name our favorite book. Mine was *The Wizard of Oz*, because it was colorful. I remember how disappointed my teacher was to learn that I was referring to the brightly colored watercolor drawings in my edition of the book. The right way to use the word "colorful" to praise a book, she explained, is to describe distinctive or memorable characters, such as the Tin Man and the Cowardly Lion, or surprising and whimsical events, such as a house falling on a witch, as being, in a metaphorical sense, "colorful." *The Wizard of Oz* was good because it was colorful, but not in the superficial way I meant it. This was the same teacher who got annoyed when, having told the class to draw a picture of spring, she observed I had drawn a metal coil. (The possibility of drawing trees and birds and sunshine did occur to me, but that seemed harder, and I am not good at drawing.) There is a flat literalism to the way I think, and there is a flat literalism to color as well: somehow, color flattens the world. The puzzle is that it also, at the same time, enlivens it.

The movie version of *The Wizard of Oz* builds a bridge between literalists like me, and sophisticates like my third-grade teacher. Dorothy starts out in the sepia-toned plains of Kansas, a world of dirt roads and open sky and old scattered farm equipment, and when the color gets turned on she is in a place chock-full of amazing, impossible wonders. The advent of color means the exit of the dull, the flat, the ordinary; with literal color comes metaphorical color. You can experience a version of the opposite when you switch the display of your phone or computer into black and white mode. Suddenly it is a much less appealing world to spend time in; you have drained it of life, even though it was never alive in the first place.

Color means liveliness, despite the absence of any correlation between how alive something is and how colorful it is: some colorful things are alive, some are not; some drab things are alive, some are not. When a given instance of color is very colorful, it is often described as vibrant, a word related to the word "vibrate," as though the color were in the business of moving rapidly, even though it is not moving at all. Arguably, color is one of the things that never moves. Things that are colored can move, and your eye can move across a field of colors, but colors are no more capable of motion than numbers are capable of emitting smells. So here we have two features of color: it is flat and it is lively. This is not exactly a contradiction, but there is some kind of tension between the reality of color as literal, as flat, as shallow, as a property of the outermost surface of things, and our sense that color is a mark of liveliness, of vibrancy, of energy, pointing us to the life that teems deep within. I want to explain why I choose color over music; to do that, I am going to have to make sense of how color vibrates without moving.

Let's start with a different question: which comes first, color or shape? You might think that this is a bad question, but Plato, a top questioner if there ever was one, disagreed. There are no fights about the chicken and the egg in the Platonic corpus, but there is one about the relative priority of color and shape. It starts when Socrates defines shape in terms of color: "Let us say that shape is that which alone of all existing things always follows color." Socrates is saying that shapes precipitate out of colors, in the sense that we identify shapes by tracking color boundaries. Socrates' interlocutor, Meno, calls this definition "foolish": what if a person came along who claimed "that he did not know what color is, but that he had the same difficulty as he had about shape?" Meno is complaining: what if I were blind? So Socrates offers Meno a second definition: "shape is the limit of a solid." But Meno is not satisfied and pushes Socrates to define color. Socrates complies: "color is an effluvium from shapes which fits the sight and is perceived," by which he means that objects emit streams of tiny shapes, which we perceive as color when they enter our eyes. At this point, Meno is satisfied. He loves this definition, "This seems to me to be an excellent answer, Socrates." And Socrates rebukes him for loving it: "it is a theatrical answer so it pleases you, Meno . . . it is not better . . . but I am convinced that the other is."

The dispute between Meno and Socrates is this: Meno prefers to define color in terms of shape, whereas Socrates prefers to define shape in terms of color. Consider trying to actually use Socrates' second definition of shape — "the limit of a solid" — in order to identify a shape. If Meno were blind, he would find the limits of solids by attending to tactile changes, but as it is, given that he is sighted, he relies on color differences. Socrates' first definition stands behind his second one. Color is what helps us find limits. You are using color that way right now, to read these words. Maybe that will be easier to see with words you (probably) can't read:

> ἔστω γὰρ δὴ ἡμῖν τοῦτο σχῆμα, ὃ μόνον τῶν ὄντων τυγχάνει χρώματι ἀεὶ ἑπόμενον.

Look closely at those marks, and pay attention to where each shape comes to an end. Notice something? You keep running into color boundaries! The limit of each shape is the place where the color changes. Color lets us see shape. And notice that it doesn't go the other way. If you look closely at the unprinted margins of this page, you'll find you can attend to an indeterminately bounded patch of white within the larger, unprinted margin. You see the color of that patch — white — but not by seeing any particular shape. Color does not follow shape, shape follows color.

If you know ancient Greek, you may have struggled to overcome your inclination to read the sentence — which gives Socrates' first definition of shape — instead of seeing its shapes. Even if you aren't able to translate the sentence, you still had to fight against your recognition of many of the letters. That struggle is good practice for our next exercise, as we move into the third dimension. You are going to lift your eyes from this page, but before you do, instruct yourself to adopt an infant mindset. I mean: try to remember that once upon a time you didn't know there were such things as books and carpets and windowpanes. Before you learned to parse the visual language of the spaces you are in, it was all Greek to you. Keeping that in mind, look up.

Welcome back. It's time to reflect on your experience. How did your eye decide where one thing stops and another starts? It looked for color changes. Once again, shape boundaries track color boundaries. That's the only way you get keyed into a new shape, at least if you are using vision. To see shape, you are forced to rely exclusively on color.

Shape is that alone of all existing things which always follows color. Every time I say this sentence to myself, it literally changes the way I see everything: instead of recognizing familiar groupings of familiar things, I find myself gazing at a sea of patterned color. If the definition favored by Socrates immerses me in the act of seeing, the one favored by Meno has the opposite effect. The shapes of which color is an "effluvium" must be so tiny as to be invisible, and when they enter my eye, they do so, in a sense, unseen. Meno is trying to get behind or underneath color experience; he is eager to move away from the vocabulary of the first person into terms that are abstract and alien, or, as Socrates puts it, "theatrical." Socrates is encouraging us to dive into our experience, to allow it to make itself intelligible on its own terms. I could tell Meno's story about color to a blind person, whereas in order to tell Socrates' story about color, I had to get you to use your eyes.

A variant of the dispute between Meno and Socrates would recur, a few thousand years later, when Goethe resisted Newton's conception of color. Newton understood color as a property of light, whereas Goethe insisted that color is a kind of subjective experience: the numerical wavelength of light might be a property of the light, but redness is a property of how things appear to the seeing subject. Wavelength is quantitative whereas red is a quality. Wittgenstein takes the side of Goethe and Socrates when he writes: "I don't *see* that the colors of bodies reflect light into my eye." Let us separate the question of what I see from the question of what happens — with light, and retinas, and tiny invisible shapes — when I see. Those inquiring into the second question will come upon all sorts of surprises, such as the surprising fact that white light can be split into the other colors of light, and surprises about whether light is a wave or a particle, about the structure of the eye, and of the brain, and so on. But these surprises are themselves unsurprising. When the journey is meant to end in a full understanding of the apparatus of seeing — the eye-brain interface, the surface, the light, and so on — we know in advance that it will be a long journey, full of alien and "theatrical" twists and turns. But if we turn our attention to the first question, the Socratic one, we don't expect the unexpected. What do I see? The answer is color, and that is the end of the story, right?

Wrong.

In 1950, a year before he died, Wittgenstein was thinking about color, and his reflections were collected into a little book called *Remarks on Color*. The question that runs like a guiding thread through his remarks is: why isn't there transparent white?

At first I took this question as proof that even great philosophers can ask bad questions, because there definitely is such a thing as transparent white. You can look down through the clouds from an airplane and see the world below through a whitish tint. And there is also frosted glass, and wax paper, and ice when it is filled with tiny air bubbles. And then I realized: those objects are not transparent, they are translucent. You can have milky white glass, cloudy glass, but the analog to that is milky or cloudy green glass, which is not the same as transparent green glass. Translucency blurs the boundaries of things, transparency does not. So I posed Wittgenstein's question to a friend, and he said, "Of course there is transparent white!" I demanded he show me some and he promised to do so. He returned, hours later, defeated. He couldn't find any, either.

Why isn't there transparent white? This question became an obsession for me, as it was for Wittgenstein, who poses it over and over again, in many different ways. For example:

> Why is it that something can be transparent green but not transparent white?
>
> "White water is inconceivable, etc." That means we cannot describe, (e.g. paint) how something white and clear would look, and that means: we don't know what description, portrayal, these words demand of us.

> Why can't we imagine transparent-white glass — even if there isn't any in actuality? Where does the analogy with transparent colored glass go wrong?

> And it does not suffice to say, the word 'white' is used only for the appearance of surfaces. It could be that we had two words for "green": one for green surfaces, the other for green transparent objects. The question would remain why there existed no color word corresponding to the word "white" for something transparent.

> "Why then is transparent white impossible? Paint a transparent red body, and then substitute white for red!"

You might be inclined to say that it is obvious why there isn't transparent white glass: a transparent medium filters out the relevant color and only lets that kind of light through, but white is all the colors, so "transparent white" glass can't do any filtering. But then perhaps a clear transparent glass should count as "transparent white"? Yet it doesn't. As Wittgenstein would say, look at it! Does it look white? ("We don't say of something which looks transparent that it looks white.")

Wittgenstein considers a potential rule for transparency: maybe transparent *X* glass, for any color *X*, has to change the colors of what is behind it so as to make white things *X*-colored, and it must make everything else appear in some shade between *X* and black. This rule does indeed work for "transparent red" and "transparent blue." But then he has us imagine that there were a glass that drained the world of color, rendering everything black and white — I suppose it is the glass you would have to look through, for the rest of your life, if you opted for music. Viewed through this "decoloring" glass, as we might call it, whites are white, and everything else is in a shade from white to black. This glass should, by the rule proposed above, qualify as "transparent white." And yet, notes Wittgenstein, we are not inclined to call it that, because whether or not something is white is not a matter of whether it satisfies some rule but, again, whether it *looks white*. Whiteness is not stipulative. But if it is not stipulative, then why would we assume that there would be a white version of everything? That is the real question.

Why *should* there be transparent white? Wittgenstein also notes that there are no luminous greys: "the fact that we cannot conceive of something 'glowing grey' belongs neither to the physics nor to the psychology of color." Moreover, "a shine, a 'high-light' cannot be black." And yet, he goes on to observe, "a flag may be yellow and black, another yellow and white." White and grey and black are interchangeable on flags, but not when it comes to flames, or transparency, or shadows. When it comes to flags, anything goes, but when it comes to shines and shadows, only some things go. We should, I propose, be less surprised by the flames and shadows, and much more surprised by the flags: how marvelously unstuck their colors are! Transparent white is the rare exception to the rule that if you pick out almost any object in your visual field you can easily imagine it being a very different color from the color that it is. Pink squirrels? Sure. Lavender grass? No problem. Color is layered very thinly on reality, which gives it a life of its own.

Contrast sound. There is no single, unified way to refer to the sonic analog to "lavender" or "maroon." We must mention both the pitch of a note — how high or low it is — and its timbre. Timbre picks out the difference between the same note played on a piano, or a flute, or sung by a human voice — each gives the note a different "coloring." Notice that in order to refer to those different timbres, I have to refer to their causal underpinnings: the most natural way for me to describe the distinctive sonic quality of a trumpet's blast is to mention the brass thing that produced the sound, namely the trumpet. The same goes for the other senses. I do not think that just anything can taste sweet — salt, for instance, cannot taste sweet. The fact that salt cannot be sweet, or granite cannot be squishy, does not induce in me the feeling of perplexity that I feel when I learn that what is transparent cannot be white. If I try to imagine a book that tastes salty or sour, I find that my mind has deposited a fine layer of salt or lemon juice on the surface of the book. The smell of a rose or the ocean is associated with a very specific thing, namely, a rose or an ocean. Against the backdrop of the causal embeddedness of our other senses, it is remarkable that we have such a concept as "red," which requires no mention of tomatoes or fire or lobsters or Coca-Cola cans or carpets used for celebrities. I conceive of red as something in its own right, detachable from any of the objects that cause me to experience it. And this is, in general, how I think of color, as something that can be peeled off of reality, as something that inhabits a strange realm called "my visual field," a mental arena to which there is no analog in any of the other senses. Is a color "patch" a piece of the world or a piece of my mind?

Had he not died a decade before it was published, I believe that Wittgenstein would have loved Josef Albers' *The Interaction of Color*. Albers was a Bauhaus painter, printmaker, graphic designer, photographer, art educator, and color theorist — in sum, a practitioner of color. *The Interaction of Color* is not a treatise about color but a workbook filled with exercises designed to teach the reader to do something she thinks she already knows how to do, namely, see colors. The thesis of the book is in its title: colors interact. The interaction of color can cause two colors that are the same to look different, or several colors that are different to look the same — it causes "the Weber-Fechner Law," which says that transparent colors must be layered upon one another geometrically in order to produce what looks like an arithmetic progression, and it causes "the Bezold effect," by which proximate colors can lighten or darken one another. But the "most exciting of all color phenomena," according to Albers, is an interaction effect that causes the vanishing of boundaries at the border between two different colors of equal light intensity. When Wittgenstein asks, "Why is green drowned in the black, but white isn't?", he is gesturing at Albers' favorite interaction effect. As an artist, Albers is most famous for his series of paintings of nested squares called *Homage to the Square*, which makes frequent use of this same effect. Albers wrote, of his series paintings, "I'm not paying 'homage to a square.' It's only the dish I serve my craziness about color in."

Early in the book Albers makes clear that he is taking the Socratic path:

> Our study of color differs fundamentally from a study which anatomically dissects colorants (pigments) and physical qualities (wave length).
>
> Our concern is the interaction of color; that is, seeing what happens between colors.
>
> We are able to hear a single tone.
> But we almost never (that is, without special devices) see a

single color unconnected and unrelated to other colors. Colors present themselves in continuous flux, constantly related to changing neighbors and changing conditions.

In an early chapter called "a color has many faces," Albers writes that "color is the most relative medium in art," but it is not until the end of the book that he dares to explain what he means by this: "The purpose of most of our color studies is to prove that color is the most relative medium in art, that we almost never perceive what color is physically." Albers is saying: we don't see the colors that are there. What we see, instead, is the interaction between colors.

If this seems like a crazy claim, the book is filled with proof. The wonderful images in his book are sadly copyrighted, so I can't reproduce them here, but here is an (inferior) example of my own construction. Take a look at this set of shapes:

FIGURE 1

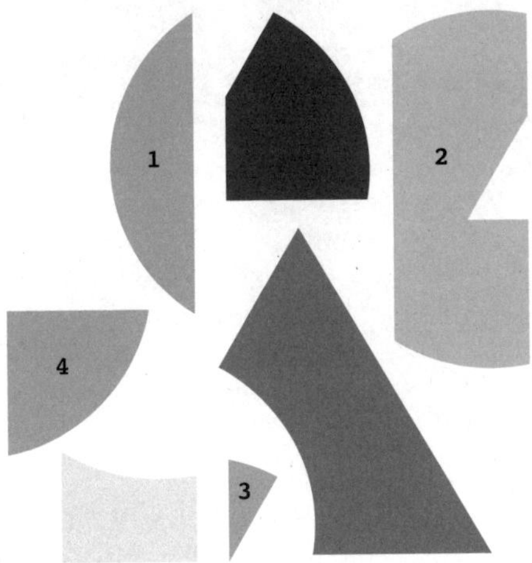

Ask yourself how hard it is to determine the relative color values of the shapes that I have marked 1, 2, 3, 4? Is 1 darker or lighter than 3? Is 2 darker or lighter than 1? Now look at Figure 2, where I have rearranged the same set of shapes. I have not adjusted their color values or even rotated them; I have simply changed their relative positions. Notice, first, that it is now easy to determine which is darker, and second, that in their new arrangement the shapes composing (what now appear as a) triangle and rectangle are transparent. Albers would chalk both of these differences up to the interaction of color. The colors in Figure 2 interact in such a way as to produce transparent color, and in such a way as to make it easy for you to tell that 1, 3 and 4 have the same value, whereas 2 is lighter.

FIGURE 2

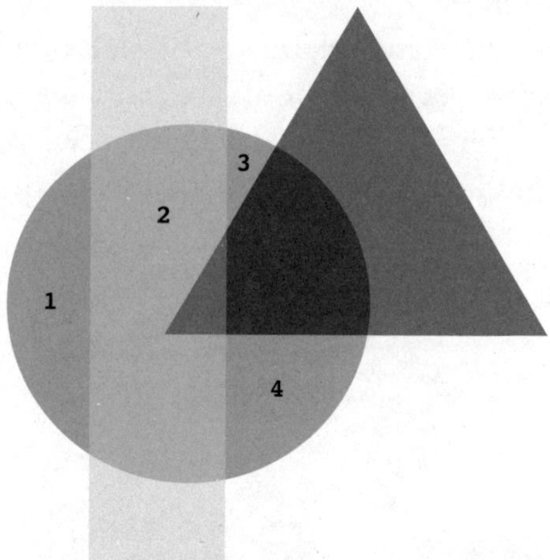

My images echo a thought experiment described by Wittgenstein:

> Imagine a painting cut up into small, almost monochromatic bits which are then used as pieces in a jig-saw puzzle. Even when such a piece is not monochromatic it should not indicate any three-dimensional shape, but should appear as a flat color-patch. Only together with the

> other pieces does it become a bit of blue sky, a shadow, a highlight, transparent or opaque, etc. Do the individual pieces show us the real colors of the parts of the picture?

Given that our color assessments are more accurate for Figure 2, why might we think that it is Figure 1 that shows us “the real colors”? The answer must be that “real colors” means “colors in the absence of interaction effects.” I believe that this is also what Albers means by “physically,” when he tells us that “we almost never perceive what color is physically.” Of course we cannot remove all interaction effects, because a color patch is always seen against some background. Figure 1 frames each grey shape in white, and in Wittgenstein’s example we must imagine that we are examining the painting fragments strewn on a rug or held up against a wall.

Still, we can remove many interaction effects by “deconstructing” an image: we can bring it about that we can no longer identify the blue as the blue of the sky, and no longer pick out items such as shadows or highlights, no longer distinguish between what is transparent and what is opaque. Wittgenstein points out that in a painting, a transparent object, such as a glass vase, will be painted using the same sort of paints as an opaque one, such as the table on which the vase rests. The “building blocks” of a transparent image will not be transparent. Figures 1 and 2 illustrate this as well: transparency is an interaction effect. We can chop an image up to the point where many such interaction effects are removed, even if not all of them, and we have the sense that this brings us closer to the “real” color. Oddly enough, the “real color” is not what we tend to see.

Once again it is worth noting that our atomism about color is unparalleled in our other forms of sense experience.

We don't instinctually decompose music or food into its component parts and claim that those components are what we are "really" hearing or seeing. That is why you didn't notice that my initial framing — comparing losing color to losing music — was guilty of a lack of parallelism. Strictly speaking, the parallel to losing color is losing pitch and timbre, whereas losing paintings and stained glass windows should be on par with losing classical and pop and so on. But when I frame it in the first way, people translate pitch plus timbre into music — they care about being able to distinguish a voice from a trumpet exactly insofar as they care about being able to hear Bach. And framed in the second way the choice is too obvious, even for me: I would pick music over paintings, because so much of my aesthetic experience of color can be salvaged. It comes naturally to balance red against Bach, turquoise against the Beatles; somehow colors are on par with much more organized experiences of sound or taste. I own a book called *The Secret Lives of Color*, which contains hundreds of pages of detailed discussions of many colors, including sixteen shades of yellow and orange (amber, saffron, minimum ginger, orpiment, gamboge) — and yet it is missing my favorite yellow-orange, ochre. I could not imagine a book called *The Secret Lives of Notes* that discusses middle C as played on a piano versus A sharp on a flute. Who cares about notes? We care about flavors mostly insofar as they are clustered into foods, and likewise for textures, but ochre shows up for me as an important citizen of reality, it stands on its own two feet. We are blasé about the existence of notes we cannot hear (a dog whistle) but we feel very differently about the prospect of colors we cannot see. (Wittgenstein: "There is, after all, no commonly accepted criterion for what is a color, unless it is one of our colors.")

In 2015, a picture of a dress worn to a wedding went viral because people could not agree whether it was blue and black or white and gold. A few years later, there was an analogous acoustic disagreement: in a brief audio recording, some heard "yanny" where others heard "laurel," shortly followed by a variant with "green needle" and "brainstorm." Notice: in the visual realm, we are torn between colors, in the auditory realm, between words.

A color is in many ways less like a sound, or a taste, or a smell, and more like a word. A word presents itself as separate from the causal structure that gave rise to it; it floats in the air, Homer observed, as though on wings. A word is also a unit — standing apart from other words — even though, as with color, we only ever encounter words in the context of other words, and the "interaction effects" are, to put it mildly, significant. When the person I am talking to is angry with me, or boring me, or I am in some way averse to the interaction I am in, the words they are saying sometimes materialize in the air in front of me. I see the words more than I hear them, and their presence comforts me, as though they were saying: you can interact with us instead.

Color both flattens and enlivens the world, and words do the same. On the one hand, it is a truism that there is much that cannot be expressed in words, that a word only conveys a whisper of the thing itself; on the other hand, when we do succeed in describing something that we previously found difficult to describe, or even just inventing a name for it, the phenomenon is thereby, in some sense, brought to life. Suddenly being able to speak something you couldn't speak before is a lot like having it jump out at you, visually, in the form of a bright gash of pink, or a garish polka-dot pattern.

Your eyes show you a world of things, immediately, and in the same glance they show you color and shape and transparency and shine. Unless I am instructing you to perform strange Socratic exercises, you see everything together all at once. In a similar way, when you read this text, you access my thoughts, what I am trying to communicate, and you access my words and sentences and linguistic style, all together. Color is packaged with things as words are packaged with thoughts, but unpacking is a task one can take up, if one is so inclined. I am, in both cases, all the time: to be literal-minded is to be attuned to the superficial liveliness that buzzes all around you, because you have accepted the standing invitation to detach the surface from what is bundled with it.

Even when I am listening to it in public, music is private. By the time I hear it, it has already been granted direct access to my core, the place where my secret thoughts and hidden feelings lie; I locate it in my interior. But my visual field and the color patches that populate it are not private — at least not in that way. They are private in the way a private conversation or a private club are private: by invitation only. Music reminds me that I am alive, that I carry life within me, but a colored world presents *itself* to me as alive, as though it were talking to me. I want both, but if I have to choose, I would rather feel less life in me and more life around me.

PAULA BOHINCE

Young Lady in 1886

after Manet

Smudge of ivory
cameo (another lady's
face, but anonymous) lists
from black ribbon.
To her, she offers
a petite bundle
of lilac. The African
grey contemplates a beyond
beyond its empty dish,
no droplet or
seed to hold its attention.
This is discipline.
The blue velvet
hair bow and red (parted,
kempt) complement
each other. At the rack's
wooden feet sits
a half-peeled orange, sug-
gesting, yes, undress.
Muse in pink
sheen, buttoned up
nearly completely, folds
fallen all to the floor
to peekaboo slip of slipper.
Listen, what music

rode the room is secret. O
but that milky pink
the freckled ones will get,
mottled with shyness.
A man's monocle,
spontaneous, over her navel
dip, cannot conceal
the memory of it
from him. In that coy
cave, what was said remains
between, a privacy.

Peaches

Born from pastel clouds and blushed as health,
each a painted infant, gessoed and reaching. Kin to Monet's
faraway "Jar of Peaches," seeded into the clay spectacular
to commune and dream and flower, achieving
at the center the divided brain of human nature:
split between the orchard's timetabled logic
and the sumptuous urge toward art, to make of any surface
a canvas and on it a peach folk-pretty and big
as a dinner plate beside a tiny pig and silo.
Held, it's sunset, almost utterance,
grave, airbrushed velveteen.
A rapture of peaches, hummed into balsa
and wire, delved from the original ochre pleasure, redden
round in the potter's terra cotta: a porch gift, a June reunion
of fruit and earth, mother flesh and child relentless.

A Photograph

How long had it languished, erotic in the stalls
of oil paintings and furs cryptic as the decrepit hutch
where rabbits are generations gone?
How well hid in the warrens of the flea market, then deeper
as if back into the camera's aperture,
suddenly abloom as a daisy in the cemetery dirt
that nurtured it. Some wan, anonymous beach, no signal
if Cap Coz or Côte des Basque, it was all her:
cuffs rolled (she must've been wearing his trousers),
grayish hair a wing, fisherman's sweater,
glimpse of cheek, a privacy signed Leo Brisbois
in grade school loops, deep pencil. He'd hung back, amber
in its black barrel rolling one frame into
the future. Waited as it bathed, gave it ivory mat.
Valium to see it, like that Janis Joplin interview, her shy
responses, her embarrassment in explaining how she sang
from "the bottom of the music." Her little girl teeth,
how softly remarkable they seem, these sincerities.

Pretty

Sculptural swan, left behind
earring sworn to the garden, as after
an encounter on a carpet, risen
then into a different person.
When a thing alights, its *missingness*
elevates prettiness into art.
All of life in the sunset-fired contours.
Your life poured into looking.

ENRIQUE KRAUZE

Munich 1919: A Precedent, A Parable

1

Sometimes the great moments of history are the small moments of history. Such is the case with the short-lived Munich Revolution. Compared to the world wars or the Russian Revolution, it seems like a footnote about a failed adventure. But its significance is far greater: it was a social earthquake whose aftershocks marked the twentieth century, and whose ideas and reasons remain pertinent to our own volatile and unjust century. It unfolded from November 1918 to May 1919 in three stages of increasing radicalism — social-democratic, anarchist, communist — until it led to a military, nationalist, and anti-Semitic reaction that gave rise to the Nazi Party. Perhaps no other European episode of its time contains a similar historical density.

It began the day after the German defeat in the Great War. Over four savage and disillusioning years, the initial exaltation, the patriotic intoxication, the promise of glory, with which the conflict began all ended in a hell of rationing, hunger, plague, and one million seven hundred thousand dead soldiers, four million wounded, and one million prisoners. While the fate of Germany depended on France, England, and the United States (Bolshevik Russia had made peace with Germany in the Treaty of Brest-Litovsk), the old order collapsed forever. In Weimar, a republic was declared on November 9, to be led by the Social Democratic Party, the SPD. But parliamentary democracy was an inadmissible outcome for the German revolutionaries who sought to emulate — and correct, and surpass — Lenin's recent feat. Several pockets of rebellion were ignited in ports and cities. In Berlin, two legendary leaders, Karl Liebknecht and Rosa Luxemburg, founded the Spartacus League aimed at creating a free socialist republic. On January 15, 1919, they were murdered by soldiers of General Gustav Noske, whose army, notable for its discipline and ferocity, included four thousand paramilitary *Freikorps*, composed of the *Sturmtruppen*, elite troops hardened in war. But by then a peaceful revolution had triumphed in Munich, capital of the independent kingdom of Bavaria.

Two months earlier, the ancient Bavarian monarchy had fallen in five days under the impetus of a peaceful mobilization of tens of thousands of workers and soldiers, led by the least likely of political leaders, a fifty-one-year-old Jewish intellectual named Kurt Eisner. Imprisoned in early 1918 for his militant pacifism and released in October, Eisner became the hero of the hour. In the squares, auditoriums, assemblies, and beer halls of Munich, his speech electrified "the masses," a key term in the vision and the vocabulary of the revolution. (It should be noted that, at the height of the revolution, those mobilized masses numbered perhaps ten percent of the population). On November 8, pending elections in the Bavarian parliament, the Provisional National Council declared Kurt Eisner the first minister-president of the Free State of Bavaria.

Suddenly that peaceful, cultivated, and dynamic city became the stage on which the twentieth century was being rehearsed. The novelty of a revolutionary government took everyone by surprise. And the effects were immediate. Eisner espoused women's suffrage and an eight-hour workday. Elated, the workers' councils, headed by intellectuals, won allies among the soldiers recently returned from the front. But the main parties from the center to the right, the bureaucracy, the middle classes, the majority press, the Catholic clergy and other religious groups (including the Jewish community), the ultra-nationalist secret brotherhoods, a significant portion of the university teachers and students, the diplomatic legations of the countries allied to Germany, and most of the farmers (predominant in Bavaria) — all saw the revolutionary government as an intolerable anomaly.

An almost unbelievable cast gathered in that Babel of ideas and ideologies. Alongside Eisner, a major presence was the great anarchist thinker and editor Gustav Landauer. (If he is remembered at all today, it is as the unlikely grandfather of Mike Nichols.) Several other prominent intellectuals, literati, and bohemians, but also economists of renown such as Edgar Jaffe, Lujo Brentano, and Otto Neurath, and pedagogues such as F. W. Foerster, would join the government, believing that the revolution was nothing less than a new dawn in history. The most fierce critic of the revolution and its leaders was

Max Weber, who dissected their political romanticism in a legendary lecture delivered to the Munich Liberal Students Union, entitled "Politics as a Vocation". Among the students in his audience were the young philosopher Karl Löwith and Max Horkheimer, who would be one of the founders of the Frankfurt School. Also attending was Carl Schmitt, who would become one of the main political theoreticians of Nazism. The hotbed of Munich included Spartacist revolutionaries and Lenin's agents, as well as several future Nazis, such as Rudolf Hess and Ernst Röhm. Nuncio Eugenio Pacelli, the future Pope Pius XII, sent back reports to the Vatican. The first-hand witnesses of the turbulence included Thomas and Heinrich Mann, Rainer Maria Rilke, Victor Klemperer, Martin Buber, and Lion Feuchtwanger. And an obscure twenty-nine-year-old veteran soldier of the war named Adolf Hitler, a failed painter, was wandering confusedly around the rallies and barracks looking for where and how to pour out his hatred. In Munich he found the answers he was looking for.

The Munich revolution was a dizzying theater of ideas — not pure ideas but armed ideas. Yet the violence was slow to break out. When Weber delivered his lecture on January 28, 1919, barely ten weeks had passed since Eisner's accession to power. The revolution was seeking its course and the republican order was being maintained with difficulty. Weber considered Eisner's government disastrous. Before addressing his audience, he remarked, "This does not deserve the honorable name of revolution: it is a bloody carnival." In fact, his rejection of the present was the measure of his anguish for the future. He was persuaded that the history of his country, and that of Europe, would be decided there and then. In 1919 in Munich, Weber saw the Aleph of the century, and was horrified. A historical drama and a personal drama came together to imbue his words with the gravity of a prophetic revelation. His lecture, designed to have an effect on political circumstances, was an enduring lesson, and one of the sacred texts of modern liberalism. It has come down to us as a warning against the converging influences of demagoguery, unchecked charismatic leadership, and ideological fanaticism.

"What is the ethical home for politics?" Weber asked. The key, as is well known, lay in the contrast that he drew between an "ethics of conviction" and an "ethics of responsibility." For Weber — who, while recognizing the gravity of the former, favored the latter — a genuine "political vocation" meant a passionate embrace of a cause, but without vanity or overflowing, with restraint and distance, and above all with a high sense of responsibility. Only a politician with such mettle deserved to "put his hand on the wheel of history."

He hastened to point out that this was not the case with the demagogues of his time, who "acting under an absolute ethic, feel responsible only for the flame of conviction, the flame, for example, of protest against the injustices of the social order." If their action does not achieve the desired end, "they will hold the world responsible, the stupidity of men or the will of God who made them so." Weber drew an analogy between the German revolutionaries and the ancient prophets of the seventeenth century confident in the imminent coming of Christ: the same sense of "orgiastic chiliasm," the same certainty in an "eschatological opening of History." Demagogues, revolutionaries, and prophets announced a radiant future that was yet to come, and in order to hasten it any means seemed legitimate. But even the most intense subjective conviction about the absolute value of the ends did not justify, much less sanctify, irresponsible disregard for the objective consequences of the means.

Nor were the pacifists — those perennial votaries of inaction — spared by the indictment. Given that the inescapable and specific means of power is force, Weber lamented "the naiveté of believing that from good comes only good and from evil only evil." Often, he said, "the opposite is true, and anyone who did not see this was a child, politically speaking." This paradox led him to emphasize the existence of "a tragic warp in the human condition," and in no activity was this distortion more evident than in politics. That is why he defined politics as "a slow drilling of hard boards." Weber did not preach quietism, conservatism, or reaction. Nor did he offer paths of salvation or recipes for happiness. He opened a passionate but realistic way to act with prudence and inner strength in defense of the highest human values. That is what the "ethics of responsibility" consisted of. The unnamed demagogues, revolutionaries, and pacifists of his lecture, emblems of the "ethics of conviction," were Karl Liebknecht, Rosa Luxemburg, and most of all Kurt Eisner. People recalled him mentioning them in his lecture, but days later, in the printed version, he omitted their names. But there was another less obvious and unnamed character in his lecture: the "pure type" of the politician who embodied the "ethics of responsibility." That character was Weber himself.

Max Weber was then fifty-four years old. Highly respected as a sociologist and social philosopher, he had a monumental, though mostly unpublished, body of work behind him. He came to Munich in November 1918 to take up academic work, which he had been forced to suspend many years earlier owing to a protracted and painful depression. His political position was difficult to pigeonhole. He had been, like so many, an enthusiastic supporter of the war. "No matter what the outcome, this war is great and wonderful," he wrote in August 1914. He was not driven by pan-German romanticism, but by a realism that revealed for him an inevitable geopolitical destiny: whereas Switzerland could be the guardian not only of "freedom and democracy but of much more intimate and eternal cultural values," Germany had no choice but to assert its power against Tsarist Russia and Anglo-American hegemony. According to Ernst Bloch, Weber used to dress as a soldier every Sunday. He would have liked to serve at the front. His consolation was to direct, with the same disciplined passion that he put into his research, the military hospitals in Heidelberg.

Very soon, though, the political, diplomatic, and military decisions seemed to him not only wrong but spectacularly stupid. He deplored the conversion of a war that he considered defensive (especially because of Russian imperialism) into a senseless expansionist enterprise spearheaded by military "madmen" and their industrial allies. He criticized annexationist measures in Belgium, and warned that submarine attacks on civilian ships would draw — as in fact they did — the United States into the war. No protagonist was up to the task, neither the Kaiser, whom he despised, nor the successive chancellors who bowed down before military stubbornness and arrogance: "There is not a single statesman, just one, to manage the situation! And to think that this man who does not exist is indispensable," he wrote in November 1915 to his old friend, the pastor and liberal politician Friedrich Naumann. For a long time, Weber thought that that statesman could be him.

In 1916 he spent time in Berlin in an attempt to put his "hand on the wheel of history," but his wishes were frustrated.

Neither his diagnoses of the economic outcome of the war, nor his plans to informally represent Germany in Poland (granting that occupied country the necessary autonomy), received the slightest attention. "It is highly unlikely that there is anything in it for me," he complained. His most devoted friends, such as Karl Jaspers, complained about the time that he wasted on such pursuits, diverting him from his work. But he regretted more his life as a vicarious politician. And although he confessed to being "fed up with bursting into people's offices to 'do something'," he did not lose hope: "Everyone knows that, if they need me, I will always be at hand."

For Weber, politics at that time had only one purpose: to secure peace in order to build the future. But not peace at any price, let alone the undignified peace that, in his view, the pacifists were proposing. The viability of the German parliamentary republic depended on the possibility of a dignified peace. This republican and constitutional option was as opposed to pan-Germanic and militaristic hegemony as it was to social revolution in any of its facets, from the "general strike" to anarchist, Spartacist, and Bolshevik insurgencies. Since the revolution of 1905 in Russia, and with greater urgency after Lenin's triumph in October 1917, Weber wrote abundantly about socialism, criticizing it in terms of practical possibility: he saw no way in which the prophecies of the the *Communist Manifesto* could be fulfilled.

Politics, he would have said, was his secret love, and would remain so until the end. But politics evaded him. If he could not advise, influence, act, or command, he could at least teach outside the professoriate, while taking up his great *Sociology of Religion*. Fortunately, there were the young people: could he bring them clarity and objectivity about the historical moment? Two years before dictating "Politics as a Vocation,"

Weber presided over two seminars at Lauenstein Castle attended by several well-known writers of various political positions and a group of students of liberal, socialist, and pacifist tendencies. What happened there — vividly recorded by his wife, Marianne Weber, in her admirable biography, which is rich in personal testimonies and letters — was the rehearsal of the generational clash that would take place two years later in the streets of Munich.

One of these young men was an intense and tortured poet named Ernst Toller. (There is a moving photograph of the young Toller looking up at a hatted Weber in a group of attendees.) A veteran of the war, seriously wounded in battle, he had gone from psychiatric hospitals to prisons because of his active pacifist militancy. His concern, Toller wrote in his memoirs, went "beyond the sins of the Kaiser or electoral reform", subjects of which Weber spoke. He and his comrades wanted to "create a new world, to change the existing order, to change the hearts of men." They respected — Marianne recalls — Weber's "controlled ethos" and his "sober incorruptibility," but they hated "that scientific mind which was incapable of offering a simple way to solve problems and which asked itself about every 'social ideal' by what means and at what price it could be achieved." Weber did not despair. He was willing to be their teacher, as long as they were prepared to "crack the hard nuts" of scientific work, to seek knowledge of themselves and the world through objective data, configurations, and connections, and emphatically not through "revelations."

Weber disbelieved in social prophecies and yet — according to Marianne's testimony — his deepest identification was not with the misunderstood fathers of science but with the prophet Jeremiah, a "titan of invective" who cried out against his king and against his people without waiting for or getting an answer, without a retinue of apostles to follow him, sure of the truth of his criticism. "He was enveloped," Marianne recalls, "by the pathos of inner solitude." What was the ultimate origin of this attitude? We would have to call it tragic realism. From a young age he knew that he was not susceptible to the spell and the comfort of religion or its ideological substitutes. He understood that spell and made it into the subject of some of his greatest work, but he was spurred by the world to its opposite — to the scientific vocation to demystify the world. In Weber's universe there was no room for fantasies or reductions: through the comprehensive sieve of his "pure types", economic forms, juridical institutions, religious ethics, the sources of political domination in the entire history of East and West, all acquired meaning. But if anything characterized the human fabric, it was the inevitability of conflict. In the face of this harsh and irreducible condition, the highest vocation of which Weber could conceive was that of the politician, because no other activity touched the tragic core of life as it did. And exercised at the highest level, it could touch people, the moral quality, even the nobility, of their existence.

This was the man who had arrived in Munich in November 1918 only to discover that the young people to whom he preached the "ethics of responsibility" were following a leader animated by the "ethics of conviction," a demagogue from out of Weber's own pages: Kurt Eisner.

Eisner was the villain of Weber's conference at Laustein Castle. Gustav Landauer, his friend and close collaborator, described Eisner thus: "this modest, pure, honorable man, who has earned his living as a precarious writer, is suddenly the spiritual leader of Germany by the mere fact that this courageous Jew is a man of spirit." A militant worker shared this opinion: "He is the sword of the revolution, he has overthrown the twenty-two kingdoms of Germany, he is our brilliant leader, I will defend him to the death." The person who recorded that worker's words was the retired sergeant Victor Klemperer, professor of ancient languages, a Jewish convert to Protestantism, and the author of one of the most extraordinary diaries of the German cataclysm. In those early days of exaltation, however, he himself drew in his diary a less flattering portrait of the leader:

> Eisner is a delicate, diminutive, fragile, corseted, small man. From his head, bald and not at all imposing, his hair hangs down to his neck, as dirty and gray as his reddish, graying beard. His gray, misty eyes look through his glasses. There is nothing brilliant, venerable or heroic in his appearance. He is a mediocre, worn-out man who looks sixty-five although he is barely over fifty. His look is not particularly Jewish, let alone Germanic. But the way he jokes around the stage (he doesn't stand behind the podium) reminds me of typical caricatures of Jewish journalists.

Eisner had even implied — anticipating Groucho Marx's joke — that he would not vote for a party that had him as a candidate. How was it possible, Klemperer wondered, that such a character could provoke such ecstasy when speaking of "the renewal of the spirit"?

Max Weber had the answer. It could be summed up in a single word: charisma. Eisner possessed that rare and non-transferable gift that the sociologist had studied in his work as one of the three legitimate sources of political authority. Charismatic leaders, he observed, flourished above all in times of exception:

> Charismatic leadership is always born out of unusual situations — especially political and economic ones — or out of extraordinary psychological states, especially religious ones; or out of both at the same time. It arises from the collective excitement produced by extraordinary events and from prostration before heroism of any kind.

Eisner, the "pure type" of the charismatic leader, alarmed Weber because he sharply represented the "ethics of conviction" which, enamored of its principles, was capable of proclaiming: "The world seems torn to pieces, lost in the abyss. Suddenly, in the midst of darkness and despair, trumpets sound announcing a new world, a new humanity, a new freedom."

Who was Eisner? He had studied in Magdeburg under Hermann Cohen, a Jewish neo-Kantian philosopher who postulated the convergence between the moral categories of Kant and the message of the biblical prophets. An inspiration for liberal and Reform Judaism in Germany, and the author of perhaps the greatest modern book on the philosophical meanings of Judaism, Cohen elaborated the doctrine of an "ethical socialism" as a possible stage of universal concord. Eisner revered Cohen and made this doctrine his own, but his vocation was far less speculative or contemplative. Long before leaping into the political arena, Eisner had been the editor-in-chief of *Vörwarts*, the influential newspaper founded by Karl Liebnecht's father and a voice of the Social Democratic Party. There he also served as a political commentator, storyteller, theater critic, and superb satirist. His hilarious articles on the sexual "peccadilloes" of the royal family brought him national fame, but led to his dismissal. During the war he earned his living as a freelance writer. He was a convinced pacifist.

Such a transition from journalism to politics did not surprise Weber, who in his political sociology anticipated a growing affinity between the two professions, while warning of the risks of moving from one to the other. Only after his investiture did Eisner come to understand that criticizing power was different from exercising it. As minister-president he became Hamlet in Munich. Politically, he would live torn between the revolutionary Workers' Councils and the Bavarian parliament. "The masses" demanded to overcome parliamentarianism (a "bourgeois relic") as a minimum step to establish a socialist regime. The parliamentarians were the representatives of the parties, ranging from the nationalist right to the left of the USDP (an independent offshoot of the SPD, chaired by Eisner), with the moderate nationalist and liberal-democratic tendency between them. The parliament, with a social democratic majority, favored social and economic reformism.

Although he was overwhelmed by his verbal hyperbole, the truth is that Eisner never departed from the convictions and the responsibilities of a social democrat: he criticized but did not nationalize the press, and he did not lay a hand on private property (which he distrusted). Still, he managed to introduce some substantial reforms aside from women's suffrage and Sunday rest, such as the ordered transport of prisoners and the end of conscription. Inspired by the anarchist philosophy of Gustav Landauer, he proposed an ambitious program of cultural and educational "spiritual renewal," which included secular education outside the powerful Church (Bavaria was mostly Catholic). But he ended up pleasing no one. His left wing pushed him toward a communitarian or communist revolution, which he considered premature. The bourgeoisie rejected his social reforms en bloc. The Church opposed his educational reforms. The Bavarian regionalists denounced his Prussian origins. And the nationalists deplored his Jewishness.

One of Eisner's boldest steps was to publish confidential documents that proved the German culpability for the outbreak of the recent war. His hope was to soften the severity of the Allies' demands for reparations, especially with Bavaria. Broad sectors of German and Bavarian society repudiated this policy. That it was a Jew who propounded such allegedly abject arguments fed the myth of the "stab in the back" that "the Jews" would perpetrate against the German fatherland, by handing it over simultaneously to the imperial powers of the West and the Russian Bolsheviks. Weber, of course, did not share in such humbug, but Eisner's program of atonement, of German repentance, seemed to him counterproductive, dishonorable, and unbecoming of a statesman. A classic example of the "ethics of conviction." Weber held Eisner responsible "for bringing peace, not war, into disrepute."

By the time Weber delivered his lecture in late January 1919, Eisner's popularity had been waning rapidly and with it his already limited power. What was most salient in German daily life was unemployment, inflation, the scarcity of basic commodities, transportation paralysis, and the like. He finally had to admit the fragility of his situation and opted to call elections. They were held on January 19, 1919, with disastrous results for his party, the USPD. Eisner promised to leave office. Nine days after, Weber spoke to the students.

2

A nation in turmoil, a polarized and feverish city, a charismatic demagogue in decline, a fragile parliament, a revolution that sought immediately to reach its ultimate apotheosis, a military and nationalist reaction that steadily gathered undetected forces: This historical and biographical situation accounted for Weber's vehemence before his young listeners, romantics of the revolution. He was a prophet-scholar crying out in the wilderness: "Whoever seeks the salvation of his soul and that of others should not do so by the path of politics, whose tasks are very different and can only be accomplished by force."

Weber's criticism of the practitioners of the "ethics of conviction" was based on recent paroxysms of violence:

> Are we not seeing that the Bolshevik ideologues and the Spartacists produce the same results as those of any military dictator precisely because they use this means of politics? How does the government of the councils of workers and soldiers differ from that of any ruler of the old regime if not in the person of the one who holds power and in his amateurism? How do the attacks of most representatives of (supposedly new) ethics on their adversaries differ from the attacks made by any other demagogue?

In Moscow, the Bolsheviks had triumphed. In Berlin, the Spartacists had failed in their assault on power. In Munich, however, the "amateur" Eisner ruled. The "attacks" to which Weber referred had been suffered by himself, when on November 4, 1918, he was interrupted at a rally by two furious representatives of "the new ethics," the literati (Weber's sardonic word) Erich Müsham and the Russian Leninist Max Levien:

> Will it be said that they are distinguished by their noble intention! Well, but what we are talking about here is the means used, and the adversaries being fought also claim for themselves, with total subjective honesty, the nobility of their ultimate intentions.

Although he planned to write a "Sociology of Revolution," which he did not carry out, in his lecture he traced the arc of degradation that he saw unfolding before his eyes. Once the leader — that is, Eisner — unleashes the passions, it is difficult to tame them. They are no longer within his control. Even if he is inspired by a pristine ideal, his action rests on the apparatus that he has formed, and that apparatus is not composed solely and mostly of pure beings, but of "the red guards, the rogues, and the agitators" who would demand internal and external rewards:

> In the conditions of the modern class struggle, the leader has to offer as an internal reward the satisfaction of hatred and the desire for revenge . . . the need to defame the adversary and accuse him of heresy.

The external rewards for the *apparatchiki* were "power, spoils, perks": "let us not deceive ourselves," he pointed out, applying Marxism to the Marxists, "the materialist interpretation of history is not a chariot that is taken and left at whim, and does not stop at the authors of the revolution."

In closing his lecture, knowing perhaps that the young listeners would be carried away by their conviction at the expense of their responsibility, he quoted from Goethe's *Faust*: "The devil is old; become old to understand him." His repeated invocation of "demonic forces" in politics had a vatic tone. He envisioned that, for various reasons, "an Age of

Reaction would be enthroned in less than ten years." And then all the noble goods to which they aspired (and which Weber confessed to longing for) would be no longer attainable. He was issuing a warning. What Germany awaited was not "the dawn of summer, but a polar night of icy harshness and darkness." His young listeners were as dismayed by his message as Toller had been in Lawenstein. Karl Löwith remembered: "Weber tore away all the veils of illusory thinking, and yet no one could fail to feel that at the heart of that clear mind beat a deep human earnestness." But they did not want to surrender the illusion. Max Horkheimer recalled: "Everything was so precise, so scientifically austere, so free of values, that we returned home completely desolate."

The illusion continued, but it was Weber who got it right. Three weeks later, on February 21, 1919, Eisner made his way to parliament to tender his resignation. He never made it. A young aristocrat named Anton Graf von Arco auf Valley assassinated him. The assassin acted to legitimize his German identity in front of the Thule Society, an extreme right-wing nationalist group that had rejected his incorporation because he had a Jewish mother. The "carnival" was just beginning to deserve the adjective "bloody." Although he did not live permanently in Munich until June 1919, Weber witnessed the beginning of the tragedy. The "polar night" was looming on the horizon.

The main eulogy at Eisner's tumultuous funeral was delivered by Gustav Landauer. He compared his friend to Jesus and Jan Huss, who were "executed for stupidity and ambition," and added: "Kurt Eisner, the Jew, was a prophet because he sympathized with the poor and downtrodden, and saw the opportunity and the need to end poverty and prostration." In the days following, Bavaria seemed to enter a state of contrition. Crowds filled the streets. People laid wreaths at the site of the assassination. Even the churches rang their bells in mourning. Eisner became a symbol — charisma frozen in time. The revolutionaries harbored a new hope. Eisner had not shed his blood in vain.

Landauer had spent months of intense activity with Eisner, trying unsuccessfully to encourage him to deepen the "revolutionary intervention", to break definitively with parliamentarianism, representative democracy, the secret ballot, all mechanisms "of the oppressive condition of the past". It was also necessary to break with the Weimar Republic in order to give way to "a union of independent republics based on direct democracy". Yet nothing was to be accomplished by violence. Bavaria could become the cradle of a "new spirit," of a "new humanity," aimed at "salvation" and "redemption." What kind of revolutionary was this forty-eight-year-old who spoke openly in evangelical tones and eschatological concepts? Among his letters from Munich, one stands out that reveals the meaning of his words and his project:

> ... if I was able to endure the horrors of war, it was because I always hoped to have what we have now ... If we have learned anything from this war, it is this: Men only do what is right and necessary when the misery has become unbearable and when it is no longer possible to do wrong. Taking this into account, they will probably not seize this opportunity to save themselves, no matter how much we push them. Rather, they are likely to rush toward disaster. But, sooner or later, the revolution will give the people impetus and fire, a blazing and intense life, the culmination of the moment and of the centuries, as well as a historical existence ... The process that has

now begun will take us much further. It will lead us to what Buddha and Jesus have already taught us: the unity of humanity.

Landauer was an anarchist thinker touched by a messianic mysticism. Like some kabbalists of yore, and like many Christian traditions ancient and modern, he believed that salvation would be preceded by the apocalypse. The apocalypse of the recent war was not enough. One had to suffer more, to die better. But always in the distance there was a flickering light, the end of history, and if it offered "openings" it was necessary to penetrate through that crack, to take advantage of it. The Munich revolution was one of those openings.

Although he spoke and wrote in biblical images, Landauer had little to do with the Judaism of his parents. His training was secular and his readings were eclectic: Meister Eckhart (of whom he wrote profusely), Hölderlin (he theorized about his poems and edited his humanist letters of 1793), Whitman (the individualistic poet of the collective American self), Shakespeare (whom he translated), and the late Tolstoy, the Christian anarchist. Later he would recognize as a mentor Martin Buber, who published his writings in his journal *Der Jude*. Buber's writings and compilations on Hasidism restored Landauer to the Jewish tradition. This heterogeneous mixture of influences and authorities somehow fused in his mind. He saw them as heralds of a possible humanity — foreshadowed in Paris in 1789, 1848, and 1871 — in which the individual and the community are united and realized on a higher, indivisible plane of love and harmony. In that future map of the universal soul there was no room for races or nations, there was room only for cultures. Two concepts abound in his writings: spirit and people, *geist* and *volk*. In his mystical interpretation (and entirely blind to the long career of anti-Semitism in Germany) Landauer saw *geist* and *volk* dialectically incarnated in two spiritual peoples, the Jewish and the German:

> My German quality and my Jewish quality do not get in the way of each other, but do each other a lot of good. Just as two brothers, the firstborn and the youngest, loved by a mother — not in the same way, but with the same intensity — and just as those two brothers live in harmony with each other, whether they have a common path or advances along his own, I experience this strange and intimate duality in unity as something precious.

He defined himself as an anarchist. Above all, an anarchist opposed to communists: "they are pure centralists, like Robespierre," he wrote, referring to the Spartacus League. "Their aspiration has no content, they only know power." The military regime for which they advocate would be the most frightful ever seen in the world. "The dictatorship of the proletariat in arms? I prefer Napoleon!"

His anarchism was essentially pacifist. As much as he was repulsed by Bakunin's violence, he agreed with the constructive models of Kropotkin (whom he knew well in London) on the convergence between the countryside and the city, between farms and factories. He envisioned the mass but voluntary exodus of workers from the city to the countryside. His utopia — an exact reversal of the Weberian state, that "legitimate holder of violence" — was a state without a state, a society of pure fraternal cooperation. The precondition to achieve it was revolution, conceived not as an act of bloodshed but as an educational process, a change in the spirit of the people so that it would recover its purity. In these ideas there was a mysticism of history that aspired to integrate the "I" into a primeval "we."

Like Proudhon, Landauer lived in the world of print: books, magazines, manuscripts, and translations. Separated from the family, from business, from the universities in which he fleetingly studied or from which he was expelled, he worked for a "theater oriented to the people" and above all for *Der Sozialist*, a magazine he edited in various periods over almost twenty years. His anarchist militancy was intense but intermittent. His natural disposition was to philosophical seclusion. *Through Separation to Community*, he titled one of his books. He was a loner who saw the realization of the individual in loving memberships, from the family and the local community to the universal community. His solitude was not that of the ascetic but that of the mystic who seeks the inner voice to announce it to the world and transform it.

In November, 1918, his wife Hedwig Lachmann died of pneumonia, leaving Landauer with their two daughters in a state of desolation that could only be alleviated by revolutionary hope. Landauer heard Eisner's call to join the Munich revolution as the herald of a new era. His charisma was different from Eisner's, more religious and ethereal. The photographer Heinrich Hoffmann, who had captured Eisner's melancholic idealism in a famous image, would do the same with the mystic Landauer. Klemperer could have written the caption when he described him in his diary: "tall, slender, with beautiful, fine features, bearded like Christ, with an energetic forehead and visionary eyes looking into the utopian distance." Before the tragic death of his friend, he had fluctuated several times between extreme exaltation and the greatest despondency. He regretted nothing more than Eisner's defeat in the January 1919 election. He was puzzled by the "overvaluation of the vote." To him, the SPD was simply a counterrevolutionary and militaristic party. Even his mystical faith in the German people collapsed: "What an exultant acclamation of the authoritarian government: in these years it has been a very dubious honor to be German, now it is even more so." Nevertheless, at the first workers' demonstration, hope was reborn.

Eisner, for all his idealism, recognized the limits and admitted the reality: they were a minority. Landauer did not. And yet they did not quarrel. Their bond went beyond politics, an activity that was basically alien to them. Two writers, two editors possessed by the "ethics of conviction": the socialist and the anarchist, the journalist and the thinker, the humorist and the mystic, the idealist and the messianic. At bottom, they were two heterodox Jews pursuing, by different paths, the utopia of universal brotherhood.

After Eisner's death, Munich was in turmoil and Landauer was at the center of events. Weeks later, the Bavarian Parliament elected a new Social Democratic government under Johannes Hoffmann, Eisner's minister of education, who had to face the same tensions, which have been exacerbated by the recent triumph of the Hungarian revolution led by Bela Kun. The deceptive tide of history seemed to favor the revolution once again. In the workers' councils of Munich — which, significantly, were no longer frequented by soldiers, students, or peasants — the voice of the Bakuninian militants was increasingly heard closing ranks with the Communist Party of Germany, the KPD, which, headed by the poet Eugen Leviné, sought to replicate the Bolshevik example. The demand of both in the general assemblies was the establishment of the Räterepublik (a Republic of Councils) equivalent to the original plan of the Soviet Republic, with all that it implied: nationalization of factories, expropriation of land, suppression of "bourgeois parliamentarianism," the judiciary, and the free press, and immediate collaboration with "the glorious pioneers of world liberation in Russia." Landauer, for whom the Communists were "tragic fools" possessed of "Marxist madness," opposed the motion, which was then postponed by "the masses."

The Hoffmann government, for its part, took its social democratic vocation seriously. The Austrian economist Otto Neurath, its prestigious minister of economics, wanted to centralize the economy, concentrate it on the generation of commodities, and — as a gesture of genuine openness towards the anarchists — to finance communes in the Bavarian countryside. The purpose was to demonstrate to the majorities that the collectivist experiment could work. Landauer, a disciple of Kropotkin and therefore a supporter of rural anarcho-socialism, favored it. The radicals did not want to depend on government handouts. They demanded political autonomy for these communes. This project was also rejected by the "masses." Finally, the tension between the government and the workers' councils reached the streets. The shadow of repression (and his own revolutionary mysticism) led Landauer to utter a memorable sentence: "In the whole of natural history, I have not encountered a creature that I find more repugnant than the Social Democratic Party."

Hoffmann opted to leave Munich and settle in Bamberg. Munich remained a revolutionary stronghold. Against Landauer's opinion, and without the participation of the Communists (who were waiting their turn), the "masses" finally, on April 6, 1919, decreed the establishment of the First Republic of Bavarian Councils, an anarchist idyll that would not shed a drop of blood and wanted to create a new world, like God, in seven days. At the head of the government would be none other than Ernst Toller. Although some members of the cabinet had a more professional profile, the highest authority was held by the dreamy Landauer, who lived the anarchist paradox of exercising power from the repudiation of power:

> I am now the people's delegate for propaganda, education, science, arts and other things. If I have a few weeks, I hope to accomplish something. However, most likely I will only have a few days and then all this will have been like a dream.

In those days, Klemperer interviewed him: "A modest man in a black overcoat, with black hair and the tone of a prophet," Landauer defined himself as a "non-political politician." He justified the Räterepublik as "the only way of 'salvation' to honor the memory of Karl Liebknecht, his murdered friend, and to put an end to the Weimar lie . . ." The comparison with Eisner was inevitable, as was his Weberian conclusion about the inexorable presence of force:

> An idealist, like him; bohemian, like him; poet like him; and like him, miles away from all real political needs . . . His hands as clean of blood and money as those of Einser. He will surely be forced, like Eisner, to engage in acts of violence himself or to resign by force, violently, by the action of others.

Toller called this anarchist dream "the amorous republic." Although there was no shortage of utopian measures (issuing money with an expiration date) or delusional ideas (declaring war on Switzerland for refusing to sell arms), the government concentrated on socializing education and the theater rather than the economy, and the person in charge of this spiritual transformation was Landauer. His priority was to reform the university, so he suspended classes until the summer. He established a Revolutionary University Council, a libertarian community of students, parents, and teachers. The cornerstone of the curriculum would be Walt Whitman: "Every ten-year-old Bavarian child will recite it by heart." He planned to promote a communal cultural life instead of the traditional isolation of artists. He planned to abolish the law faculty (which would be dedicated instead only to training public servants) and to legislate socialist teaching, "so long muzzled in the universities." The professors of economics were to be all socialists. Naturally, Landauer wanted to close the doors to the "arch-reactionary Max Weber".

His coercive measures were neither light nor democratic nor liberal, but compared to those of the Bakuninian anarchists they were merely pious, almost cosmetic. A mystic to the end, Landauer had no thought of destroying capital or church by the violence of the state, which he considered inherently illegitimate, inhuman, and immoral. His utopia was to be reached by the cultural evangelization of "the people," who would find in the spirit of communal life its true and full realization. On April 12 he wrote to a colleague:

> Although it is possible that our lives will be short, the wish I have, and it is a wish you share with me, is that we leave lasting effects in Bavaria . . . so that we can hope that, when authoritarianism returns, among discerning circles it will be said that we did not have a bad start during the Räterepublik and that it would not have been bad if we had been allowed to continue our work. This is in case we collapse.

They collapsed two days later.

On Palm Sunday, April 14, the Second Räterepublik was declared in Munich. The third period of the "bloody carnival" had arrived, the time of "the Russians," as they were known from their country of origin: Comrades Eugene Leviné, Tobias Axelrod, and Max Levien. (Leviné and Axelrod were Jews, Levien was not.) The first had participated in the revolution of 1905 in Russia and in the founding of the Spartacus League. The latter, an expert in information and intelligence work, was such a close collaborator of Lenin that he had traveled with him on the famous sealed train to the Finland Station. Dr. Levien, an intellectual and military man, an early Spartacist and also close to Lenin, was the toughest of the three. When Klemperer complained about the shortage of milk in Munich, he heard him remark that "he was indifferent" because "it nourished above all the bourgeois children, and their survival was of no interest to us." At another point Levien bluntly stated: "The middle class and the capitalist bourgeoisie in Germany does not number more than one hundred thousand people. Their representatives in the National Assembly keep the people in ignorance and stupidity. To spill a little more of their blood makes no difference."

None had any doubts about the justification of the means to achieve the end. After what they called the "impostor republic" of the anarchists, the dictatorship of the proletariat was at last opening the way. Their plans were radical: "in every house where there are twelve bourgeois, we will immediately install twenty proletarians". The expectations were even greater: "There will be no more prostitution because only the bourgeoisie is guilty of its existence." The measures were categorical: property was confiscated; cars, jewelry, bank accounts were seized; the free press was shut down so that there was no news from abroad, only the newsletter of the Central Committees. As a consequence, Klemperer noted in his diary, "postal services and trains, industry and trade were almost completely stopped." Munich was under siege.

Although he never changed his opinion of the communists — "their aspiration is power" — Landauer offered them cooperation in confronting the counterrevolution. After two days he would exchange a letter of "mutual repudiation" with them and withdraw, but Klemperer managed to visit him in his office. They did not talk about French literature (their shared passion) but about the aborted educational redemption. He was struck by Landauer's fastidious disdain for the practical affairs of his office: "he had thrown all the day's correspondence into a laundry basket next to his desk: a high school was asking permission to devote a day to sports; the gymnasium of a girls' school needed repairs; a preparatory school needed to replace its recently deceased prefect." The liberal Klemperer — a perceptive psychologist — concluded that Landauer was less equipped for politics than Eisner himself, and judged him in Weberian terms:

> He is an entertainer, a journalist, gifted with great talent but a childish talent. But even the most talented child can inflict harm when he plays irresponsibly with adult objects. He is a child, and I hope for his sake (and for all of ours) that no one ends up turning him into a martyr.

By then civil war had broken out. The Leviné government appointed his predecessor Toller as Minister of War, who marched to confront, with temporary success, Hoffman's troops. (Toller refused to execute the defeated.) But Hoffman would eventually win the support of Berlin. The army of General Noske and the *Freikorps*, which included several future Nazi officers such as Rudolf Hess and Ernest Röhm, intervened in an offensive against Munich.

The final battle began on April 27 and was resolved in a few days. Everybody revealed their true character. The "Russians" Levien and Axelrod fled, leaving their troops without courage or defense. Leviné went underground. Toller, the brave pacifist-turned-general, learned with horror of the imminent execution of ten prisoners, several of them belonging to the ultranationalist Thule Society. He was unable to stop it. "Once the crime had been committed," Klemperer noted, "they could not expect forgiveness." The revenge would be atrocious. More than a thousand people were executed, most of them innocent or alien to the government.

Among them was Gustav Landauer. His friends implored him to leave Munich. He had the chance to go to Switzerland and join his two daughters, Charlotte, twenty-four, and Brigitte, thirteen, who lived in a nearby town. Revolutionary hope never left him, but evidently it did not include his own survival. After the assassination of Karl Liebknecht and Rosa Luxemburg, he sent his daughters a remarkable letter:

> It is because of you, my daughters, that I remain alive. I will not yield. It is for my *Ethos* and my hopes for humanity that I oppose the methods of violence and revenge, and that I work instead for the passionate but peaceful creation of socialism. Do not fear at all! I will continue on my path, as I have done up to now.

When the civil war broke out, Landauer urged his family to take refuge with an uncle, who "would gladly receive them."

On May 1, shock troops raided the house and seized him. The next day some soldiers executed him, after insulting him ("dirty Bolshevik"), humiliating him, and torturing him mercilessly. Some testimonies report that he said: "I have not betrayed you. You do not know the terrible degree to which you have been betrayed." Others affirmed that his final words were: "So kill me. And to think that you are human . . ." In 1925 the anarcho-syndicalists in Munich erected a monument to Landauer, with an epitaph taken from his own work: "It is time to create a different martyr, not heroic but discreet, an unpretentious martyr, who offers an example of life." The Nazis destroyed the monument in 1933.

All the revolutionary leaders in Munich died in a similar way. Leviné was executed in June 1919, shouting, "Hail to the Revolution" in front of the firing squad. The poet Erich Müsham, who founded the anarchist magazine *Kain*, was jailed for fifteen years and then brutally murdered in a concentration camp in 1934. Axelrod and Levien died in Stalin's purges. Toller, jailed until 1925, became a successful exponent of Expressionist theater, but was exiled after Hitler's seizure of power in 1933, and in 1939 committed suicide at the Mayflower Hotel in New York. Only one of the main protagonists would survive: Ret Marut, the editor of the anarchist magazine *Der Ziegelbrenner* (*The Brick Burner*). Under different identities, he would end up living a secret life in Mexico, writing novels of high social and revolutionary content, many of them about the indigenous people of Chiapas, that were widely read in Mexico; we remember him now as B. Traven, who wrote the screenplay for *The Treasure of the Sierra Madre* based on his own novel. The paradox of the Bavarian Revolution was to conclude in the country of a revolutionary peasant who was an enemy of power and communism, a Mexican figure so close to anarchism that Landauer, years before, had written about him: Emiliano Zapata.

Weber also was to die before his time. Back in Munich since June 1919, after very brief and unsuccessful incursions into politics, he witnessed the virtual takeover of the university and the city by xenophobic, nationalist, militaristic, and anti-Semitic authorities, all driven by the passions that he detested. Setting himself up as an example of the Protestant ethic that he was then researching, he tirelessly returned to writing, lecturing, issuing liberal and unpopular opinions that earned him the (unfair) label of "godfather of the Soviet Republic." (And all this in the context of family dramas unbearable even for a man of his stoic temper: the suicide of his widowed sister, who left four children, and his tortured love affair with Else Jaffe, a former disciple, wife of his colleague Edgar Jaffe, with whom he edited the legendary journal *Archiv für Sozialwisenschaft und Sozialpolitik*.) Weber was particularly offended by what he described as "the mad anti-Semitism" that poisoned even his colleagues. And to show his moral independence, he acted nobly towards his former adversaries. "The great philo-semite" — as Leo Löwenthal, a future founder of the Frankfurt School, described him — successfully defended Otto Neurath in the courts. He did the same with Toller, arguing that "in an act of rage, God made him a politician." (Thomas Mann also testified on Toller's behalf.) Moreover, he publicly recognized Eisner's good faith and decisively defended several other imprisoned leaders, explaining before the judges the meaning of the "ethics of conviction." It was for that reason that he had not included his name in the printed version of "Politics as a Vocation."

Weber's prophecy was more than fulfilled. The Munich revolution, with all its generosity and idealism, proved that, indeed, "good does not follow good, but often the opposite." Demagogues, socialists, pacifists, anarchists, communists, many in good faith, had committed the greatest political sin: the sin of unreality. No, "the masses," i.e. the working masses, were not even remotely in the majority in Bavaria, nor in Germany. No, the political vocation did not consist in devising plans of salvation by neglecting the annoying practical problems. No, the factories did not conform to the socialist order but to capitalist continuity, under other bosses: bureaucratic and military. No, not all the followers of Eisner and Landauer were idealists like them: many quickly changed sides and sought their "internal and external rewards" at the side of the new winners on the ultra-right. No, the real enemy of the dreamers of the revolution was not the Social Democratic Party — which they condemned as lukewarm and reformist — but the pan-Germanic militarism whose reaction Weber foresaw but the revolutionaries did not. As for the young students who would create the Frankfurt School, they announced the definitive decline of the West, but to save themselves they migrated to the United States, where they freely consolidated their school of thought, in many ways contrary to the economic order of the country that hosted them. The revolutionaries preferred to believe that the liberal, constitutional, and parliamentary order proposed by Weber (along lines similar to his friend, the Austrian-Jewish political and legal philosopher Hans Kelsen) had been forever liquidated. But by attacking and banning the "arch-reactionary Weber," they opened the door to the real reactionary: Carl Schmitt.

And yet, granting the political unreality that blinded those Romantic revolutionaries, was Weber entirely right in his condemnation? I think so, but with nuances. There were gradations among them that Weber failed to recognize. Eisner, the socialist, was a German Kerensky, never a German Trotsky. Neither was the anarchist Landauer, a utopian mystic who detested the will to power of the Marxists. In political terms, one might ask: was Eisner's pacifist stance so irresponsible? If it persisted, wouldn't it have softened the punitive clauses of the Treaty of Versailles? On the other hand, were Landauer's communal living projects unrealizable, at least on a small scale? (Consider the young kibbutzim in Israel.) In his lecture "Science as a Vocation," delivered in 1917, Weber had assumed the impossibility of restoring "enchantment" to the secular post-Enlightenment world. Eisner and Landauer, on the other hand, stuck with enchantment, in the form of their utopian hope. Eisner and Landauer practiced the "ethics of conviction" to the limit. They sacrificed their lives for it.

Weber died in June 1920, a victim of pneumonia. Fury against the Treaty of Versailles (where he was present) and political exhaustion were not unrelated to his end; though he never lost his inner strength, the loneliness of the battle surely weakened him. He did his part in defending a constitutional and parliamentary path for Germany from the forces of unbound revolutionary passion and crude dictatorship. But even he could not foresee the diabolical extremes to which both forces would converge in the totalitarianisms of the twentieth century. Was this the "polar night" he foretold?

3

There was something else that those radical leaders did not see: the centuries-old monster of the German hatred of the Jews. Weber did see it, since the beginning of the revolution: "separatism is raising its head," he wrote to Else Jaffe, "and it is going to embellish itself with anti-Semitism." In Munich, especially in the wake of the failed revolution, that hatred reached insane proportions. That is the subject of *Hitler's Munich*, the admirably researched and deeply saddening book by the historian Michael Brenner. His subject is not so much the Munich Revolution as the tragedy of its leaders, almost all of them Jews, and the turning of that revolutionary dawn into the human pyre of Nazism. Brenner seeks to answer three questions: What was the relationship of these leaders with Judaism? How did Bavarian society react to their rise? How did Munich develop from a liberal and "healthy and lively" place into a city that Thomas Mann — by then the famous author of *Buddenbrooks*, who was gradually awakening from his Apollonian apoliticism — described as "blood poisoned by anti-Semitic nationalism"?

Given the pervasiveness of the old anti-Semitism in that city and that time, Eisner's attitude is puzzling. As he experienced the revolution as the awakening of humanity, his office received an avalanche of vexatious letters. The predominance of Jewish leaders in the movement unleashed an ominous propaganda that grew after the crushing of the revolution: graffiti in synagogues and cemeteries, cruel caricatures, editorial commentaries, all riddled with the old commonplaces of anti-Semitism — the Bolshevik Jew, capitalist, exploiter, usurer, stateless. The Jew was the "enemy within" who had stabbed Germany in the back, bringing about its defeat in the War. Eisner and his comrades despised all this; but as Brenner shows, they awakened the beast. The tragic fact is that their movement changed the historical place of the "Jewish Question": although Jews constituted only around one percent of the population, the anti-Semitic waves that had broken out in 1819 and 1848 came to occupy the center of the Bavarian stage in 1919, never to leave it again — until, that is, the defeat of the Third Reich in 1945.

As Brenner documents, blaming Eisner and his collaborators for the bloody outcome of the revolution was the predictable reaction of various sectors: the victims, not the victimizers, became responsible for their own deaths. Max Weber did not concur in this widespread judgment. A student of ancient Judaism, he found inspiration in the Prophets, the Psalms, and the Book of Job. He lived surrounded by Jewish colleagues, disciples, and friends. Sociologically, Weber attributed the revolutionary proclivity of some Jews to the ancestral condition of belonging to a "pariah people" yearning for redemption. There is a grain of truth in this, but only a grain. The Jewish revolutionaries of Munich were not acting as Jews but as people with a universal vocation. They represented a minority, a marginal and heterodox fringe, what Isaac Deutscher later called the "non-Jewish Jew."

In Brenner's vivid and moving portraits of the revolutionaries, this heterodox factor is decisive. Despite their ideological differences, what characterizes the two main figures, Eisner and Landauer, as well as Mühsam, Levien, and Toller, is the secular eschatological aspiration that was typical of many Jews on the margins of Judaism, all of them heirs of Spinoza, Heine and Marx. "The Jewish Messiah is the moral humanity of the historical future," Eisner had written to his teacher Hermann Cohen. In November 1918, Landauer had asked Martin Buber to study Jewish participation in the revolution. He was convinced of its significance: "The prophets are more relevant today for understanding the Jews than the momentary experiences of their brittle lives." Speaking of the revolutionaries he was speaking also of himself. For all these reasons, when, days before Eisner's murder, Buber met him and Landauer in Munich, his presentiment on leaving them was one of theological desolation:

> As for Eisner, to be with him was to peer into the tormented passion of his divided Jewish soul; nemesis shone from his glittering surface; he was a marked man. Landauer, by dint of the greatest spiritual effort, was keeping up his faith in him and protected him, a shield-bearer terribly moving in his selflessness. The whole thing, an unspeakable Jewish tragedy.

The secularization of messianism, however glamorous it now seems, was by no means the prevailing temper in German Jewish life. Brenner provides irrefutable evidence for this. The Jewish community of Munich — a very small minority, eleven thousand out of a total of six hundred thousand inhabitants in Bavaria — felt as German as the Germans, and created companies such as the Löwenbrau Brewery and soccer teams such as Bayern Munich. It was they who were most concerned about the effects of the revolution. "The Trotskys make the revolution and the Bronsteins pay the price," they used to say. Consequently, the communal authorities and their publications publicly distanced themselves from the Räterepublik; the rabbis supported the conservative party; and in the extreme, there appeared cases of anti-Jewish Jewish intellectuals possessed by what Theodor Lessing called in 1930 *Judische Selbsthaas,* or Jewish self-hatred, whose twisted and influential trajectory Brenner records in painful detail. Eisner's murderer, a half-Jewish far-right nationalist, was not alone in being ashamed of his roots and acting accordingly. Brenner cites the case of Rahel Lydia Rabinowitz, a famous Jewish doctor who published a repudiation of Eisner in which she pointed out that Jews should have no more political representation in Bavaria than that corresponding to their minuscule demographic weight. This text was so influential that in 1942

Hitler remembered it: "In 1919 a Jewess wrote 'what Eisner is doing now will be passed on to us Jews'." With clear reference to the systematic murder of the Jews then in progress, Hitler added: "This is a rare case of clear-sighted foresight."

Several decisive figures of the twentieth century crystallized their ideas, convictions, and prejudices in the stormy days of Munich. For Heinrich Mann, "the hundred days of the Eisner government brought forth more ideas, more joys for reason, more animation of the spirits, than that of fifty years before." His brother Thomas disagreed — in those years he was a political work-in-progress that he later documented in *Confessions of an Unpolitical German* — but the events shook him enough to dust off the manuscript of *The Magic Mountain* and begin to rework it. Brenner records the case of the Vatican nuncio Eugenio Pacceli, who sent regular reports of the changes in Germany that ominously foreshadow his indulgence of the Nazis decades later as Pope Pius XII: Eisner he described as "a Galician Jew who was repeatedly sentenced to prison for political crimes," and the revolution as part of the "Jewish-Bolshevik global conspiracy" based on "the idea of a Jewish world government." And just one year after the events Carl Schmitt published *Dictatorship*, his vindication of an executive power capable of suspending the constitutional order at will to deal with exceptional circumstances, such as revolutionary threats. It is difficult to imagine his rabid and permanent anti-Semitism, his hatred of "Jewish debaters" (beginning with "Spinoza, the first liberal"), without the Munich experience.

But perhaps the greatest disaster of the Bavarian revolution was the appearance of Hitler. He had arrived in Munich in November 1918. Several biographers have dated the origins of his anti-Semitism to his youthful years in Vienna; others, such as Ian Kershaw, locate its beginnings in Munich. Hitler electrified the crowds in the very same locations where Eisner had electrified "the masses" months before. Was the fascist demagogue emulating the socialist demagogue? Weber's theory of charisma was now vindicated by both extremes. Is that Hitler in the blurry photographs of Eisner's funeral? Between September 1919 and November 1923, Hitler gave one hundred and eighty-eight speeches, one hundred and thirty-two of them in Munich. In July 1923, in the run-up to Hitler's ill-fated putsch, Thomas Mann remarked that Munich is "Hitler's city." One of those bewitched was Heinrich Hoffmann, the author of the Eisner and Landauer images. He became Hitler's official photographer and in 1925 captured his delirious gesticulations in front of the mirror. The pathetic photographer of charisma.

Just as the assassination of Eisner foreshadowed that of Walter Rathenau in 1922, the experience of 1919 heralded the collapse of the Weimar Republic and reverberated in various times and countries, when the contempt of the various left-wing currents for parliamentary politics outweighed their sense of alertness to the advance of militarist and ultranationalist reaction. History repeated itself in Spain, where ideological hatreds and disdain for liberal democracy — identical to the anti-democratic contempt of Landauer and the Communists — weakened the republic and strengthened the nationalist right, leading to the triumph of Franco, who reigned for four decades. In Latin America the pattern was replicated several times, notably in Chile in the 1970s and in Venezuela in the 1990s.

And the cycle is not yet spent. Who would have believed

that our liberal societies would now be faced with dangers of which Munich 1919 is a cautionary example? But here we are, drowning in what is politely called populism. The Weberian category of the charismatic authoritarian leader is ubiquitous. (I suppose I should exempt Putin, who represents the uncharismatic authoritarian leader.) Regardless of their ideological sign, tinged to different degrees with charisma, convinced of the purity of their convictions or secretly cynical about them, Chavez and Lopez Obrador, Trump and Orban and Modi, do not correspond to the strong democratic president bounded by parliament (Weber's conception) but to the dictator of the Schmittian friend-enemy thesis. Some countries that have not yet entirely forgotten the lessons of World War II (France, England, Italy, Germany) have so far resisted the autocratic temptation, but not by much, and the United States, shockingly, is in real danger of succumbing to it. 1919, 2025: Who would have imagined that the postwar warnings of Adorno and Horkheimer, German students in Munich during the convulsion, in *The Authoritarian Personality* would become valid in the run-up to the two-hundred-and fiftieth anniversary of American independence?

Populist leaders are not the only ones who now regard politics through the flattening and darkening and polarizing Schmittian lens. It is shared by many university students in the United States and Europe, imbued with a new and more inarticulate version of the "ethics of conviction." But which convictions? Unlike the revolutionaries of 1919, who impatiently dismissed Weber's message because they sought to build a world of social and economic justice, today's students seem to confuse altruism with narcissism. Those young people joined the revolution and, like Eisner and Landauer, many of them died for it. What risks do the insurrectionists of the

Ivy League run? (They demonstrate for their own amnesty!) Other students of 1919 turned away from active politics, not to escape their responsibility as intellectuals but to elaborate a theoretical construction of social utopia. What is the utopia of today's youth? They display nothing more than the ecstasy of their own sensibility: what is good for what I feel is good for humanity. As David Rieff has written, "the political emergency merges with the psychological emergency."

But there is one cause that obsesses them the most. It is the Palestinian cause, a perfectly legitimate cause were it not for the fact that it drifts too easily into support for Hamas and anti-Semitism. The tents and the banners in the quads can seem merely like an expression of sensibility, except that there is nothing merely symbolic about the global eruption of contemporary anti-Semitism: if contemporary anti-Semitism does not justify looking away from the carnage in Gaza, neither does the carnage in Gaza justify looking away from anti-Semitism, not to speak of the Hamas pogrom itself. All this is yet another serious echo of 1919. If the idealists of Munich believed that the triumph of their revolution would open an era of universal concord that by itself would dissolve the ancient hatred of the Jews, we, the postwar Jewish generations, believed with a similar naiveté that the Holocaust — the reality of it and the memory of it — would overcome the millenarian prejudice or at least open an indefinite truce. It did not happen for many reasons, because of the hostile and murderous response to the establishment of the State of Israel. The Nazi inspiration of many Palestinian leaders, religious and secular, has been abundantly documented. In the decades since, there has been progress toward peace, with the conclusion of peace treaties with Arab states and the current work toward a grand bargain with Saudi Arabia — but the Israeli-Palestinian conflict remains trapped in atavisms and hatreds. In that conflict the Schmittian perspective grows larger, not least for the addition of theological animosities.

A long time has passed since 1919, but not long enough. Weber's "Politics as a Vocation" is now a twenty-first-century document, as valid now as when he spoke the words in the castle. It is a call to keep reason and a clear head in volatile times like these, in times of confusion and despair. It helps us to recognize that the apocalypse is not a historical inevitability but a choice. Only heroic spirits, said Weber, filled with a conviction guided by responsibility, could overcome the polar night that he foresaw. Fortunately for our recent ancestors, there was no shortage of heroes in the democracies of the West, who dared to look "the tragic warp of history" in the face and brought the dawn with them. Who are the heroes now? Must Volodymyr Zelensky lead us all? As I strolled the streets of Munich recently, I noted occasions for hope: its memorials to Eisner and Landauer, for example, and the Munich Documentation Center for the History of National Socialism, with its exhibits about the Munich Revolution, its hopes and its horrors, which now stands near the place where the headquarters of the Nazi Party once stood. And in the immediate aftermath of October 7, in the midst of the war in Ukraine, I saw people in its main square listen to a troupe of Jewish singers intoning melodies in Yiddish while in the Old Town Hall of Marienplatz the flags of Germany, Ukraine, and Israel fly together. All is far from lost. But the struggle against a new polar night is far from over.

JAMES TRAUB

Is There Any Excuse for Honesty?

As part of the research for a book that I am writing on civic education, I recently interviewed Dr. Matthew Spalding, the dean of the Van Andel School of Government of Hillsdale College, the conservative Christian institution that has supplied much of the intellectual heft for the war against "woke" education. I wanted to talk to Spalding about *The 1776 Report*, a highly patriotic account of America's founding principles which the Trump administration had commissioned as a counter-blow to *The 1619 Project*, which places slavery and racism at the heart of the American story. (I find both insupportable and tendentious.) Spalding was the document's chief author. I had been pursuing Hillsdale officials for the six months since I had written to Larry Arnn, the university's president. I had done so in my own peculiar way, which often involves the hope that I can disarm with candor. "I will say, not to be coy," I wrote, "that I do not share Hillsdale's politics, but I do share a good deal of your pedagogical principles." That was true: Hillsdale also runs a network of "classical" charter schools, which use an old-fashioned Great Books curriculum to which I am very much drawn. I share Hillsdale's view of how to teach, though not of what to teach. And since even the most cursory Google search would have revealed my politics, I felt that it was in my interest to admit the obvious and then use whatever credit I would gain for honesty to demonstrate my bona fides. In the ensuing months I sought to persuade Hillsdale's chief of communications, sincerely, that I was the liberal most likely to give Hillsdale a fair shake. Apparently I succeeded. As I prepared to interview Dr. Spalding, I was feeling rather proud of myself for having trolled the waters so laboriously and finally hauled in a prize fish. More would come; this was to be the first of a series of interviews.

Dr. Spalding and I spoke by Zoom for slightly over an hour; the head of communications hovered silently and invisibly in the background. We found much to agree on: that the great defect of progressive schooling was not its ideological content but its lack of content; that most teachers want to teach, not to indoctrinate. Dr. Spalding told me about his graduate U.S. History class, in which, he said, he "tried to understand history as it was understood by those who were there," rather than by imposing contemporary understandings on the past. We seemed to be getting along swimmingly.

Now, going back over my notes, I can see, at approximately the forty-minute mark, where our conversation began to go off the rails. Spalding was talking about the natural law tradition upon which the Founders had drawn — the view that truths inhere in "nature" and are thus permanent and universal. Cultural conservatives argue that America lost its way when twentieth-century progressives abandoned natural law for "relativism." One of the contributions that *The 1776 Report* makes to this debate is the bizarre and almost mischievous claim that John Calhoun, the theoretician of racial superiority, was the polluted fountain from which modern identity politics springs — because he thought rights inhered not in nature but "in groups or races according to historical evolution." I said to Dr. Spalding, "Do you *really* think all this goes back to Calhoun?" My notes show: "Yes, defends Calhoun." Then I asked Spalding if he believed, as the report implies, that the ubiquity of slavery in the eighteenth century should govern our judgment of our slaveholding Founders. My notes report, "Yes, palliating that slavery widespread" — that is, we should not judge these men harshly for doing what so many others did at the time.

In short, I argued with my subject. I mistook the strategic candor that had enabled me to overcome skepticism or suspicion for the kind of unguarded exchange that is fraught with danger. I *knew* that. I had told myself beforehand that I must not do what I so often do in this kind of situation. I should instead show curiosity, pose open-ended questions, murmur ambiguously. If I argued adversarially, as I knew from painful past experience, I might snap the thread I had so laboriously tied with Hillsdale's publicist. And that is exactly what happened. After the interview, she went silent. No more interviews with Spalding or any of his colleagues. I had done it again. Why? Why would I give a sharp yank on the pole when I knew it might let my fish off the hook?

In *The Journalist and The Murderer,* which appeared in 1989, Janet Malcolm famously described misrepresentation, including lying, as a dark trade secret of her profession, too perilous to admit in public but too precious to abandon. She described the journalist as "a kind of confidence man, preying on people's vanity, ignorance or loneliness, gaining their trust and betraying them without remorse." I still remember how I recoiled when I read that. Betrayal, I thought, was a choice, not an imperative. Everyone has a justifying ideology to excuse self-serving behavior. Ours — the pursuit of truth — may have been the best of them, but we were still giving ourselves license to behave in a way that, as Malcolm readily conceded, would be regarded as inexcusable in almost any other context. And yet . . .

In almost half a century as a journalist, I have let so many fish off so many hooks. In the days that followed my interview with Dr. Spalding, I began to ask myself the opposite of the question I had asked before: what, for a journalist, at least one in my line of work, can justify not lying, or at least not temporizing in a way that achieves the same effect? Malcolm had offered a worldly pragmatism that I could neither fully accept nor convincingly refute. As I thought back over my own work, I realized that I had migrated across the borderlands of honesty in a way that I could not make sense of morally and could only dimly grasp as a matter of personal choice. I was, in fact, a much better liar than I let on to myself. But in other settings I seemed to choose — no, not choose but adopt — an almost suicidal candor. Different settings seemed to provoke different intuitive reactions.

I have not consulted with other writers about this strange, semi-conscious question. But I cannot believe that I am alone in my perplexity. What Malcolm presented as a matter of perverse moral courage must surely be a perpetual negotiation for most of us, a bargain with ourselves about what is permissible in the name of truth-telling. Or maybe it is a negotiation between ambition and fear, or between a truth-telling impulse and guile. It is certainly an equation without a solution — including, I think, Malcolm's. Perhaps the best I can do is to open up my own life to inspection.

In 2005, Condoleezza Rice, then George W. Bush's Secretary of State, agreed to talk to me about UN Secretary General Kofi Annan, about whom I was then writing a book. We had never met before; perhaps she did so as a favor to Annan, then reviled on the right for his opposition to the war in Iraq. We met in a lovely yellow parlor adjacent to her office. The Secretary, a product of the extremely rectitudinous black middle class of Jim Crow-era Birmingham, sat perfectly erect, her hands folded in her lap. She rapidly disposed of most of the questions that I had planned in advance. The upshot was, no, there was no tension between the United Nations and the Bush Administration. Finally I raised the delicate issue of UN Ambassador John Bolton, a professed UN-hater widely rumored to have been appointed over Rice's objection. I knew that Bolton had been doing everything in his power to wreck efforts at UN reform. Did he, I asked, have "his own agenda?" Rice stiffened — or, more precisely, stiffened further. "This is silly," she said. *She* was Secretary of State.

It would have been a dereliction of professional duty not to have asked Rice about Bolton, even though it would have been equally unprofessional for her to have given me an honest answer. That is why so much high-level political reporting feels ritualistic. But now I had the bit in my teeth — or perhaps I had run out of questions with time left in the interview. What's more, I had been living inside the UN, where everyone hated Bolton. And more, I am an argumentative person. I pelted Rice with questions about Bolton's role. Was it true that Bolton had been holding back-channel conversations with other opponents of reform? "These are not conversations that I am party to, have time to be party to, or have any desire to be party to," Rice said — the equivalent, for her, of a tirade, though she had not raised her voice by a decibel. The interview didn't so much end as die out. I was dismissed and sent to a vestibule to be escorted downstairs. There — for the first time and only time in my life — I literally banged my head against a wall.

When I ask myself why I have conducted so many fruitless and self-defeating arguments where circumspection and suavity would be in my interest, I come up with a number of different answers, some more embarrassing than others. I consider the one that I think applies to Rice relatively excusable: I appear to hold the belief that arguing shows that you take the other person seriously. People who operate in the realm of ideas should look forward to a vigorous truth-seeking discussion. Wasn't that Socrates' implicit premise? Isn't that how we advance the truth? In a profile of Larry Summers, I once wrote that the then-president of Harvard "says he has always believed that the best way to show your respect for your fellow man is to argue with him, generally until one or the other of you is forced to admit the error of your ways."

Of course the abrasive Summers makes a poor role model for someone in my line of work — or possibly his own, since the Harvard Corporation finally tired of the fights he picked with his own faculty, among many others, and forced him out of office. Many people, like Condoleezza Rice, regard arguing as a breach of politesse. Perhaps, if I can indulge in an ethnocentric generalization, journalists need to be especially on their guard with Gentiles. I cannot call to mind any instance in which I got in trouble arguing with a Jewish subject — Summers, Richard Holbrooke, even Abe Foxman, the volcanic former head of the Anti-Defamation League. The whole arguing-with-God thing does seem to have some basis in sociological fact, and it is certainly conducive to valuable journalistic interviews. I thought that Dr. Spalding and I were doing just fine. But leaving aside the somewhat dubious matters of ethnic predisposition, Dr. Spalding would have had every reason to be on his guard as he fenced with a certified liberal. As he sat at his desk in his suit and tie with his PR person lurking offscreen, I had the distinct impression that he had not expected to be put to the test, did not very much enjoy it, and possibly resented the effort he was having to expend when he had a graduate school to run. Or, to be perfectly honest, that thought occurred to me later; perhaps I would have sheared off if I had noticed it in real time.

It is also true that every so often candor proves more effective than seduction. Malcolm describes this approach as "the higher ingratiation," but I am thinking of actual artlessness, which has a seductive power of its own. For my very first book, about a ludicrous Reagan-era scandal involving a company called Wedtech, I went to San Francisco to interview the company's lawyer, a very odd character who spelled his name in lowercase — e. robert wallach. We met in the North End cafe where wallach hung out. Suspicious, for good reason, wallach interviewed me. Where had I grown up, where had I gone to school, what had been my life path? Characteristically, I didn't think to adjust my life story to whatever expectations he might have. That night wallach called to say that my pedigree implied elite scorn for his hardscrabble background. He would not cooperate. I was nonplussed, and I said, "I don't think you have any obligation to talk to me, and I'm not going to hold it against you that you won't." Was that the higher ingratiation at work? Maybe, though I wouldn't have said so then. The next day wallach called me back and said that he had changed his mind. We spoke for hours. By contrast, Wedtech's CEO and the chief perpetrator of the scandal proved to be such a mooncalf that he spoke to me without conditions — the journalist's unearned gift. I'm guessing that neither was very happy with the outcome.

I do think that wallach was reacting to something real. It is very hard to say whether the reason that I am not comfortable misrepresenting myself is that I am a literal-minded person who lacks the talent for it or whether I lack the talent because I have an inner compunction against lying. Although the first is plainly true, the second is my most effective counter to Malcolm's accusation. I was born in 1954; my political consciousness began to dawn at the age of fifteen. I was just young enough to escape the draft, but old enough to go to Washington to attend the Moratorium to End The War in Vietnam in November, 1969. I was a political person; we were all political persons. Very few of the aspiring writers my age became novelists; we became journalists because we wanted to right wrongs. It wasn't only that we wanted to tell the truth — many of us, most of us, really did — but that we wanted to tell the truth about politics and policy rather than the far more ambiguous truths about human nature which were the domain of an older generation. Malcolm had a novelist's awareness of the elusive nature of truth, a Balzacian sensitivity to the ways that each of us is deluded by vanity or ambition or desperate need. I read novels at night, but for my day job I used to write about schools and race and welfare policy; later, the UN and foreign affairs; today, civic education. Perhaps I am both more literal-minded as a person and less ambivalent about my pursuit of what I regard as the truth.

Of course these questions do not always arise. I have spent much of my life plunged into situations that I barely understand, dependent on my subjects to enlighten me. The questions that I asked the soldiers with whom I was embedded in Afghanistan while writing about "counter-insurgency theory" in 2010 — or for that matter the ones I posted to the great Mariano Rivera of the New York Yankees when I wrote about him that same year — were neither artful nor pointed; they were efforts to learn. But unless you are a newspaper reporter, which I was not, you write with, or towards, a set of beliefs. And those beliefs often conflict with those of your subject.

For my book on the United Nations I spent a year essentially living inside the institution, attending high-level meetings, traveling with Kofi Annan, wandering untrammeled around the floors of the Secretariat Building where he and his staff worked. This "insider" status offers the most insidious temptation to the writer, who over time gains the confidence of his subjects, hears their confessions, and knows that he must not compromise his precious access by awakening suspicions about his actual views. Yet Annan had good reason to grant me this exalted status. I had already written extensively about both him and his institution and was regarded as what is known around Turtle Bay as a "critical friend." A kind of implicit compact of high seriousness obtained: since I was a liberal internationalist who faulted the UN for failing to live up to its own professed values, I could be trusted to write honestly about those values and those failures. Showing my own hand was part of the compact. Every month or so I would do battle with Sir Kieran Prendergast, Annan's rather grandiose head of political affairs, a devout institutionalist who considered NATO's war in Kosovo immoral because it had not been authorized by the Security Council. Many of his colleagues felt safe confessing their fears and frustrations to me because they understood that I shared their principles. I would say, even with hindsight, that I was able to enjoy the almost illicit thrill of insiderdom without either betrayal or surrender.

But what happens when the writer changes his mind? At the core of Malcolm's essay is a libel trial that pits a convicted murderer, Jeffrey McDonald, against the journalist Joe McGinniss. During his trial McDonald had allowed McGinniss to report from inside the defense camp, certain that the journalist would recognize that he had been unjustly accused. McGinniss would be a kind of critical friend. By the time Macdonald was convicted, however, McGinniss had concluded that he was, in fact, guilty, and described him in his book, *Fatal Attraction*, as a heartless monster. McGinniss had changed his mind and then lied about it to maintain his access. Malcolm's McGinniss is a boldly, even recklessly, transgressive figure — a type of Promethean writer prepared to steal the sacred fire of the gods in the name of truth, or at least of narrative. I am a tamer guy, and I wonder what I would have done in a comparable situation. I doubt that I would have blown my cover. Would I nevertheless have had the courage — or is it shamelessness? — to betray people who had trusted me with their deepest beliefs?

And if I had balked at doing so, wouldn't I have been betraying something else even more precious — my implicit contract with the reader to tell the truth as I understand it?

This raises a larger and even more troubling question. Was the real reason why I had not squarely faced the issue of betrayal in the past not, as I told myself, because I had argued myself out of stories rather than artfully finessed my way in, but rather because I had been all too willing to accept — or to dispute or satirize within acceptable limits — the narrative to which the diplomats, politicians, and institutional leaders I had written about were committed? Had I been too reluctant to pierce the self-constructed world of Joe Biden (then vice president) or John Kerry (then senator) out of a timorous respect for position? Or, more likely, had I simply taken for granted the rules whereby high politics are conducted — a failure of imagination rather than a failure of nerve? I would like to think that, as with Kofi Annan, I had shared their basic framework of ideas and chose to engage them within the confines of those shared values.

Insiderdom is typically corrupting not because it engenders duplicity, as with McGinniss, but because it encourages deference, both because the journalist wants to keep his access and because he grows habituated to his surroundings. The journalist gradually deludes himself into surrendering his own narrative and becoming the instrument of his subject. I wrote regularly about Rudolph Giuliani during his tenure as mayor of New York, and I see now that while I constantly challenged him, my tone was often needling rather than actually provocative. Isn't it true, I asked, when he was considering running for the Senate, that you are less fitted for the U.S. Senate than almost anyone else on earth? Nah, he said. Don't you regret any of the terrible things that you have said, including about fellow Republicans? Nope. So I satirized Giuliani, but within acceptable limits. Was that a failure of nerve on my part? I would say in my defense that the Giuliani of 1995, unlike the pitiful lying flunky of today, deployed his brutality for a good purpose. As I wrote at the time, he convinced many of us of something that we hoped was false: that bullying works.

Yet I did once have a version of the Joe McGinniss experience. I changed my mind in the middle of a book. When I began researching a book on the City College of New York in 1990, I felt that its tumultuous experiment with "open admissions" twenty years earlier had been a qualified success. I began spending time at City during the summer, when remedial classes met. I saw that many of the entry-level students lacked the reading skills to understand even fairly simple texts. Their teachers, though dedicated to their students, knew that very few of them ever made it into City's regular curriculum, much less graduated. City simply could not do for them what it claimed that it could. I didn't think that anyone could, and I said as much to the teachers and the administrators who shared this view — but not to the very dedicated entry-level English teacher whose class I sat in on almost every day, and certainly not to her students. If I had, I would have been branded an enemy. I no longer would have been welcome and would not have been able to write in a fully human and fully persuasive way about the inherent limits of this noble enterprise. I did not mock, or insult, or even blame the people I had come to know. The book was written in sadness rather than in vindictive ideological triumph. Yet it enraged many of City's teachers and students; some must have felt betrayed by me. Can I justify my "betrayal" by virtue of the seriousness of my goal, or the empathy of my treatment?

That's not all — far from it. While I may have argued with Dr. Spalding, I did no such thing last fall when I visited an elementary school in Illinois whose principal had helped to develop the state's "culturally relevant teaching" standard. I was sufficiently familiar with this practice to know that I considered it a bad idea; there was no way that I could say "I share your pedagogical views." The principal turned out to be a thoroughly admirable figure, intelligent and thoughtful, a big man with a gentle voice and a warm demeanor. When he raised his commitment to "CRT," I asked him, in all innocence, to tell me what the doctrine entailed. And when he explained that children of color have been shaped by a culture that prizes "orality" rather than the abstract acts of reading and writing, and thus need to be taught through talk, song, and chant, I made noncommittal murmuring sounds as I bent over my notebook. I respectfully took down the title of the inane book on the subject that had inspired him. The reward for my strategic tact was permission to attend a fifth-grade science class in which the teacher labored mightily to persuade a group of Hispanic children that they would never have a place in the scientific community until society became "anti-racist" — the kind of drivel that gives progressive education a bad name. As if that weren't enough, one innocent little striver, who had completely failed to get the message, told me that he was sure that he could become a doctor because "my parents always say that we should follow our dreams." That was the cherry on top. I felt almost giddy with triumph. Also guilty? Not very, so far as I can recall.

Despite all my fine protestations about hapless candor, under certain circumstances I resort to strategic misrepresentation with barely a second thought. Should I at the very least have felt more guilty about the deception that made my triumph possible? I had not told a lie, of course; I simply made the kind of noncommittal noises that a reasonable if unwary person would have construed as signs of agreement, the way we all do when trapped with a bore at a cocktail party. I cannot speak for my colleagues, but I assume that most journalists behave in this manner when confronted with a potentially refractory subject. That is quite different, of course, from the cascade of lies with which Joe McGinniss stayed in Jeffrey Macdonald's good graces. Janet Malcolm would proclaim that we are deceiving ourselves: McGinniss' gross duplicity, she contended, was only a "grotesque" version of the standard journalistic transaction. That may be logically, and even morally, correct, but I am guessing that most people feel differently. I do not believe that five out of six members of a jury would find me guilty of libeling City College, as they did McGinniss for libeling Macdonald. In the realm of betrayal, as in all bad acts, there are felonies and there are misdemeanors.

Yet that still leaves a very large perplexity behind. What rule, characterological if not moral, determines whether I resort to duplicity or plunge into the icy waters of candor? Is it a rule that deserves to be generalized? I think I can illustrate the triggering mechanism with another story. In 1991, I spent a few weeks with the hundred or so folk who gathered daily at the Apollo Theater in Harlem to watch the taping of "The Gary Byrd Show," a kind of neonatal ward for the birth and nurturing of conspiracy theories about racial mistreatment in New York. Despite the politics, it was a pretty polite crowd, and I could have challenged some of the crazier details about, say, the Tawana Brawley case with no danger to myself. But since my goal was to explain how these legends were born out of a very real sense of grievance, I kept mum and gathered the material for a piece titled, "A Counter-Reality Grows in

Harlem." That was news in those days; today counter-realities have almost crowded out reality.

With this experience in mind, I launched on a profile of C. Vernon Mason, a black lawyer who specialized in fanning the flames of real or imagined racial incidents, including that of Brawley, a young black woman who had briefly riveted the country with a lurid and completely fabricated tale of rape and abuse. He agreed to meet in his office in Harlem. I needed to be very much on my guard: given how supremely suspicious he would have been of any mainstream white journalist, almost anything I said could have convinced him that I meant harm — which, of course, I did. (Several years later Mason would be disbarred for gross failure to provide adequate representation.) While I had no hard feelings towards the crowd at the Apollo, I did towards Mason. I no longer have my notes and I cannot recall what I said — maybe, "Do you still think Tawana Brawley was raped by a white cop?" — but whatever it was, we had no second interview.

I cannot possibly claim that I was giving Mason the-respect-that-comes-with-argument, since I regarded him as a rank propagandist. Yet plainly at some level, which I wish had been more conscious than it was, I felt called upon to challenge him in a way that I did not with the ordinary civilians who acquired their worldview from people like him. I could not, or would not, or in any case I did not, fully mask my feelings. Mason had power, or at least a platform; they did not. The combination of wrong-headedness and power seems to cue my imp of disputation. I would like to defend this as a moral proposition, but I don't need Janet Malcolm to tell me that as a journalistic posture it is simply inexcusable. What I should have said to C. Vernon Mason was, "Tell me what it was like growing up as a black man in Georgia in the 1950s." After all, Mason had agreed to talk to me; apparently he wanted a mainstream auditor. Oh well.

I recognize, then, that while I feel absolutely no regret for whatever modest impostures I have committed in order to make people believe that I was on their side, I do feel regret for letting fish wriggle off hooks instead of reeling them in with craft and guile. I seem to have come around to the side of Malcolm, who advises writers to shed no tears over a practice they cannot do without: "Hypocrisy is the grease that keeps society functioning in an agreeable way," she writes. "You do it and shut up about it." Well, no. I cannot swallow that Rochefoucauldian cynicism, though I have no better rule to apply. I would only say that some deceptions really are worse than others; some truths seem more worthy than others of the betrayals committed in their name. Surely if doctors and lawyers and accountants have an obligation to scrutinize their justifying ideologies, the responsibility for writers, with their professed commitment to truth, goes much deeper.

A fine moral distinction — but possibly irrelevant. My subject is not really justice, after all, but character, choice, instinct. I draw my lines after the fact, not before. Of course I am angry at myself about Dr. Spalding, and losing the other interviews at Hillsdale; but really, how could anyone stand that sophistry about John Calhoun and identity politics?

JAROSLAW ANDERS

Farewell to Greatness

A few years before his death, Zbigniew Herbert, the prominent Polish poet, published a slim volume of nineteen poems titled *Elegy for the Departure*. Many of the poems had a clearly valedictory theme. The title poem, "Elegy for the Departure of Pen Ink and Lamp," is particularly significant: it seems to announce the end of Herbert's lifelong project as a poet. The poet bids farewell to three companions of his childhood that might have set him on his literary path: the pen, the "outlet of the critical mind, messenger of soothing knowledge;" the ink of "wise depths" smelling of "a gentle volcano / the call of the abyss;" and the oil lamp, "a bright allegory / a spirit stubbornly battling / the demons of gnosis," yet also familiar with "the surf of passions" and able to call up "landscapes of a savage city repeated in water."

Elegy for the Departure was not Herbert's last book. The poet had still eight more years of life and three more poetic volumes ahead of him, but he was already very ill, tired, and aware that his best days were behind him. What he was bidding farewell — apologetically, as if the departure was his fault — in these three objects was both his turbulent life and his poetry based on the struggle of reason and light against the "demons of gnosis" and the "gentle volcano" of existential mystery. It was not a gentle farewell. The last line sounds like a door slammed shut in anger: "and / it will be / dark."

Reading this poem again thirty years later, I cannot resist the feeling it is also a farewell to a whole poetic epoch, or to a certain type of poetry that had prevailed in Eastern Central Europe in the postwar decades, especially after the relative relaxation of the political and aesthetic strictures of Communism around 1956. It was as if the poet felt that after his departure, and the departure of several members of his generation, no one is going to write like them. He expected a literary extinction.

This is exactly what happened. The young Polish poets of the 1990s, those born in or around the 1960s, loudly foreswore the legacy of the giants of the previous generations. And a similar revolution was taking place in practically all the countries of the now post-Communist region. This was not surprising, considering the immensity of social and cultural change that occurred with the end of the Communist regime. But what was the era that had so spectacularly ended with the victory of the dreams of all the postwar generations? Did it have to end? And was it replaced with anything that promises equally lasting value?

The first of these questions may be the most important and also the most difficult to answer. In the postwar decades the poetic scene was dominated by a handful of great names scattered throughout the region subjugated by the Soviet Union after the Second World War: Czesław Miłosz, Zbigniew Herbert, Tadeusz Różewicz, Wisława Szymborska, and Adam Zagajewski in Poland; Vladimír Holan and Miroslav Holub in Czechoslovakia; János Pilinszky in Hungary; Vasko Popa and Ivan Lalić in Yugoslavia. The list may be longer, but it is certainly not shorter.

What, if anything, links all those poets? For a start, they shared a tragic time and tragic circumstances. Most of them were born in the 1920s. They were teenagers when the war broke out and young adults when it ended. There were the older ones, like Miłosz or Holan, who started writing and even gained prominence before the war, and younger ones, born after the war, such as Adam Zagajewski. But most of them grew up during the Nazi atrocities, sometimes as members of the resistance and sometimes as helpless witnesses. After the war, they faced the momentous political disruption in the form of the Soviet Communist takeover. Some of them, such as Herbert, met it with inner resistance, some with hope, or resignation, or even, like Szymborska, with enthusiasm.

In every case, however, the political and social transformation must have been a moral and psychological jolt. Those who were favorably disposed towards the new order were usually quickly disappointed, leading some of them to open opposition, but more often to poetic resistance against the ideological and aesthetic vulgarity that surrounded them. During the years of the strict and forcefully imposed doctrine of socialist realism, they were often reprimanded and sometimes silenced by the monitors of official culture for their pessimism or alleged obscurity. With very few exceptions they staunchly refused to write "for the masses" in the prescribed propagandistic mode. In many cases, their true poetic debuts took place in or around 1956.

Many of these poets knew and respected each other, met or corresponded, formed friendships or practical alliances, and generally felt a bond of fraternity, a certain "genetic attraction" to each other. They constituted what is called a "biographical" literary generation linked by a set of historical facts and private experiences that defined their lives. It would be hard, however, to call them a literary school, or group, or movement. In the strictly literary sense, there are few similarities and much diversity among their particular poetic idioms. At first glance, what can link Miłosz's elegantly versed declarations, meditations, and "treatises" on poetry, philosophy, and theology with Popa's rich, oneiric, near-surreal imagery, or with Różewicz's stripped-down, unfigurative, deliberately un-poetic style, or Herbert's ironic anecdotes, and perfectly balanced "classical" lines with the texture of ancient marble, or with Holub's tongue-in-cheek philosophizing and free use of scientific language, or with Pilinszky's prison-camp tableaus, where realistic description flows into a set of metonymies so accurate that one can easily take them for plain speech? (Upturned faces of hungry prisoners pulling a heavy cart seem "strained for a scent / of the far-off celestial trough.") Is it possible to talk about all those very different poets as a common literary phenomenon?

When, in the 1960s, the works of these poets were discovered in the West, mainly in the English-speaking world, among others by Ted Hughes and the poet and translator Daniel Weissbort, the editors of *Modern Poetry in Translation*, or by the British critic Al Alvarez, the editor of *Penguin's Modern European Poetry* series, and a bit later by Seamus Heaney and the Irish poets from the North, it was soon noted that the voices from East Central Europe were similar in that they were quite different from what was happening at that time in the English language. "This poetry is more universal than ours," declared Hughes in a letter to Weissbort. It was more "insistent," and could "stimulate poetry-making in this country." In his introduction to a selection of Pilinszky's poems, Hughes mentions the Hungarian's "simple, unambiguous, direct" language, but also notes something reaching beyond poetic style. "Critical judgment cannot rest in the aesthetic excellence of his work: it inevitably ends up arguing the ethical-religious position of Pilinszky himself." Speaking about Holub, the poet Andrew Motion observed that poets from the East managed to express in language "the great humanitarian breakdown, including the breakdown of language, that occurred in Europe in the first half of the twentieth century." The Northern Irish poet Tom Paulin saw in Holub's poetry "the art of a prison-camp society, of a closed world where poetry is written without hope but with an obstinate integrity that negates as it creates." Donald Davie, the indefatigable campaigner for "purity of diction" in English verse, observed that the experience of living under oppressive regimes confirmed those poets "in their values, in the value of the poetic act, in the act of the imagination." In the United States this poetry was greeted especially by poets like Anthony Hecht, W.S. Merwin, Philip Levine, Robert Hass, Edward Hirsch, and Charles Simic, who positioned themselves outside the then dominant "schools" of American verse: the confessionalism of Berryman and Lowell, the programmatic mundanity of the New York School, and the loud strident protest of the Beats.

It was evident that the voices from East Central Europe possessed a form of grandeur and dignity that seemed to have been banished from postwar English language poetry. They could combine dispassion with urgency and pathos, irony with seriousness and conviction. They showed that modern poetry was still able to talk about great subjects without sounding quaint and pretentious, and could engage critically with reality in a calm, deliberate, and rigorous way.

Perhaps the most complete analysis of what separated Eastern Central European poets from their English-language colleagues can be found in Seamus Heaney's book of essays *The Government of the Tongue*, in which he pays tribute to Miłosz, Herbert, and Holub. He noted that this poetry ran contrary to many "orthodox assumptions" of the poetic practice of the time. It eschewed "inwardness," and "cadences that drink at the spot of time." It was full of "aerated adjectives" and great abstract words. Through its "laconic accuracies" this verse laid bare "the shape of relationships, politics, history; the rhythms of affection and disaffection; the ebb and flow of faith, hope, violence, art." It was analytic rather than sympathetic. It "aspired to deliver what we had once long ago been assured it was not any poem's business to deliver: a message." Most of all it reminded the Irish poet that all the "things forbidden within an old dispensation" pointed towards the very origins, the mystical source of poetic expression. Can it be, wrote Heaney, that "the shortest way to Whitby, the monastery where Caedmon sang the first Anglo-Saxon verses, is via Warsaw or Prague?"

The Eastern European, or, more specifically, the Central European "wave," did leave some rather direct traces in the English language poetry of the time. Critics noted Pilinszky's and Holub's influence on Hughes' "Crow" cycle. According to Paulin, he and other Northern Irish poets discovered in their Eastern colleagues a shared "invisible reference" to "the idea of being dominated by a foreign power." The chilling sequence "Legion" by the English "minimalist" David Harsent, a disturbing account of an anonymous, seemingly endless war, sounds sometimes like Pilinszky's realism and sometimes like Herbert's mythical allegory. Sometimes the influence took the form of direct borrowings or paraphrases: Ken Smith's "Cogito at the British Museum" not only borrows Zbigniew Herbert's poetic persona ("Mr. Cogito") but also the Polish poet's unique ironic-reflective style. The English-language poet perhaps the closest to the mood of Eastern Central European poetry was Geoffrey Hill, the author of "Ovid in the Third Reich" and "Two Formal Elegies for the Jews of Europe," who acknowledged the influence in his "Triumph of Love" sequence. It can be seen also in English-language poetic works that addressed the Holocaust and Nazi atrocities, such as Anthony Hecht's dispassionate yet horrifying poem "More Light! More Light!" (It contrasts favorably with Hughes' similar attempt in "Lines about Elias," where music played by prisoners before they are marched to gas chambers rather absurdly transports and unites the inmates and their guards, making them "Innocent all equally / Innocent equally and defenseless.")

Those various homages hardly arrange themselves in a coherent definition of Eastern Central European poetry and its uniqueness in the eyes of Western poets and critics, but they touch upon some important characteristics responsible for its appeal in their own countries and abroad. What strikes the reader first is a similar approach to language, which is often an indicator of a larger poetic philosophy. This approach can be defined as restorative and protective rather than innovative and disruptive. It is visible in the predominantly straightforward, clear, and direct diction — neither lofty nor pedestrian, free of grammatical disjunctions, phraseological idiosyncrasies, and semantic games. It was what Eliot called "The common word exact without vulgarity, / The formal word precise but not pedantic." The choice of this idiom was as much ethical as aesthetic. In his "Dedication," addressed to those who did not survive, Miłosz pledges to use "simple speech as I would be ashamed of another." "I speak to you with silence like a cloud or a tree," he continued.

It was during the war that poetry of the region started to turn away from its dominant French — that is, symbolist and surrealist — influences and towards a more reflective Anglo-Saxon brand of modernism. "The symbolists discovered the idea of a poem as an autonomous, self-sufficient unit, no longer describing the world but existing instead of the world," wrote Miłosz, the translator of Eliot's "The Waste Land." According to Miłosz, poetry's *raison d'etre* rests "somewhere outside poetry itself — in the spiritual and interhuman domain." Not everybody would go as far as Miłosz, who linked the symbolists' linguistic license to the "sack of cities," and found a connection between "theories of literature as *écriture* and the growth of the totalitarian state." But many would agree with Miłosz that such poetries were "not prepared to cope with those catastrophes." Even those who were ardent symbolists in the interwar period, such as the Czech poet Miroslav Holan, felt the inadequacy. "How to live? How to be simple and literal?" he asked in a poem titled "How?" After what happened, could reality be disregarded as an obstacle to a free play of individual imagination? (There were such attempts in the post-war poetry of the region, and they were treated as politically innocuous, and with a good measure of forbearance by cultural bureaucrats, but the great poets of the time would have nothing to do with them.)

Language had fallen victim to power as much as people and cities. It was now to abandon its flights of fancy and come down to earth. It could no longer pretend to be a separate, self-sufficient universe parallel to and competing with reality. It suffered immensely at the hands of ideologues and propagandists and should be healed rather than experimented upon. It was also faced with the challenge of expressing the inexpressibility of violence, and in order to be even marginally suitable for this task it should undergo, to use Paul Celan's words, the purification of "terrible silence." This was one of this poetry's main goals.

Another often noted characteristic, obviously linked to the directness of language, was its preoccupation with the objective, the demonstrable, the empirical. It can be argued that all poetry is the expression of the subjective, of the poet's self. Where else can a true poem germinate, unless it is a stylistic exercise or a work on assignment? But in this poetry we see a constant effort to objectify the subjective, to give it an impersonal character, to turn it (in Herbert's words) "into a person or a thing," something located safely outside the self, with clearly delimited borders, that can be regarded from a distance and analyzed with a degree of cool detachment. Hence the frequent fascination with, even envy of, inanimate objects, perfect essences, never alive and therefore immortal, with no business whatsoever with the vagaries of human existence. The motif of a conversation with a stone can be found in Herbert, Popa, and Szymborska. Herbert's pebble appears as "a perfect creature / equal to itself / mindful of its limits / filled exactly / with a pebbly meaning." Popa's stone-hero of the cycle "The Quartz Pebble" "listens to itself /

Among the worlds a world." Szymborska's arrogant stone refuses to open his door: "You may get to know me but you'll never know me through. / My whole surface is turned toward you, / all my insides turned away."

Objects often rebuke people but their presence, their inviolable sameness, is also a source of reassurance, a strategy of perseverance. For Herbert, objectivization of our volatile, paradoxical existence into "a person or a thing," locking it in a sculpture, a piece of architecture, or a myth is the very essence of culture, a source of aesthetic delight but also a strategy of survival. And in his introduction to Vasko Popa's collection *Homage to the Lame Wolf*, the American poet (and Popa's translator) Charles Simic writes: "One might be reading Euclid on the triangle here. He is so deadpan. The usual drama of the self is completely absent. The archetypal forms that emerge are employed for cognitive ends. Popa meditates on myth. He talks to it, and it talks back." It is probably owing to this "deadpan" objectivity among the greats of Eastern Central Europe that whenever the poetic "I" appears we are often forced to ask who it is, who is actually speaking. The tone makes us suspect a persona, whether or not openly introduced, like Herbert's Mr. Cogito, which puts a distance (but what distance?) between itself and the poet's voice. What is more, persona, even in the singular, often sounds like a voice of a collectivity: a chorus, a generation, a nation, or maybe, as in Herbert's "Envoy of Mr. Cogito," the whole civilization. Quite definitely not Herbert's "small broken soul with a great self-pity."

And there is still another seminal paradox. Having assumed the immense burden of speaking in the name of many, this poetry is constantly skeptical about its expressive powers. It dwells in the shadow of Adorno's famous warning that writing poetry after Auschwitz would be "barbaric." It answers that after Auschwitz it would be barbaric not to write poetry, but it must be a very different poetry, stripped of all "poetic" trappings, it would have to be poor poetry, an anti-poetry using non-poetic tools and sources: hard, unsentimental, clear-sighted, and relentless, responding to existential rather than esthetic needs. "You are asked again and again why you write poems. To find out why you are alive — that is why you write poems," declared Popa.

The poet who went furthest in this direction was Tadeusz Różewicz. It is said that he read his poems in a monotonous, almost apathetic tone, as if reading from a newspaper. "I regard my own poems with acute mistrust," he said in an interview. "I fashion them from the great rubbish dump, the great cemetery." Michael Hamburger observed that Różewicz and other poets of his generation "have made themselves at home in the silence." "Should someone ask, what, after all, is my poetic language," said Pilinszky, "in truth I should have to answer: it is some sort of lack of language, a sort of linguistic poverty. . . . I would like to write as if I had remained silent." Silence is a frequent trope in Holub's poetry, as in the poem "The Lesson" where it is "cutting like a knife" through the drone of voices from the loudspeakers.

Silence and understatement come to the rescue of constantly threatened language. Was it a political stratagem, a way to avoid censorship and let the readers fill in the gaps? Perhaps, but such evasions were not to the detriment of the poetry itself. Also, although born out of a certain political situation, it was not, by and large, political poetry, although it was often presented as such. When read today, even poets who were publicly engaged as citizens, such as Herbert and Holan and Holub, seem to be preoccupied with ethical and metaphysical problems rather than pointless squabbles with the regime.

It is true that almost all of them, from time to time, were tempted to write something that sounded like political satire or an Aesopian comment on current events. Herbert, with his mythical allusions, comes to mind, as does Zagajewski in the early stage of his career when he was a member (with Stanisław Barańczak, Julian Kornhauser, and Ryszard Krynicki) of the poetic group called the New Wave, advocating for a more direct involvement of poetry with the social and political "here and now." These were usually not their best productions, although they were adored by their readers and passed around like Masonic handshakes. In my youth it was habitual to look for contemporary political innuendos almost everywhere. Al Alvarez called it the favorite Polish game of "Find-the-Allusion." (The proclivity was unfortunately shared also by censors, who often suppressed quite innocent poems in case they were "wrongly" understood.) For the most part, however, poetry aimed much higher than just sticking it to the regime, and Zagajawski openly repudiated those efforts in his extraordinary essay "Solidarity and Solitude."

Yet the shadow of history, both the memory of the war and the reality of Communist strictures, was always reflected in their writing. They were poets of ruins, of a disintegrated and debased world, of broken human relations, philosophical confusions, and moral uncertainties. In that, they resembled the moderns of the Eliot generation, except that they were moderns whose anxieties and dark premonitions had been most cruelly actualized. Their wastelands and their hollow men were not metaphors. They were part of the physical reality that surrounded them. Where the great moderns of the past suffered from ennui, alienation, and the indefiniteness of their lives, the postwar moderns from the East saw terror, dehumanization, moral collapse, and ever-present threat. Eliot's protagonists dwelled in Limbo, "without infamy or praise." His East-Central followers saw man descend into the lower rings of Hell. Their world ended both in a bang and a whimper.

The older moderns believed that they had reached an end, but the question of what comes next, though disturbing, could still be thrilling. It posed an intriguing aesthetic challenge, the task of inventing new styles and literary forms to express it all. The East Central Europeans knew that what comes next may be annihilation. For them, searching for the right word was a moral rather than an aesthetic task, the expression of their need to find a path among Różewicz's "great rubbish dump, the great cemetery." This is, perhaps, how we should understand Popa's dictum about writing in order to know why one still lives.

Yet the great poets never succumbed to total despair, or its smirking nihilistic twin called "postmodern irony." Even the writing of Tadeusz Różewicz, who in his early poetry seems to abandon all hope, is an unending quest to prove himself wrong. Herbert, by contrast, temperamentally an enemy of pessimism, stubbornly invoked "the old incantations of humanity," which do not promise victory but at least keep the human person from dissolution. Miłosz finds nourishment and hope in his repeated returns to his "native realm" in pre-modern Lithuania and tries to restore the human universe that had been destroyed, in his view, by the "scientific outlook," while Holub's sharp scientific eye takes apart facts and events and then puts them back together to prove that objective truths can be extracted from the sea of doubt and confusion. And Popa peruses cryptic Balkan yarns and fables in an effort to find the source of what he calls "word-keys" that give the human soul a fighting chance "when the very existence of this tiny, fertile star — whose shine should be mankind itself — is in question."

This poetry was never far from the last things, even when it spoke from agnostic or atheistic positions, never far from the human drama even when speaking about stones, wooden cubes, onions, or, like Holub, about "ugly, grunting creatures" of the microbial world. And even at the most apolitical, it was never far from history, because, as my poet-friend Michael March helpfully suggests, it often originated as "civilized resistance to circumstances." It spoke with urgency, as if what it had to say was of real and general importance. It was concerned with ideas, sometimes expressed directly but more often through a particular blend of thought and feeling, not unlike in Eliot's definition of the metaphysical poets of sixteenth-century England. It was poetry of unmistakable grandeur and power, though often wry and self-ironic.

Is it possible to sum it up in a neat phrase that would gather it all? Was it a poetry of "ardor," to borrow Zagajewski's term from one of his essays, or a "wisdom project," from Susan Sontag's essay on Zagajewski? Or, to use the German theologian Paul Tillich's term, was it a "concern about being?" (For Tillich, those who deemed being — their own, everybody else's, and Being in general — as worthy of concern were already on the side of faith, even if they defined themselves as atheists.) Or was it — in the awkward, unscholarly term — a poetry of greatness? Greatness is something quite different from "excellence," which is akin to what Eliot called "word mastery," a virtuosity that in his view can push out everything else, especially insight into the human soul. (He used Dryden and Milton as cautionary examples, although Milton at least got Satan's soul right.) An excellent poet can excel in anything he or she endeavors — grand or trivial, true or conceited, wise or silly — and leave us in awe of his or her craft. Poetic greatness, on the other hand, is entirely a matter of soul.

Excellence can be described and analyzed with the ever-expanding toolbox of supposedly precise academic terms and definitions to show how a poem "works." It can be evaluated according to various, often conflicting, critical approaches. Greatness is much more mysterious, elusive, difficult to grasp; but given the right sensitivity, it is usually unmistakable even to the uninitiated. It is about a largeness of vision that includes and unifies all strata of human experience — from the empirical to the intellectual, from the individual to the collective, from the historical to the ethical and the metaphysical. Greatness properly understood is not, as Hughes rightly observed about Pilinszky, an exclusively aesthetic phenomenon. A great poem is more than a verbal construct of considerable beauty and complexity. It stands with one foot outside its own text. It requires the encounter of a poet and a reader who are both interested in more than poetry.

The three long decades between 1956 and the late 1980s were definitely the era of poetic greatness in East Central Europe. Then, abruptly, a reaction came. The young poets, born in the 1960s, proclaimed that they were sick and tired of this sort of greatness. They wanted a clear break from it, and from their venerated elders. A Polish poet of this generation, Andrzej Sosnowski, born in 1959, declared in his programmatic poem "What is poetry?":

> Certainly not a strategy of survival,
> or a way of life. Your insistence is droll

when you invoke mystic lakes,
rustling forests or abysmal caves where voice
can echo forever. The caves
of Sybil?

He might have been addressing Miłosz ("What is poetry which does not save / Nations or people . . .") or Herbert, or maybe one of their younger followers, such as Zagajewski. For Sosnowski, such salvific ambitions are "droll." What really matters, he continued, were little stones you can play ducks and drakes with. A tiny room in a tenement house can be more interesting than a magical cave. This is what our world is made of — small everyday facts, common objects waiting until the draft of poetry picks them up and scatters them "like confetti."

It was a rather elegant sendoff, and one that ended on a consolatory note. The young poet asks his exalted colleague not to leave in offense, to stick around and listen, because the new poetry of leaves and stones may also carry a grain of knowledge, may "suddenly say / about peoples and wars, struggles and sea voyages / about how things are and how the business goes." There were, however, much more violent attacks. A Polish critic found it necessary to declare the formation of the League to Defend Polish Poetry from Herbert. "The poetry of slaves feeds on ideas, / Ideas are watery substitutes of blood," inveighed Maciej Świetlicki, one of the young poets, mocking poetry where "even trees have crosses / — inside under their bark — made of barbed wire. . . ." Even older poets who chose, or were chosen, to be the mentors of the young rebels, added their quotient of invectives. "Words huge like beans and as hard to swallow," said one of them in a poem. This poetry was "not beautiful, but suddenly all reach for their hands / And clap, so it must be right." (Piotr Sommer,

"Liberation in language.") And another one (Bohdan Zadura), known for subtle lyricism and formal refinement, fulminated in a prose diatribe (possibly ironic, but I cannot be sure) about "toothless gums of empty rhetoric," and the "vanity and shittyness" of "the old and infirm, and only youth is allowed to be vain."

Hardly anybody tried to be fair, thoughtful, or to use the standard language of literary criticism. It was mortal combat and the point was to hit, and hit hard, no matter where. Most of the assaults were based on crass misreadings or directed against straw men with little resemblance to the alleged targets. The attacked poets hardly used "words large like beans," or pretentious symbols like "crosses made of barbed wire." But the characteristics that so enraged the poetic newcomers were the perceived loftiness, abstraction, intellectualism, didacticism, and ethical rigor (Herbert's "yes, yes, no, no"). They were calling into question the very aspiration to poetic greatness.

The clash was most raucous in Poland, but similar battles were taking place throughout the region. What was supposed to replace the poetry of great subjects and high concerns? Everything that was its direct opposition. The new poetic idiom had to be down to earth, open to chaos, to the contingency and the banality of daily existence. It should be personal, even autobiographical, focused on details and eschewing abstractions and grand ideas. Its language should step down to the level of street talk, common speech as practiced by the young generation, including vulgarities and slang. It should constantly remind the reader of its awkwardness as a tool of serious communication. The poet should address the reader as an equal, that is, as someone equally confused, bored, or annoyed by "all that." High cultural references — those eternal myths and timeless masterpieces — should be replaced by mass culture tropes. Poetry should accept its inevitably marginal status, something to be enjoyed in a close circle of friends rather than on a national stage. In sum, it was a general lowering of poetic register and narrowing of the range of interest to things observed "outside the window."

The change began a few years before the miraculous year 1989, in the gloomy and uncertain time, anxious and lethargic, when it was obvious that Communism was finished but it was by no means clear what was going to replace it. When the breakthrough finally came, the intoxication with new freedom quickly gave way to disappointment. The post-communist countries did not turn overnight into mature and stable liberal democracies. Where the older generation saw a lot of unfinished work, the young ones noticed vulgarity, emptiness, primitive consumerism, economic uncertainty, frenetic money chasing, and rapid commercialization of culture. That was their world. The older poets kept writing, but it seemed that they completely overlooked these realities and talked above the heads of the crowds that not long ago listened to them in rapture.

One of the reasons for the pique of the younger generation might have also been the extremely elevated, almost prophetic status that the great few enjoyed in the post-war decades. Especially, but not exclusively, in Poland, great poets were treated, often against their will, as moral arbiters, spiritual guides, guardians of their nation's soul. They were asked to read in churches and at secret gatherings where the public eagerly "reached for their hands" to attest that this poetry was not only beautiful but also "right." What passed for literary criticism of their work often amounted to blatant hagiography, while rare attempts at respectful critique were suspected of a nefarious political agenda. In other words, they were forced into the old Romantic role of "unacknowledged legislators of the world." Inevitably, this kind of reception simplified and diminished their poetic message. During these mystery rites the devotees heard what they wanted to hear. The powerful echo drowned the original tune. Such spectacles could provoke jeers from the more skeptical in the audience. Was it time to blaspheme against the gods, to be naughty, and finally to break some things?

Interestingly, the new generation of poets from Eastern Central Europe sought inspiration primarily among English-language poets — not among their contemporaries but those one or two generations older: the New York School, especially Frank O'Hara (in Poland, "Oharism" became a handy critical term); English "minimalists" (Tony Morrison, David Harsent) with their attentive, unadorned descriptions of everyday life; the "Liverpool poets" (Brian Patten), with their penchant for pop, humor, and performance; the British "New Fantasts" or "Martians" (Craig Raine) searching for strange and "denaturalizing" perspectives on familiar objects and situations; and also poets from Northern Ireland (Seamus Heaney, Paul Muldoon, Andrew Motion, Derek Mahon) cultivating, at least at that time, their provincialism and treating the political drama in their own realm with a tad of detachment. Some of those "influences" were merely imitations and unwilling parodies. In some cases, however, the young apprentices managed to turn them into a fresh, personal idiom. One of the Polish "Oharists," Marcin Sendecki, can draw in few quick lines a brilliant image with a small intriguing point:

> Shadows glow from billboards. After
> Crossing the tracks the boy stops

To rush the dog. Do not expect
A miracle from a factual photo. This
Is a chair. This is a table.

Or,

The dust seems lighter, the leaves
Breathe: slowly, carefully.
We made love and now we talk
To each other. Bronze drops swell and
Fade with every flap of the lids.

Andrzej Sosnowski evolved into probably the most hermetic poet in his generation, fond of intertextual games and sudden surrealist riffs, as in this impression of a watch left on a beach:

And moisture will be able to dream about a museum
Wandering among springs and stones
And steaming under a golden watchcase
Till the end of the sea and time.

The young rebels of the 1990s are now in their sixties. It is they who are now the leading generation in their countries. They gather awards named after their once-rejected elders. There are already younger ones, who try to add something new — references to the digital world, social media, cyber- and hyper-textual experiments — although they usually stay within the same zone of the quotidian, the domestic, the private, and within the same colloquial registers. Their gift of observation can be impressive. I have recently read — with pleasure — a poem by the Polish poet Sara Akram about a young "girl in golden sequins" vomiting and undressing in a metro station, while her amused companions take pictures and post them online. As Eliot said, "the possible interests of a poet are unlimited."

The question I hear sometimes, "So what is happening now in Central European poetry?" is simple to answer, but the answer is usually unsatisfactory. There is absolutely everything there: conceptual poetry, intertextual poetry, language poetry, surrealist poetry, lyrical poetry, confessional poetry, poetry about death (a lot of it), poetry of social criticism (mostly anti-consumerist), feminist poetry, queer poetry, and environmental poetry. But greatness, at least as I have tried to define it here, is nowhere to be found. The question that often follows, impatiently, "So who, in your view, are the three best poets writing today?" is not only impossible to answer, but somehow beyond the point. Critics have frequently noted that in the new poetic environment hierarchies got flattened. It is as if reaching too high, trying to be too different, was somehow undemocratic, or impolite towards one's fellow poets. The field is full, even crowded, but at the same time it looks empty. Within their particular niches, poets sound strikingly similar to each other and similar to their contemporaries in other countries. It would be hard to distinguish a poem written today in Poland or the Czech Republic from one written in the United States, or Great Britain, or Germany. The poets of the region have finally joined the world and "softly and suddenly" vanished in it.

An era has ended. All eras have to end. Perhaps this is exactly as it should be. After all, as Auden declared, "poetry makes nothing happen." But few care to read on in Auden's poem: poetry "survives, / A way of happening, a mouth." Poetry does not change the world (for that we need real muscles and good politics), but it is a part of what happens, a way of seeing the world and articulating it. So we must ask ourselves some more questions. Have we really put all the "great narratives" of humanity behind us? Is it not obvious that, for all the astonishing transformations of our time, the world has not completely changed? Are we not living again in times when (to stay with Auden's "In Memory of W. B. Yeats") "intellectual disgrace / Stares from every human face?"

History teaches us that poetry does not remain for long satisfied with marginality and dispersion. Is it not the pursuit of greatness that kept this strange, some say unnatural, art alive as "a part of what happens" for millennia? True, much of its intensity comes from the intensity of its times, from the often terrifying historical drama within which it is composed, and no one should wish for more historical tragedy, for another bout of madness, to "hurt us into poetry." But tragedies are never too far away. In fact they are happening right now, in Europe and elsewhere. It is possible that the stimulation that Hughes saw in Eastern Central European poets will come from parts even farther east. There is something happening in contemporary Ukrainian poetry, suddenly confronted with existential questions — individual and collective — that not too long ago seemed like the songs of the past. A Belarusian prose writer and poet, Alhierd Bacharevič, called his recent novel *The Dogs of Europe*. Yes, the same dogs that bark in Auden's poem. We already hear them, too, but they sound louder in the darker peripheries. Their poetry, too, may prove "more universal than ours."

GARY SAUL MORSON

Thinking Thoughtlessly

In *The Gulag Archipelago*, Aleksandr Solzhenitsyn described the moment he realized that he did not really believe what he had always professed. It happened during a conversation with another *zek*, or prisoner, named Boris Gammerov, a "yellowish youth, with a Jewish tenderness of face." After exchanging biographies they passed to politics. Gammerov "began to question me" in a peculiarly intense way new to Solzhenitsyn, who had always lived in a world where educated people agreed on fundamental issues. Recalling "one of the prayers of the late President Roosevelt," he "expressed what seemed to me a self-evident evaluation of it: 'Well, that's hypocrisy, of course.'"

To Solzhenitsyn's surprise, Gammerov furiously countered: "Why do you not admit the possibility that a political leader might sincerely believe in God?"

Solzhenitsyn could hardly believe that someone born and educated under Soviet rule could utter such words. He suddenly became aware that he was less than certain about what he had said — and about the system of thought that his remark presumed.

> I could have replied to him very firmly, but prison had already undermined my certainty, and the principal thing was that some kind of clear, pure feeling does live within us . . . and right then it dawned on me that I had not spoken out of conviction but because the idea had been implanted within me from the outside. And because of this I was unable to reply to him, and I merely asked him: "Do you believe in God?
>
> "Of course," he answered tranquilly.

"Implanted in me from the outside": evidently there is more than one way to have convictions. They can be accepted and professed, quite sincerely, only because one has never doubted them. They can seem like an intrinsic part of oneself, even when they are not. They can be nothing more than the impact of an external influence, a contagion, a surrender to conformity. But authentic convictions, by contrast, derive from lived experience. One must have seriously examined, tested, and revised them, and be prepared to do so again.

Beliefs "implanted from outside" are accepted passively, while authentic ones demand effort. If ideas are simply learned, the way one memorizes the kings of England, they remain inert. Their truth seems beyond question only because one has not questioned it. Authentic beliefs exhibit what Mikhail Bakhtin called "ones-ownness"; they are "inwardly persuasive" because we have worked on them. Having gone through a complex process of examination and assimilation, they have acquired our own unique tonalities, which are themselves always changing in response to outer and inner experience. "One's own word," Bakhtin observed, remains "unfinalized." "Its creativity and productiveness," he writes, "consist precisely in the fact that such a word awakens new and independent words, that it organizes masses of our words from within, and does not remain in an isolated and static condition. It is not so much interpreted by us as it is further, that is, freely, developed, applied to new material, new conditions."

Inwardly persuasive words often conflict with other inwardly persuasive words. They enter into dialogue with each other, they "struggle" and undergo change. Out of these inner dialogues we construct a self. Our point of view on the world develops "in just such an intense struggle within us . . . among various verbal and ideological points of view, approaches, directions, and values." So long as one lives, these dialogues continue. Inwardly persuasive discourse is therefore "not finite, it is open; in each of the new contexts that dialogize it, this discourse is able to reveal ever new ways to mean." Yet sometimes inwardly persuasive discourse begins to lose its persuasiveness. It begins to feel more than half "someone else's," or, in Solzhenitsyn's words, "implanted from the outside." Once one becomes conscious of a belief as "implanted," one acquires a kind of double vision. With effort, one can still see the world in the old way, but can never wholly banish the way one really sees it.

Communism posed questions about belief especially

starkly, but the most profound Soviet thinkers consciously developed insights from Tolstoy, Dostoevsky, and other great pre-revolutionary Russian writers. One could almost say that the central question of Russian literature for the past two centuries has been: what does it mean to believe something? That question leads to several others. How can it be that one believes what one does not really believe? What process leads us to accept inauthentic beliefs?

In his autobiography *Child of the Revolution*, Wolfgang Leonhard — with whom I studied Soviet history as an undergraduate at Yale — described how, as a young German refugee growing up in the USSR, he was delighted to be admitted to the Komsomol even though his mother, friends, and teachers had not long before been arrested. "Somehow I dissociated these things, and even my personal impressions and experiences, from my fundamental political conviction. It was almost as if there were two separate levels — one of everyday experiences, which I found myself criticizing; the other of the great Party line, which at this time, despite my hesitations, I still regarded as correct, from the standpoint of general principle." What exactly does Leonhard mean by "dissociating" these two realities? When (or if) one at last "associates" them again, what happens to one's consciousness, to one's self?

Does contemporary America raise similar questions? One can hardly live in a university environment — or in some other professions, such as journalism — without being aware that one cannot say all one thinks, that students express political opinions that they know their teachers, neighbors, and parents expect, and that self-censorship is routine — not only of ideas but also of words, idioms, even grammatical forms that are hard to avoid without constant vigilance.

I often wonder whether my colleagues really believe what they profess. If so, are their views accepted because they were "implanted from outside"?

Writing about the nature of dialogue in the 1930s, Bakhtin clearly had in mind the emphatically non-dialogic Soviet view of beliefs. For the Soviets, the right answers to all important questions were known. Everything else was simply wrong. Any attempt at individuality, any departure from the "ready-made truth" accepted by the properly informed collective, amounted to a dangerous error.

Socrates, Bakhtin stressed, proceeded from the opposite assumption — that the more certain we are about something, the less likely we are to have examined it closely. Theaetetus expresses delight at the unanswered questions that Socrates poses: "It is extraordinary how they set me wondering whatever they can mean. Sometimes I get quite dizzy with thinking of them." Socrates replies: "The sense of wonder is the mark of the philosopher. Philosophy, indeed, has no other origin." And wonder expresses itself in open-ended dialogue — for Bakhtin, that is why Plato chose the form — whereas certainty is expressed "monologically," as categorical and indubitable propositions. The plot of Soviet socialist realist novels often centers on a well-intentioned young man who learns that not he, but the Party, possesses the truth, and so he must act not on his own initiative but at the Party's direction. In Soviet terms, he must recognize that "consciousness" (that is, Party doctrine) is superior to "spontaneity."

Like Socrates, Konstantin Levin, the autobiographical protagonist of *Anna Karenina*, relentlessly pursues the truth, even when it indicates that he has behaved wrongly. We see him stop in mid-sentence to ask himself how he can profess some high-minded doctrine when he has behaved quite differently. Levin has trained himself to look for counter-evidence. Honesty, Tolstoy suggests, entails a lot more than not telling a conscious lie. It demands that one actively determine whether what one thinks or says is actually true.

The last thing Levin would do is thoughtlessly adopt a "ready-made truth." His friend Stiva, by contrast, favors fashionable beliefs no less than good taste in wine, cuisine, and conversation. Keeping up with the latest opinions, knowing what has just become passé and what has replaced it, becomes not only a mark of sophistication but also a delightful game that Stiva plays adroitly and with ease. The right opinions must seem to have come effortlessly — and, in Stiva's case, they really do: Stiva "had not chosen his political opinions or his views; these political opinions and views had come to him of themselves, just as he did not choose the shapes of his hat and coat, but simply took those that were in style. And for him, living in a certain social environment, where a desire for some sort of mental activity was part of maturity, to hold views was just as indispensable as to have a hat." Stiva, of course, reads

> a liberal paper, not an extreme one, but one advocating the views held by the majority [of his circle]. And in spite of the fact that science, art, and politics had no special interest for him, he firmly held those views on all these subjects which were held by the majority and by his paper, and changed them only when the majority changed them — or, more strictly speaking, they seemed to change of themselves within him.

What does it mean to hold "firmly" beliefs one has not really considered? Clearly, it does not mean that those beliefs reflect one's unique experience or train of thought. The "firmness" of Stiva's opinions derives not from any serious attempt to examine the grounds for them, but from his life among a certain social class. So far as evidence is concerned, these opinions might just as well have been quite different. And they do, in fact, become different over time, not because Stiva has changed them — no agency is involved — but because they "change of themselves within him." In sum, Stiva thinks thoughtlessly.

If one chooses beliefs for their truthfulness, which one takes pains to verify, then one is bound to amend them as the evidence warrants. They will not always coincide with those of the "majority." That is what Levin does, as we see the moment he begins to converse with Stiva. "Aha! You are in a new phase, I see — a conservative," Stiva remarks with his "scarcely perceptible smile." As the novel progresses, we see Levin change his mind about several questions, especially the one that most concerns him: how can one make Russian agriculture more productive and so improve the wretched life of the peasants? Levin has tried the method favored by up-to-date thinkers: copy what the English do. Since well-educated liberals routinely — almost instinctively — treated imitating the West as the answer to every problem, their recommendations for agricultural productivity required no special knowledge of how farming actually works. But painful experience, and an empirical frame of mind, has taught Levin that copying Western methods never improves and sometimes actually harms productivity. Import an expensive English threshing machine and somehow it always breaks. Levin's English seed oats have unfortunately been, in his bailiff's understated phrase, "a little scorched." For reasons no one can specify, the peasants seem unable to follow new practices.

These problems are foremost on Levin's mind when he visits his friend Sviazhsky. Tolstoy focuses primarily not on what but on how Sviazhsky believes. Levin is puzzled that Sviazhsky can sincerely profess liberal principles contradicted by his own conservative way of living. "Sviazhsky was one of those people, always a source of wonder to Levin, whose convictions, very logical though never original, go one way by themselves, while their life, exceedingly definite and firm in its direction, goes its way quite apart and always in direct contradiction to their convictions." Although Sviazhsky "despised the nobility and regarded the government of Russia as so bad that he never permitted himself to criticize its doings seriously . . . he was a functionary of that government and a model marshal of the nobility, and when he drove about he always wore the cockade of office." Like a good Westernizer, Sviazhsky "considered the Russian peasant as occupying a stage of development intermediate between ape and man," yet no one was readier to shake hands with peasants "and listen to their opinions." Believing "in neither God nor the devil," Sviazhsky nevertheless "took special trouble to keep up the church in his village."
An extreme feminist advocating women's right to labor, "he arranged his wife's life so that she did nothing and could do nothing but share her husband's efforts to make her time pass as happily and agreeably as possible."

Some might have dismissed Sviazhsky as a fool or a scoundrel, Tolstoy observes, but Levin knew that his friend was admirably intelligent and thoroughly decent. Regarding Sviazhsky as a "living enigma," Levin wanted to "get at the foundation of his life," but whenever he "tried to penetrate beyond the outer chambers of Sviazhsky's mind . . . he noticed that Sviazhsky was slightly disconcerted; faint signs of alarm were visible in his eyes . . . and he would give him a kindly, good-humored rebuff." What's more, Sviazhsky takes an interest in matters of no relevance to his life or to his other intellectual concerns. Why does he care so much about new discoveries about the eighteenth-century partition of Poland, Levin wonders — but when he asks "'Well, what then?,' there was nothing to follow. It was simply interesting that it had been proved to be so and so. But Sviazhsky did not explain, and saw no need to explain why it was interesting to him."

Tolstoy suggests an explanation for some of these enigmas. What matters most to Sviazhsky is being a good host, welcoming and entertaining. His finely expressed liberal views, along with his interest in questions about which no one could feel strongly, make the time his guests spend with him admirably pleasant. His concern for peasants, noblemen, and clergy reflect his kind-heartedness. In a sense, Sviazhsky's life and views do cohere, not because they are consistent with each other but because they all foster convivial entertainment. Though inauthentic, they make sense in the economy of Sviazhsky's personality.

To make his point unmistakably clear, Tolstoy portrays another of Sviazhsky's guests, described simply as "a reactionary landowner" with whom Levin disagrees. Again, Tolstoy wants us to focus on *how* the landowner has arrived at his views:

> The landowner unmistakably spoke his own individual thought — a thing that rarely happens — and a thought to which he had been brought not by a desire of finding some exercise for an idle brain, but a thought which had grown up out of the conditions of his life, which he

> had brooded over in the solitude of his village, and had considered in every aspect.

In his later works, Tolstoy portrays inauthentic thinkers much more harshly. Those whose beliefs and behaviors unthinkingly conform to ready-made norms — who aspire to be perfectly *comme il faut* — have surrendered their souls. They live "unconsciously." "And if the whole complex lives of many people go on unconsciously," Tolstoy recorded in his diary, "then such lives are as if they had never been."

That is the horrible discovery made by the eponymous hero of "The Death of Ivan Ilych" as he is dying. A "virtuoso" of conformity, Ivan Ilych has made his self coincide more and more completely with his social roles, in both his profession and private life. In law school, he was "already what he remained for the rest of his life: a capable, cheerful, good-natured, and sociable man, though strict in the fulfillment of what he considered to be his duty; and he considered his duty to be what was so considered by those in authority." You could not call him a toady, Tolstoy acidly observes, because he cultivated people of authority without hypocrisy or premeditation, but "as a fly is drawn to the light, assimilating their view of life" completely. Like them, "he succumbed to sensuality . . . and latterly among the highest classes to liberalism." When Ivan Ilych is promoted, he easily finds a new house that perfectly suits himself and his wife. "It might have been specially built for them." Ivan Ilych chooses the wallpaper, furniture, and knickknacks according to his own taste, but because his taste conforms exactly to the prescribed pattern, the result "was just what is usually seen in the houses of people of moderate means who wish to appear rich, and therefore succeed only in resembling others like themselves."

When Ivan Ilych falls ill, however, he begins to discover his unique self. After all, his roles will continue when he is gone. They are immortal, but he will die. And that is especially dreadful because he has not really been alive. The sicker he gets, the more he suffers an unspeakable terror of death. "'Maybe I did not live as I ought to have done,' it suddenly occurred to him. 'But how could that be, when I did everything properly?' he replied and immediately dismissed from his mind this, the sole solution of all the riddles of life and death, as something quite impossible."

At last Ivan Ilych realizes that he lived not just "improperly," but exactly contrary to the way he should have lived. What he deemed good was bad, and vice versa. In childhood, before he had lost his self to conformity, there was still real life. He recalls particularities: the smell of a striped leather ball and "the raw shriveled French plums of his childhood, their peculiar flavor, and the flow of saliva when he sucked their stones; and along with the memory of that taste came a whole series of memories of those days." In short, "the further back he looked the more life there had been," but the closer he came to the present real life disappeared ever more rapidly, "in inverse ratio to the square of the distance from death." At last Ivan Ilych realizes that "my whole life has been wrong." Everything now confirmed the "huge deception which had hidden both life and death."

If conformity is death, then a single genuine action is life. No one recognizes the authentic feeling with which Ivan Ilych forgives his wife and blesses his son, but in doing so he transforms his dying. "To him all this happened in a single instant, and the meaning of that instant did not change" in the two hours he had left. At last he hears someone say "it is finished," but he is content to die having regained life.

"'Death is finished,' he said to himself. 'It is no more.'" The story of Ivan Ilych was to haunt Western existentialists and, still more sharply, Soviet Russians who strove to conform to official norms.

Unlike Tolstoy, Dostoevsky focused on the political dangers of adopting ready-made beliefs or, in his words, wearing "a uniform." In his great novels we encounter enthusiastic copy-cat radicals who believe just what they should. He describes Lebeziatnikov, a minor character in *Crime and Punishment*, as "one of the numerous and varied legion of dullards, of half-animate abortions, conceited, half-educated coxcombs, who attach themselves to the idea most in fashion only to . . . caricature every cause they serve, however sincerely." Lebeziatnikov trips over himself voicing all the approved nihilist doctrines: the denial of free will ("it all depends on the [social] environment"), the condemnation of charity (which distracts from attacking root causes), the uselessness of art, and the duty of husbands to applaud the infidelity of their wives.

In *The Possessed*, a novel about the Russian terrorist movement, Dostoevsky illustrates how such buffoons can be dangerous. As Lenin was to show, a few thoughtful revolutionaries can seize power if others follow whoever is considered most radical. As the conspirator Pyotr Stepanovich explains, we can get such people to do anything if we only tell them they are not progressive enough. Those who do not actually commit violent acts will excuse, justify, or even applaud them, as the Russian liberal party, the Kadets, actually did, only to be the first people Lenin liquidated.

"Do you know how many we will catch by little ready-made

ideas?" Pyotr Stepanovich asks. Those eager to accept prevailing beliefs will spread them and shame each other into obedience. "Ha, ha, Listen," Pyotr Stepanovich explains,

> I've reckoned them all up. . . . the lawyer who defends an educated murderer because he is more cultured than his victims and could not help murdering them . . . is one of us. . . . The juries who acquit every criminal are ours. The prosecutor who trembles at a trial for fear he should not seem advanced enough is ours, ours. Among officials and literary men we have lots, lots, lots, and they don't know it themselves.

"When the radicals hold a meeting," Dostoevsky writes, "they compete to voice the most up-to-date ideas and decide that the revolution will entail 'a hundred million heads.'" The most frightening moment in *The Possessed* occurs when a major, who has stumbled into the meeting accidentally, accepts this bloody theory. "I confess I am rather in favor of a more humane policy," he asserts, "but as all are on the other side, I go along with the rest." Once people are eager "to go along with the rest," they can be brought to agree to anything.

As they did: the famous *Black Book of Communism*, which appeared in 1997, calculated that the various countries under Communist rule murdered at least a hundred million people. Many have wondered at Dostoevsky's astonishing accuracy in this and other predictions about what radicals in power would do, but the reason for his prescience is not far to seek: as a former member of a revolutionary group, he understood the psychology that could have led him to commit foul deeds deemed humane.

Dostoevsky understood that many people become

conformists not only from fear, but also to free themselves of the burden of individuality. In *The Brothers Karamazov*, the Grand Inquisitor maintains that although people praise freedom, almost all want to surrender it. Free choice entails guilt and regret. Since we can never be certain of what is truly moral or even of our own motives, there is no escape from conscience. Craving certainty, people eagerly worship authorities claiming infallibility. "I tell Thee that man is tormented by no greater anxiety than to find someone quickly to whom he can hand over that gift of freedom with which the ill-fated creature is born," the Inquisitor explains. "But only one who can appease their conscience can take over their freedom." To do so, authorities appeal to the desire to surrender individuality. Worship is not sufficient if one worships alone: people "are concerned not only to find what one or the other can worship, but to find something that all would believe in and worship; what is essential is that they all may be together in it," since where people differ, doubt is always possible. Left unsatisfied, "this craving for community of worship is the chief misery of every person individually and of all humanity from the beginning of time."

"From the beginning of time": Dostoevsky's point is that humanity always faces a fundamental choice between freedom, individual conscience, and doubt on the one hand, and authority, conformity, and absolute certainty on the other. In various periods, each alternative affirms different theories. For Dostoevsky, the Inquisitor's view of life takes the form of socialism, which promises to unite mankind "in one harmonious ant-heap."

The Soviet Union was, in this sense, entirely "inquisitorial." Its fundamental tenet, as Lenin insisted, is that there is no such thing as "extra-class morality." Whatever serves the interests of the proletariat (that is, the Party) is good, whatever aids the bourgeoisie is bad. It follows that the Party cannot be wrong because its actions are right by definition. To imagine that there are standards by which the Party might be judged is to adopt a counter-revolutionary bourgeois philosophy. As Arthur Koestler's *Darkness at Noon* correctly illustrates, one reason that Party leaders purged by Stalin confessed to imaginary crimes is that they believed in the Party's infallibility. Had not they themselves justified executing other leaders on these very grounds?

Nadezhda Mandelstam explained that the word "conscience" almost entirely disappeared from Soviet discourse, which replaced it with "consciousness" (as in "class consciousness"). So long as people followed Party commands, they could not be behaving immorally. In 1976, in his memoir *To Be Preserved Forever*, Lev Kopelev described what it felt like when he enthusiastically agreed that to achieve Communism "everything was permissible — to lie, to steal, to destroy hundreds of thousands and even millions of people." And so Kopelev helped to enforce the terror famine, in which millions of peasants were deliberately starved to death. "I took part in this myself, scouring the countryside, searching for hidden grain . . . stopping my ears to the children's crying and the women's wails. . . . I saw women and children with distended bellies, turning blue, still breathing but with vacant, lifeless eyes." Not cruelty but devotion to the Party motivated Kopelev's actions. "To hesitate or doubt . . . was to give way to 'intellectual squeamishness' and 'stupid liberalism.'"

In Solzhenitsyn's novel *In The First Circle*, Klara expresses dismay at the countless deaths entailed by collectivization and purges. Her friend Gorbunov replies "gently but firmly": "Who is doing these things? Who is it who wants to do them? It is history. History does what it wants. You and I sometimes find it horrible, Klara, but . . . what matters most is the conviction that the process itself is necessary and inevitable." Not individuals but "history" — understood not as the totality of past events but as an impersonal agency in its own right — does what it cannot help doing. No one is responsible. Bakhtin referred to this idea as "living representatively," that is, imagining that one can avoid all personal responsibility by acting as the agent of government or some other collective. Such "representation" seems to provide an "alibi," but the fundamental fact of ethical human life, Bakhtin insisted, is that "there is no alibi."

Soviet education instructed people to overcome their conscience, their "squeamishness," and their "liberalism." They were instructed to aspire to the loss of their individuality and become perfectly functioning cogs in the machine. (Stalin famously offered a toast to "the cogs.") Ideally, they might achieve the highest Bolshevik virtue, *partiinost*, or Party-mindedness. As Getmanov, a devoted Communist in Vasily Grossman's *Life and Fate*, reflects, "the attitude of a Party leader to any matter, to any film, to any book, had to be infused with the spirit of the Party; however difficult it might be, he had to immediately renounce a favorite book or a customary way of behavior if the interests of the Party should conflict with personal sympathies."

Complete Party-mindedness demands still more: "a true Party leader simply didn't have personal likings or inclinations. He loved something only because, and only insofar as, it expressed the spirit of the Party. . . . true Party spirit showed itself when a sacrifice was not even necessary, when no personal feeling could survive even for a moment if it happened to clash with the spirit of the Party." In sum: what Ivan Ilych came to reject — the absolute loss of individual selfhood — is precisely what constituted the Bolshevik ideal.

And how does one learn to overcome individuality? In 1953, in The *Captive Mind*, written when most Polish intellectuals (and many other Western intellectuals) still regarded Communist rule as progressive, Czeslaw Milosz identified "the intellectual's feeling of belonging" as the key motive for conformity. As they concluded that their work could be significant only if they renounced outmoded ways of thinking, so American humanists I have known assiduously practiced the new paradigm and expository style. As Milosz explains, life becomes "acting, with the exception that one does not perform on the theatre stage" but everywhere. "Such acting is a highly developed craft that places a premium on mental alertness. Before it leaves the lips, every word must be evaluated as to its consequences." Eventually a person "grows into it [his role] so closely that he no longer differentiates his true self from the self he simulates, so that the most intimate of individuals speak to each other in Party slogans."

To be sure, Milosz continues, full identification with official thinking rarely happens. "A large residue of unassimilated matter remains" and people preserve a consciousness of having two selves. Since even ardent intellectuals cannot entirely rid themselves of their former personalities, they become "schizophrenics." And occasionally the private self reasserts itself. When doubt assails Krymov, another devoted Communist in *Life and Fate*, he questions whether he really believes what he has always thought he believed. He wonders:

"Why have I never found the strength to say, 'I really don't believe that Bukharin was a saboteur, provocateur, and assassin?'" If, as he tells himself, he always believed what he professed, why had he sometimes felt that his words "went against his deepest feelings"? "What is it I'm trying to say?," he at last asks himself. "That I am a man with two consciences? Or that I am two men, each with his own conscience? But then that's how it's always been — for all kinds of people, not just me."

In their fight for human rights, Russian and East European dissidents above all valued personal integrity and an undivided conscience. They wanted to break through the theatricality — the lies — of Soviet life, which is why they hit on the strategy of citing the Soviet constitution and insisting that it be observed in fact. When arrested and tried, they would demand that the authorities observe the code of criminal procedures. Make words mean what they say!

Westerners often wondered about the point of a public demonstration of protest that would end instantly with arrest. For the dissidents, however, such cost-benefit reasoning was a fundamental mistake: it fostered subservience and pretense. The point was to act honorably regardless of the cost. As the contemporary philosopher Vladimir Zelinsky has explained, human dignity — the "fundamental concern" of the movement — demanded "inner freedom." Dissidents sought "self-liberation from conditional, almost inborn ideological reflexes." They therefore struggled against "the degenerate, reflexive herd mentality that inevitably arises when people are bred . . . in 'incubators of opinion.'"

Is it any wonder that dissidents often cited Hans Christian Anderson's "The Emperor's New Clothes"? Andrei Amalrik compared himself to the child who says the emperor is naked. Even if others remain prudently silent, it is vital for some honest people to say what they see. "Behind any public protest," Zelinsky explained, "is an individual's attempt to break through his own social adaptation, through his own double think, and find himself. When young people enter into hopeless political conspiracies for which they are subsequently sentenced to ten or fifteen years, they do this because they want to possess their own identities among the surrounding masks." They wanted to make the public self coincide with the private self.

In his autobiography *Never Alone*, Natan Sharansky described growing up in a world in which "life was a perpetual loyalty test." To escape that life and the Soviet Union's ever-present anti-Semitism, Sharansky, like so many Jewish boys, escaped first into the chess world and then into science. Admitted to the prestigious Moscow Institute of Physics and Technology, "I had reached the double thinker's summit, as far as I could go as a Jew." Professors advised that "with our smarts and our work habits, we could live a full intellectual life . . . All we had to do was stay focused on our orderly inner world of scientific theories and mathematical theorems [and] ignore the ever-changing pseudo-truths of politics."

Was all the theatricality worth it? Already a doubter, Sharansky was struck by the dissidents' bravery. He was especially impressed with Andrei Sakharov's sacrifice of his position as the leading Soviet scientist to demand intellectual freedom. It was as if Sakharov's words were meant for him personally: "You want to run away from your life of doublethink and fear by making a scientific career, but that's impossible. There's no scientific breakthrough you can make that will free you, as long as you're enslaved to this immoral doublethink. . . . Either you overcome your fear and stand for truth, or you remain a slave to fear, no matter how fancy your titles, no matter how big your dacha."

Sharansky realized the falsity of the view that so many Americans today take for granted, that life is about individual happiness. So long as one thinks that way, one will never make sacrifices for anything higher. "When getting ahead professionally is the most important thing in life," Sharansky explained, "you become too willing to go along with everything. Why take risks? . . . To become free, to transcend doublethink, you must first overcome the fear that is always with you. There must be something more important than your career." Earlier this year, a reporter asked Sharansky why Andrei Navalny returned to Russia: did he not know he would be arrested and probably killed? For Sharansky, this question betrayed the Western assumption that the point of life is individual well-being. He described his retort as "pretty rude": "You're the one who does not understand something. If you think the goal is survival — then you are right. But his true concern is the fate of his people — and he is telling them: 'I am not afraid, and you should not be either.'"

Gradually, the young Sharansky learned inner freedom. "My doubts were growing, but I wasn't yet ready to abandon my — and my parents' — dream of finding refuge in science. The longer I stayed paralyzed, the more self-respect I lost." When he finally took the irrevocable step of applying to emigrate to Israel, "my life as a loyal Soviet citizen ended." Sharansky's scientific career was over, and his life as a refusenik and human rights activist had begun. He served thirteen years in prison and a labor camp, but he was spiritually free. "Now

I could say what I thought, do what I said, and say what I did. Finally, thirteen years before my release from prison and my move to a free, democratic Israel — I was liberated."

Until his "liberation," Sharansky had lived in two worlds, but many Soviet citizens, devoted whole-heartedly to the reigning ideology, had not even progressed to double-thinking. The main character of *In The First Circle*, Innokenty Volodin, gradually evolves from a sincere believer in Communism to a political prisoner rejecting it. First, he recognizes that in his job as a diplomat, "you need a double wall in your chest. Two thicknesses of skull and two separate memories." When he discovers his mother's pre-revolutionary diaries and favorite books, he comes into contact with a wholly different way of experiencing the world.

"Goodness shows itself first in pity" and compassion, she wrote, but he had been taught to reject such outmoded and "shameful" feelings. When Volodin reads her admonition to "respect other people's opinions even when they are inimical to yours," he thinks: "That was pretty old-fashioned, too. If I have a correct worldview, can I really respect those who disagree with me?" Even the words his mother and her friends used were "outdated. In all seriousness, they began certain words with capital letters — Truth, Goodness, Beauty, Good and Evil, the Ethical Imperative." Volodin was accustomed to words easier to understand, such as "progressiveness."

Vigorous cultural debates characterized Volodin's mother's pre-revolutionary world, whereas he routinely attends some "pompous assembly where everybody would unreservedly agree with everybody else." Hers was a life of open-ended dialogue, where you actually had to consider counter-evidence and contrary opinions. Volodin at last realizes that "he was a savage" who does not know what real reading is. Having read only those books "that were warranted sound . . . he had got into the habit of believing every word, of submitting without question to the author's will." In his mother's library he encounters books that contradict each other. "What he found most difficult of all was to lay down his book and think for himself." As Volodin views his life through his mother's eyes, he realizes that he has conducted it on a false principle. "The great truth for Innokenty used to be that we are given only one life" and therefore, since nothing higher exists, we should get as much pleasure out of it as possible. "Now, with the new feeling that had ripened in him he became aware of another law: that we are given only one conscience, too."

What does it mean to rediscover conscience? For Vaclav Havel, it meant refusing to affirm what one knows to be untrue. Yes, the system pressures people to lie, Havel wrote, but the pressure only works because people are all too willing to live that way, a willingness marking their "own failure as individuals." In each person, Havel continued, lives a longing "for moral integrity . . . and a sense of transcendence. But there is also in everyone . . . some willingness to merge with the anonymous crowd and to flow comfortably with it down the river of pseudo-life." Havel argued that conditions in Eastern Europe were in fact an extreme version "of modern life in general." The temptation to conform and to avoid risking the pleasures of consumer society does not require Communist rule. Havel therefore asked whether East Europeans "do not in fact stand . . . as a kind of warning to the West." Solzhenitsyn was sure that they did.

What do these principles of modern dissent have to do with us? Alas, a great deal. For many Americans, it seems as if we are living in an age of prescribed and proscribed beliefs. American students, for example: on March 10, 2022 *The New York Times* reported on a survey "of over 37,000 students at 159 colleges [showing that] 80 percent of students self-censor at least some of the time. Forty-eight percent of undergraduate students described themselves as 'somewhat uncomfortable' or 'very uncomfortable' with expressing their views on a controversial topic in the classroom." Faculty are similarly reticent. Like Havel's fellow citizens, they almost always tolerate this state of affairs. Why?

On July 4, 2020, a letter signed by hundreds of Princeton University faculty demanded not only requirements for "anti-racist education" and credit for "anti-racist" activism, but also a faculty committee to "oversee the investigation and discipline of racist behavior, incidents, research and publication on the part of faculty. Guidelines on what counts as racist behavior, incidents, research and publication will be authored by a faculty committee for incorporation into the set of rules and procedures." Did the faculty who signed this letter really want other faculty deciding on what they were allowed to research and publish? Twelve days later, an article by the Princeton professor of classics Joshua Katz identified four reasons that so many faculty signed. A few of them, he conceded, believe every word. Others told him that they signed the letter without reading it. Still more "felt peer pressure to sign." The most numerous group signed because "they agree with some of the demands and felt it was good to act as 'allies' and bring up the numbers even though they do not assent to everything themselves." Endorsing — whether automatically, under peer pressure, or to ally oneself with the right people — what one does not believe, including something as unprecedented as disciplining faculty for their research: how different is that from Eastern Europe?

To explain such behavior, wherever it occurs, Havel cited the example of the Czech greengrocer who placed in his window a "Workers of the World, Unite!" sign, not because he believed it or had even considered whether he believed it, but to convey "a subliminal but very definite message [that] 'I, the greengrocer XY, behave in the manner expected of me. I can be depended upon and am beyond reproach.'" How many people whose email signature contains an "indigenous land acknowledgment" or preferred pronouns resemble that greengrocer? Most likely, the overwhelming majority of professors do not favor censorship, cancel culture, or policing of views and language. But they let those who do speak in their name and so remain, like that greengrocer, "beyond reproach."

Beyond the campus, the crisis of authentic thinking is no less grave. Supinely accepted conspiracy theories abound. Regardless of where one is on the political spectrum, if one makes sure to hear only voices that exclude contrary evidence and does not allow for the possibility that decent people may disagree, then one is choosing to think inauthentically. By ruling out the possibility that one's allies may be mistaken, one demonstrates a quasi-Soviet disregard for truth. "Let us at least refuse to say what we do not think!," urged Solzhenitsyn in his famous article "Live Not by Lies!" Let us, indeed. People do not do so, they refuse this refusal, partly because they cannot imagine placing themselves outside the right group and partly because they do not wish to take any risks. Cowardice comports nicely with thoughtless thinking. "There is no loophole for anyone who seeks to be honest," Solzhenitsyn insisted. "And as for him who lacks the courage even to defend his own soul: Let him not brag of his progressive views . . . Let him say to himself plainly: I am cattle, I am a coward, I seek only warmth and to eat my fill."

If we Americans would stop finding reasons to believe what we are supposed to believe and begin developing the courage to resist conforming to our group's preferred views, we might avoid a terrible future. If one confines oneself to information from a single point of view, then one values something other than the truth. Real thinking takes work, and when everything confirms what one wants to believe, one can be sure that one's thought is counterfeit. So let us practice open-ended dialogue, learn to consider opposing beliefs seriously, and to affirm only what we have genuinely considered. We may thereby regain the power to think not thoughtlessly but thoughtfully.

KENDA MUTONGI

The Use and Abuse of Magical Thinking

Recent reports in *The New York Times* and the *Guardian* have noted that at least one-quarter of Gen-Zers believe in the idea that you can attract the things you want — luck, money, love, anything you want — by repeating certain mantras. The practice is called "manifesting." Most of these believers are devoted adepts of Rhonda Byrne's self-help mega-seller *The Secret*, which appeared in 2006 and has been translated into fifty languages. Byrne urges them to understand the "hidden untapped powers" within, and pledges that these latent powers will help them to "eradicate disease, acquire massive wealth, overcome obstacles, and achieve what many would regard as impossible." Ask, Believe, Receive — so goes the mantra. Answers are available within you; you need only will them into existence. My Gen-Z daughter, a thoroughgoing skeptic, tells me that I should check out something called *witchtok* (a subdivision of TikTok), where people of her generation "do witchcraft" to prevent bad things from happening to them. The keyword has over six million posts and over fifty-five billion views — many of which were apparently made during the Covid-19 lockdown when this kind of magical thinking flourished. Occult practices, it seems, are not primitive or medieval, but a large part of modern society everywhere: Ask, Believe, Receive.

On almost every telephone or electricity pole in Nairobi or Mombasa, on almost every bare scrap of wall, hang slapdash advertisements promoting the services of a *mganga*. The crude ads, usually printed on cheap office paper and pasted to any bare surface, confidently offer sources of help for any ailment, physical or otherwise — they promise cures for the sick, business boosts, love potions, help in resolving land issues or recovering stolen items, even remedies for erectile dysfunction. If you're suffering from bad luck, an antidote is available.

Waganga (plural) is the umbrella Swahili word for diviners, spiritual healers, traditional herbalists, or night runners. If, for instance, you think you have been bewitched, the *mganga* you would most likely consult is a diviner (pejoratively referred to as a "witch doctor" in the *lingua franca*), someone who could — ideally — mobilize supernatural powers to undo whatever malevolence might trouble you. If, more prosaically, you simply feel sick or depressed, you would seek out a *mganga* who practiced spiritual healing or traditional herbalism, someone whose remedies rely less on the occult. For the most part, though, the kind of *waganga* who peddle the services advertised on the roadside posters claim to be diviners, and their remedies rely on the cryptic and the uncanny.

The ads that the *waganga* have plastered everywhere have succeeded in making the citizens' pathologies public. In fact, they have become primary documents of urban culture and have drawn the attention of serious Kenyan artists. For example, Onyis Martin, in his series of paintings on Kenyan urban life, "Talking Walls, 2021," incorporates the boastful promises of the *waganga* onto the surfaces of his paintings. Worn away, covered with graffiti or other makeshift notices, the remnants of the ads still surface in his paintings to remind us of the *waganga*'s guarantee that they can heal our modern problems. The textures of Onyis Martin's paintings are gritty, thick with roughly applied impasto that reflects the cluttered walls of the urban landscape. The colors tend to be muted greys, tans, and browns, and the canvases are strewn with fragments of printed text, spray-painted numbers, slogans, and torn portraits. Occasionally a child's eyes stare out from a tattered ad, beseeching us from the scraps of text. Overall, the canvases present us with a palimpsest that records the indecipherable chaos of the streets; each is an archeological site of sorts, an archive, and the more we try to piece together the fragments of the worn *waganga* fliers, the more we can see the changing nature of Kenyan politics, economy, and culture over the last three decades.

Onyis Martin was born in Kisumu and raised in Nairobi, and for some time now has been collecting *waganga* posters for his art. "I remove a whole bunch every day, but there are lots of fresh ones the next day. So, someone must be responding to the message in them," he told me last year. "People are desperate. The government doesn't provide basic needs, so people go to a *mganga* for help." But the *mganga* is rarely the first resort, according to Martin. "People in distress start off by going to church, thinking that God will solve their problems. They pay the God-damned preacher who claims to be connecting them with God. When God doesn't respond favorably, they turn to the *mganga* who promises to link them with magical powers." He continued, shaking his head, "But, unlike God, this *mganga* is a real person, so if you are desperate, you end up paying him, hoping that he will solve your problems. But as soon as he takes your money, he disappears. It's about hope and desperation."

It is hard not to share Onyis Martin's cynicism. I, too, wonder why these ads have become more and more visible over the last few decades. Kenya is not the only place where the *waganga* business is booming. I have seen similar ads in almost every African country that I have visited — Uganda, Tanzania, Malawi, Cameroon, South Africa, and Senegal — so enough people must be responding to justify the ads' continued presence. *Waganga* seem to be drumming up enough business to cover the continent with their posters. Surely, all these *waganga* can't simply be conmen, and it is tempting to scoff along with Onyis Martin. But it is still the case that a quarter of Kenyans, both Christians and Muslims, "believe in the protective power of charms or amulets, and that they consulted *waganga* on a regular basis" — at least according to a Pew report published in a local daily newspaper in Kenya in 2014.

The phenomenon has not gone unnoticed by academics — according to scholars such as Adam Ashforth, James Howard Smith, Kate Luongo, Peter Geschiere, and Jean and John Comaroff, the number of people who take part in occult practices has increased throughout much of Africa over the last three decades. Generally, they have attributed this increase to neoliberal economies that have, in the name of free markets, torn apart communities and eroded many traditional relationships, and made material life more precarious for most people. As Adam Ashforth tells us, witchcraft has become "one of many complex ways in which Africans are creating modern societies as well as understanding modern changes in their socio-worlds and how the changes are connected to the rest of the world."

I don't disagree with such assessment, but there are other causes, too. If the recent appeal of witchcraft in Kenya can be traced to the contradictions of the modern world, and if we are probably right to blame neoliberalism for producing lives that are increasingly circumscribed and frustrated, there is also the mismanagement of the economy by elites and politicians, and the increase in population, and the corresponding rise in rural-urban migration — all these factors have rendered everything up for grabs. It is reasonable to argue, then, that the demands of the isolated self have become paramount, and life has become more and more about survival of the fittest — and as always, the rich are getting richer and the poor poorer. And many of those who do not succeed in the new economy attribute their failure to occult factors.

You can read James H. Smith's book from 2008, *Bewitching Development: Witchcraft and the Reinvention of Development in Neoliberal Kenya*, to learn how this works. If, for example, your neighbor's business is thriving and yours is not, surely your neighbor's evil eye must be causing your bad luck, and a diviner may just be the person you want to consult for a remedy. If a powerful politician is trying to steal your property, a diviner's spell might thwart the crook. If you cannot find a job, or someone steals your wallet in a *matatu*, a diviner's magic will surely help you locate them. So call Prof. Okafo or Dr. Swahib or Dr. Gombe for a ready solution — call someone with power to provide you with an intimate space and an interim answer that will help you heal. Call someone who will give you the sense that you are being taken care of, someone who will provide a place where you can suspend your disbelief and find whatever relief you are looking for. Call the good doctor and find a place that champions magical thinking. Ask, Believe, Receive.

When I was in Kenya last year, I photographed a few of the advertisements out of curiosity. It was my intention to call one of the advertised phone numbers and find out how the relationship between the *waganga* and their clients work; I wanted to understand for myself how exactly this place of magical thinking is created and performed. I braced myself with a cup of tea, stiffened my backbone, and began to make the call — but it immediately occurred to me that I had not invented a problem for the *mganga* to help me solve. It couldn't be anything too maudlin or melodramatic — I wasn't confident enough in my ability to maintain the fiction. I settled on "property rights," since it seemed the least personal kind of problem, and also the most intractable. I would invent a problem about land ownership.

It might seem a relatively straightforward topic, but it was a loaded issue. Fraudulent land appropriation and the illegitimate use of eminent domain have become endemic in Kenya in the last few decades, especially in the cities. One reason is that the Kenyan government has taken advantage of loans from China and used the money to build new roads and airports in

Nairobi, Kisumu, Mombasa, and Eldoret. All these improvements require land which gives the government the opportunity to claim the right of eminent domain, take over the land, and offer paltry compensation. The perils of land ownership are further complicated by the fact that all the improvements in infrastructure have led to drastic increases in rural-to-urban migration, and a corresponding rise in the value of urban real estate. In 2020, for example, real estate contributed 17.8% to the country's GDP compared to a mere 2.5% in 1994. It is no surprise that, as real estate speculation has rapidly increased, so too has land-grabbing by private developers and dishonest politicians. Though private property rights and zoning codes governing urban housing do exist, their enforcement has been sporadic and ineffective. Government officials have failed, for example, to keep up with the issuing of title deeds, owing to the high number of real estate transactions. Regrettably, these delays have made it possible for powerful individuals to grab the untitled land of ordinary citizens. As a result, every vacant lot in Nairobi bears a sign proclaiming that the LAND IS NOT FOR SALE, usually accompanied with a threat of prosecution. It is unclear whether or not the signs have any effect, other than preventing people from squatting on the land and claiming it as theirs.

All told, the troubles regarding land were tangible and familiar — the perfect topic with which to confront a *mganga*. Again, I stopped dialing. This time I hesitated over doubts about whether or not it was ethical for an academic to obtain data like this, by stealth. What value would any of the information have if I had lied to obtain it? But curiosity quickly vanquished any scruples. In any case, the *waganga* had shamelessly declared themselves doctors or professors of unspecified disciplines. Mine was a lesser offense.

It turned out that reaching a *mganga* was not quite as simple as I had hoped it would be — I had to dial at least five different numbers before a call was answered.

"Hello, hello. Is this Dr. Sangoma?" (Sangoma happens to be a term for "diviner" in South Africa.)

We started talking in Swahili.

"Yes," replied a husky voice like that of an old man just woken from a nap.

I told him that I was calling for help with a dispute over a piece of land I had bought for a prospective house.

He asked me where the land was.

"Near Thika Road," I lied.

He asked me where I was calling from.

"From Umoja," I lied some more.

When he inquired as to whether my dispute was with the government or an individual, I assured him it was with an individual and that I planned to take the case to court but was worried about the probable aggravation and delay. Without hesitation, Dr. Sangoma instructed me to go to the land, gather some soil, and wrap it in a white cloth and take it to his office in Kajiado, just outside of Nairobi. There he would prepare some medicine to mix into the soil, which I would return to the land and sprinkle it around. The medicated soil would solve my land dispute. "*Itakuwa vizuri kabisa*," he reassured me — everything is going to be fine.

The fee for the magic powder would be ten thousand shillings (equivalent to a hundred American dollars — about a monthly salary for most Kenyans).

I said I would find the money and call him back.

"Please call me any time if you have any questions."

I thanked him and hung up. Dr. Sangoma had played his part convincingly, much to his credit. He sounded like a kindly old man, someone who could be trusted — he was neither pushy or ingratiating, and his voice carried conviction. He had even revealed his location. Perhaps if I had an actual problem Dr. Sangoma's prescription for medicated soil might have had some appeal. Who's to say? Perhaps an attentive listener with a reassuring plan is all that is required by someone frustrated by the loss of land, and fed up with the time and money wasted in the land office at the behest of some crooked bureaucrat. Perhaps it would be twice as bad to be twice swindled, but I could begin to see how the receptive calm and confidence of a *mganga* might invite one to suspend their disbelief long enough at least to entertain the idea of a supernatural remedy. When everything else fails, the preternatural might prevail. It could at least for a while permit one to enter a different kind of space, a space where one could unapologetically chase away their vexations and indulge in magical thinking. This, I imagine, is a space where one goes when one has been made thoroughly desperate.

It is likely that the approximately twenty-five percent of Kenyans who consult the *waganga* do so out of similar desperation. Consider a *matatu* driver by the name of Patrick, who sought the advice of a *mganga* to help "tame" his stubbornly wayward wife. "I decided to protect my wife from *mafisi* [hyenas]," he told a reporter for the *Standard* newspaper, "by visiting a *mganga* in Lang'ata who applied some stuff on my SIM card for a fee and told me no one will ever touch my wife." Convinced of the efficacy of the cure, he boasted to the reporter that "it's been nine months now, and I am sure no one is eyeing her." I admired Patrick's faith, though I hoped he had a nearby piece of wood to knock on (a figure of speech that awkwardly exposes my own occult thinking).

And yet, however much I might suspect the surety found

in the SIM card, it is at least plausible that Patrick might believe that magical power could be found in a cell phone. These devices, that seemingly came out of nowhere, now connect Kenyans everywhere, invisibly and inexplicably. Millions of Kenyans had never made a phone call, and now, suddenly, it was possible to contact anyone, to send pictures, and to transfer money with a glowing palm-sized gadget. Kenya was the first country in the world where phone banking and money transfers were used widely, through the magical MPESA app, so if you had a phone you could miraculously receive and send money to people in the remotest parts of the country. It's not much of a leap, then, to believe that doctoring a SIM card could work magic. And so Patrick believed: the doctoring "locked" his wife from predatory hyenas. That, at least, is his reality. Perhaps we should be happy for him. Many of us pay far more for our peace of mind.

This kind of conjuring was no less real for Jane, who also visited a *mganga* to prevent her spouse from cheating on her. Jane's story, as told by a friend of hers to the *Standard*, was, shall we say, a bit more scandalous: "I almost fainted when Jane . . . confessed that she had sex with the *mganga* so that the 'medicine' would make it impossible for her husband to sustain an erection with another woman." The idea that Jane's infidelity — with a *mganga* — would disable her husband's sexual aptitude left her friend bewildered, especially since they were both "devoted members of a popular church along Mombasa Road." Jane's cuckoldry was not a casual affair, to say the least. She was so desperate to bring her husband back, and so convinced of the *mganga*'s competence, that she allowed herself to be persuaded that sex with the good doctor might unlock some kind of deep magic. That Jane's wrong would make right her husband's wrong was an instance of wishful thinking that could only be possible in her state of mind. To go along with the witch doctor's connivance, she had to be so fearful and vulnerable as to believe that her own infidelity could be homeopathic. We don't know whether or not it worked. But who can say that they have never acted out of fear or vulnerability? It is not just Africans such as Patrick and Jane who believe that thought alone can influence the objective circumstances of one's life. This kind of thinking appears to be universal — we have our crystals and our *witchtok*, our internet health cures, our billions of Rhonda Byrne devotees, and certainly our conspiracy theorists. They all nod at the occult.

Predictably, the "manifesting" mantra doesn't always work for everyone. Consider Natalie, who consulted a *mganga* because she suspected that her husband was having an affair with another woman. "He [the *mganga*] asked for [my husband's] boxers, took them, smelt them, then put them in a bowl and poured a brown liquid," said Natalie in an interview with the *Star*, another popular Kenyan newspaper. "He started chanting and after a minute, he told me to drink the liquid. At first, I told him I couldn't, but he said if I wanted to have my husband back, I had to take it." Natalie finally gave in and drank the vile liquid, after which the *mganga* chanted a little bit more, applied oil on her hands, and finally blew some chalk dust towards her face. As Natalie left, he gave her a small bottle containing more of the foul liquid and told her to add two drops to her husband's drink. She followed the instructions, but to no effect. She tried calling the *mganga* to complain, but he had disconnected his phone.

What went wrong for Natalie? Perhaps she had failed to manifest sufficiently what she had asked for; perhaps she had not believed enough. Perhaps the *mganga* had not invested enough emotional energy into her client to get her to "believe" — recall the masterful rhetorical skills of Jane's *mganga*, who talked her into sleeping with him in order to block her husband's infidelity. In any case, she received little more than embarrassment and disgust. Her *mganga* was, like most, a charlatan. A fly-by-night *mganga*; the kind of *mganga* that Onyis Martin describes, the kind that takes your money and runs. Having received their money, and fearing retaliation, they quickly disconnect their phones and disappear, until they can buy another burner phone and circulate a new number and a new name on posters pasted over the old ones.

What distinguishes these charlatans from the *waganga* who might be considered "legitimate" is that they do not make an effort to create a space of healing. They don't tell you where they live, as Dr. Sangoma did when I talked with him: "call me any time," he said to me (though whether or not I would get an answer is unknown). In other words, they don't hold up their end of the bargain by facilitating, for however short a time, the belief that a solution is forthcoming. They offer neither sincerity nor solace; they are just out to make a quick buck. Still, there are worse things than getting duped by a fly-by-night *mganga*. You could encounter an abusive one. Ciku, a cybercafe attendant, experienced a far more disagreeable encounter. Six years into her marriage she had not yet conceived a child. "I was desperate," she told the *Standard*, "I could have done anything." She consulted a *mganga*, was asked to visit his office, and when she arrived was immediately asked to strip off her clothes: "Then the witchdoctor tried to undress me, I slapped him and ran out of his 'den'." Surely, it is not possible that Ciku's *mganga* assumed she wanted to be impregnated right then and there. Surely, she was not proposing to "manifest" quite so unexpectedly or so literally. One may consult a *mganga*, and even believe in him, but it is important to be wary of what one receives.

I decided to make more calls. Since my pleasant experience with Dr. Sangoma differed so much from those I was reading about, I wanted to find out if there were anything but charlatans to be found. I was getting bolder. I planned to tell the *mganga* that my husband had run away with another woman. It seemed one of the more common problems.

I started dialing. Once again, I dialed about seven different numbers before the phone was picked up. A man with a gentle low voice said, "Hello"

"Hello," I responded, and we began to chat in Kiswahili.

"How are you?"

"I am okay. Are you the *mganga*?"

"Yes, I am Dr. Gombe."

"I have a problem. I want you to help me."

"What problem do you have?"

"My husband has run away with another woman. And he has refused to return home. And he does not even support me or our children."

"How many years have you been married?"

"Seven," I replied.

"How many children do you have?"

"Two children."

"When did he run away?"

"Two months ago."

"Is it the first time he has run away?"

"Yes."

"Have you consulted another *mganga* about this problem or am I the first one?"

"No. You are the first one."

"Do you want me to return him back home today or tomorrow?"

"Today."

"He will return," he said confidently. "But this is what I want you to do. Get a square piece of white cloth. Write your husband's name on each corner of the cloth. And then write your name in the middle. Then place an egg on your husband's name and another one in the middle of the cloth where your name appears. Then randomly spit on the piece of cloth six times. You will invoke a curse, saying the following words: 'I am cursing you, my husband. Not because of bad intentions but because I love you. I want you to return home.'"

I listened carefully, and then asked him how much he charges.

"On your part," he began, "you will have to send me your names plus seven thousand six hundred shillings [seventy dollars]. The money will assist me to get what is required to do my work, which is two chickens and incense. You will pay me five thousand shillings [forty dollars] upon his return."

"Okay," I said.

"Are you ready, so that I can embark on my work?"

"Yes, I am ready," I said politely, using the appropriate Kenyan colloquialism, as though I am receiving a blessing from God.

"Are you ready so that I can assemble my *mganga* paraphernalia? If so, send me your name and your husband's, plus seven thousand six hundred shillings, by phone. Then just give me thirty minutes. After I do my work, your husband is going to call you. He is going to apologize to you. He will start supporting you and your children financially." He was insistent: "He is going to call you today right away, and will be back home to you by seven o'clock. Are you ready for him to return home?"

"Yes, I am ready."

I told him that I was going to look for an MPESA agent and then send him the money. I hung up. The whole conversation took about three minutes. I had enough; I never called back. But I was not off the hook. Dr. Gombe called me a few minutes after our conversation, and he kept calling. Unlike Dr. Sangoma, he was aggressive, even bullying. Eventually I blocked his phone. But even that was not enough — he contacted me one last time using another phone number to send me an abusive text: "You prostitute stop blocking my number."

I couldn't help but smile. I suspected Dr. Gombe would never become a successful *mganga*, though his aggression might have been a reaction to a perceived lack of conviction on my part. Perhaps I had not granted him the authority that he felt he deserved; perhaps he might have been less abusive had I called him back as promised, and sent the money. Perhaps it was my fault.

Conmen or not, it is important to note that diviners, or witch doctors, are in fact illegal in Kenya. There is a history behind this. When the British colonized Kenya in the late nineteenth century they dismissed witchcraft stories as mere superstition, because many of the accusations were the consequence of personal grudges. Many alleged witch doctors died as a result of local rancor and resentment. And worse, as far as the colonizers were concerned, it challenged the state's monopoly on legally authorized violence. In the same way, the colonizers tried to suppress *tabibu wa dawa za kiasili*, traditional herbalists —

the local men and women understood to have a special knowledge of healing plants. In fact, colonial officials did not make a distinction between the two groups; they were both simply referred to, derogatorily, as witch doctors (granted that there were some people, as is still the case now, who claimed to do both). Yet the official efforts to stamp out *waganga* did not succeed. People continued to give credence to witchcraft narratives, and they continued to visit diviners and traditional herbalists during periods of crisis — prolonged drought that led to crop failure, for instance, or after the death of livestock. Or when a friend or relative was seriously ill or died suddenly.

In the early 1980s, however, traditional herbalists in Kenya started pushing the government to legalize their trade, as had been done in other African countries, most notably in Ghana and Nigeria, but also in places such as China, Vietnam, and Korea. Their efforts have been largely successful. By 2011, Kenya had about forty thousand registered traditional practitioners, including herbalists, birth attendants, bone setters, and faith healers. In response to the decriminalization of traditional herbalists, the diviners came forward and demanded that their businesses also be legalized. To no avail. The officials of the post-colonial government, like their predecessors, feared their authority would be undermined and that accusations of witchcraft would result in retributive murders.

Although outlawed, diviners continue to do their business, and allegations of witchcraft rarely end up having any repercussions, despite the fact that accusations of witchcraft have increased (particularly in the rural areas) along with retributive murder of supposed witches. Older widows are the usual victims of the murders since they present especially inviting targets — as has almost always been the case. Unattached, without a role in the villages, they are easily scapegoated; inexplicable misfortunes are easily attributed to their supposed "evil eye" and they are less able to retaliate with violence. This kind of targeting is hardly unique to Kenya. But the large increases in population have put a lot of pressure on the need for land and people want some kind of pretext to legitimize their claims. It is not uncommon, for instance, to see the relatives of widows' deceased husbands accuse their widows of witchcraft so that they will be kicked off their land. People who suffer from dementia, Alzheimer's, or Parkinson's often meet the same fate. Their diseases are often misunderstood (partly due to the fact that people are living longer and subject to diseases previously unknown in the villages). Since most rural people do not recognize the physical and mental changes caused by these diseases, the afflicted are considered strange and abnormal. "She acts like a witch," a thirteen-year-old boy from my village once told me, referring to a neighbor with Parkinson's disease whose spasms brought to mind the supposed behavior of witches. Once stigmatized and declared a witch, the sick widow is forcibly removed from her land and the accusers claim it. It is not unheard of for widows or the sick to be murdered.

It is important to know that diviners in the rural areas do not advertise with posters the way the diviners in the urban areas do. Like the local herbalists, diviners are usually people known in their communities as having an exceptional knowledge of plants or supernatural powers. Such people often belong to certain clans and their healing (or harming) powers have been in their families for generations. People in their communities know who they are and when to consult them. In the early 1980s, I remember vividly, my sister Linet contracted Hepatitis A from drinking contaminated water at her boarding school. Though my mother took Linet to several nearby hospitals and clinics in western Kenya, they were unable to diagnose her symptoms — fever, malaise, loss of appetite, diarrhea, nausea, abdominal discomfort, dark-colored urine, and jaundiced eyes and skin. She missed school for almost a year. Villagers who saw her eyes and her skin told my mother that Linet had been bewitched. As an ardent Quaker, my mother had never been to a witch doctor, but as Linet developed a blood clot in one of her legs due to a prolonged infection, my mother became desperate and gave in. She contacted a well-known diviner in a nearby village. Accompanied by my aunt Leya, a well-regarded traditional herbalist in our village, she selected two chickens and filled a basket with maize to take as payment. My sister, now able to look back with a triumphant chuckle, dramatized the story for me recently by mimicking the solemn witch doctor slaughtering one of the chickens and making her stand in the pooled blood as he chanted in an unknown language.

Sadly, it did not work. Even the herbs he gave her had no effect. Perhaps my mother, the staunch Quaker, had not "manifested" enough magical thinking to cure my sister. Even though she was desperate, she may have been too pragmatic and too practical in temperament to allow the diviner to "unlock" her mind long enough for her to believe that his magic could heal Linet. Ask, Believe, Receive. For her it was difficult, and probably impossible, to believe. She received nothing until a well-known medical doctor from my village helped her get a referral for my sister to Kenyatta Hospital in Nairobi. There the correct diagnosis was made; my sister was treated and she recovered.

It is undeniable that the diviner whom my mother consulted was recognized in our community, and even though his prescriptions failed to heal my sister, my mother never felt that he was a charlatan. He continued to be considered a legitimate diviner who had successfully treated many people. Sometimes mistakes are made, something unforeseen occurs in the treatment process, much like an error might occur in a Western-style operating room. We don't doubt the efficacy of the operation itself. Once in a while an unsuccessful outcome is inevitable, a consequence of human error, or fate.

For better or worse, consulting a diviner in our household was always the last resort. When we got sick, when we contracted the flu or malaria or had skin rashes, my mother would ask aunt Leya to treat us first. Leya would go into the woods, gather herbs (peppermint, sage, eucalyptus, African wormwood), add them to boiling water, and then ask us to cover ourselves with a blanket and breathe in the steam. Rashes were treated with concoctions made from aloe, periwinkle, and climbing oleander. She would combine the herbs by chewing them and then smearing the mixture on the afflicted areas. Within a few days we were cured. If the rash or flu persisted, our mother would take us to the local dispensary to be examined by a Western-trained doctor. Only when we were defeated and vulnerable would we consult a diviner. Only when we had given ourselves over to fate and stepped into the realm of magical thinking.

In the urban areas, by contrast, there are few community-sanctioned witch doctors. As the urban communities are often in flux, it is not easy to establish with certainty who operates in good faith, who at the very least offers a story or a spell that can, for a while, contain a possibility — a possibility that makes up for the gaps and the inconsistencies in the social systems or provides some ephemeral hope for the ill. It is exactly this ambiguity that encourages the hustlers and con artists whose ads adorn the walls and fences and telephone poles in the cities. They claim to have the powers of a diviner, but they do not have the trust of the community. When people in desperate situations in the urban areas don't know whom to turn to, they call the numbers on the posters and fail to get help. Without the good faith of the community to sanction the diviners who advertise in posters or to punish them, they can simply disappear when they are unsuccessful, and all they need to do to get back into business is buy a new phone, adopt a new name, and glue up new ads over their old ones.

The charlatans are a real problem for the traditional healers and herbalists. As Lydia Matoke, the president of the Herbalists Society of Kenya, has noted, the people who advertise on those posters "lack medical ethics and damage the reputations of genuine traditional healers." Matoke wants the government to step in and arrest the charlatans. "People in my community know who I am," she said. "My family, since my great-grandmother, has been using herbs to treat diseases for many years. The medicine is in the family and people in our communities know who we are, so we don't need to advertise on posters."

Yet the advertisers remain vigilant and inventive. They craftily deploy the stereotypes of diviners in Kenya by posing as someone from the Kenyan coast. (Traditional lore in Kenya has it that coastal people have powerful medicines due to their associations with djinns, and so the quacks will adopt Giriama or Swahili/Muslim names to lure their clients.) Often they use coastal Kiswahili while speaking to their clients — when I called Dr. Gombe, for example, he kept saying *naam*, or "yes" in

Arabic and coastal Swahili, instead of *ndio*, for "yes" in Nairobi Swahili. Many of them also claim to have been trained in Tanzania, since Kenyans believe that Tanzanians have particularly strong traditional medicines. The Kamba are also known for having strong *waganga* (as noted by the historian Kate Luongo, who has spent years studying witchcraft in Kenya), so some charlatans will claim to hail from Kitui, a town in Kamba known for exceptional *waganga*. In an interview conducted by one of Kenya's daily newspapers, one *mganga* who called himself Doctor/Professor Bwayo, explained that "I use the title Doctor because Kenyans easily connect to holders of big names." The title "doctor," he noted, was adopted because his services are meant "to offer a remedy, just like our brothers in conventional medicine do." When asked what makes him think that he is a professor, he asked, incredulously, "what other prefix should I use before my name?" He declined to disclose his level of education, but argued instead, "*masomo haisaidii, ni talanta kama hii niliyorithi kwa babu*" — "education is nothing compared to talent like the one that I inherited from my grandfather."

The irony seems to escape them. They want to be seen by the "modern" world as legitimate, so they appropriate its titles in their advertisements. To have any chance at success, they need to appear as accredited as the Western-educated professionals practicing in their vocations. But what they claim to offer is something altogether different. The doctors and the professors who advertise on the streets hope to capitalize on a different mode of knowing: the powers of the occult. But they do so by invoking a professional context whose practices would undermine their claims to that power.

Yet the irony isn't lost on everyone. Some towns have carried out campaigns to remove posters. In February 2021, the mayor of Nyeri, a town north of Nairobi, asked that the posters be removed and burned. According to the *Star*, the mayor said that "Nyeri people are God-fearing and will not entertain witchcraft." The people who advertise on posters, he went on to say, "are not diviners but con artists who are after fleecing residents." The real diviners had to be protected from the fake. Similarly, in August 2014, James Marwa, the leader of a county on the Kenyan coast, asked his workers to remove all the posters advertising *waganga*, saying that the advertisers were "thugs masquerading as diviners." He told the *Star* that he had "received several complaints of residents who are furious with the mushrooming of the posters and signboards in the town . . . that the posters had created a feeling of superstition in the area . . . and were an eyesore and not good for tourism as well as for children." Interestingly, when Marwa tried to arrest two of the *waganga*, some of the residents were not happy and claimed that the witch doctors were very helpful and that the posters should not be removed. According to one resident, "traditional herbalists had solutions to quite a number of problems and ailments that cannot be treated in hospitals."

Some people are cynical about the status of the charlatans. They think that the con-artists should be left alone to do their thing. Tom Kamau, a street vender, says that he knows that "some witch doctors are conmen, but they should go on with their trade, just like pastors do." To Kamau, "witchdoctors are just like pastors and priests, they reinforce superstition and fear," he said in an interview with the *Standard* in 2020. And perhaps he is right. It is sometimes possible to see that witch doctors and pastors in Kenya are offering similar services: magical intervention in order to bring luck, to make other people do things you want them to do, to resolve problems, and so on. All it takes is a certain degree of objectivity to recognize that prayer is often used as a way of asking God to bend the laws of nature to solve your personal needs. "Faith is the substance of things hoped for, the evidence of things not seen" (Hebrews 11:1–6). It would be cruel to deny suffering people the relief that they can obtain from psychological placebos; illusions sometimes have positive consequences, just as the truth can be crushing.

Anyway, the world is full of religious charlatans who profit from people's desperation just as readily, and with similar promises of rescue and salvation, as quack diviners. It is hard not to argue that the purveyors of the "prosperity gospel" in America work in precisely this way: they ask for your money, command that you believe, and promise that you will receive a tenfold reward from God. Perhaps in Kenya, and in other African countries, there is a kind of three-way cross-fertilization between Western medicine and the Gospel and the indigenous systems of healing provided by traditional herbalists and diviners.

Yet the popular media in Kenya still abounds with skeptics. On radio talk shows the guests regularly mock the diviners. "Who can treat the lack of a girlfriend?" asks a guest on one of the radio shows. "How is that even a condition? Who can treat *kukosa kazi* (unemployment), *kukosa mke* (lacking a wife) to *kukumbana na nuksi* (dealing with general bad luck)? They are treating the untreatable." And, of course, there are contemporary Kenyan artists such as Onyis Martin who strongly feel that those who advertise in posters are fakers. In several of his paintings he portrays the faces of children who appear as if they are emerging out of, or being erased from, the layered remnants of the *waganga* posters. The eyes of the children are innocent and hopeful and seem to plead for help, or at least recognition. The haunted faces look lost and vulnerable. They seem to be pleading for rescue, but are at the same time buried by the forces that pretend to offer them relief.

When I walk through the streets of Nairobi and see the *waganga* posters everywhere, I cringe. But when I return home and turn on my computer and google *witchtok* and scroll through over six million videos of Gen-Zers playfully "practicing witchcraft," I cringe even harder. Occult thinking is inescapable; it seems to be a symptom of modern urban life, stemming in part from its omnipresent "market rationalities" and its anxieties. Maybe fantasy and superstition are the only alternatives to the callous regimentations of economic rationality. Occultism is not — as is often presumed — a holdover from some archaic or primitive backwater. The primitive does not always represent some obscure atavism: here it is, everywhere among us, the West included. What is occultism if not the attribution of efficacy to forces that one cannot understand? Occult economies are at the heart of modern capitalism today — so mysterious to some that they turn to diviners to ease its ravages. Maybe the wizards of Silicon Valley, the priesthood of digital engineers, are the most powerful occultists who ever lived, even if the long-term effects of their miracle are beginning to seem less than magical.

PASCAL BRUCKNER

Victimhood, Pain, and Virtue

On December 8, 2015, French President François Hollande announced plans to posthumously award the Legion of Honour to the one hundred and thirty victims of the terrorist attacks of November 13 at the Bataclan concert hall and the surrounding area. The institution's Grand Chancellor disagreed. Since its creation on May 19, 1802, by Napoléon Bonaparte, the *Légion d'honneur* has rewarded service members and civilians for distinguished service to France. The innocent people barbarically slain in the name of jihadism deserved France's respects, but in a thousand other ways than by awarding them a medal reserved for acts of heroism. In the end, Hollande backed down and, on July 1, 2016, created the National Medal of Recognition for Victims of Terrorism, the fifth highest decoration in protocol order of precedence.

The news of this award was received coolly by some of the public and within the armed forces. It meant that those hurt or killed by fanatics were afforded higher honors than those bestowed on people who fought to defend France. Here were more symptoms of a very contemporary confusion that already sparked debate in the immediate post-war period between members of the Resistance and those sent to the camps: Is suffering torture more worthy than performing feats of valor? Are the unfortunate more heroic than the brave? In another example of this conflation, the municipal government of Paris wanted to honor Arnaud Beltrame, the police officer who offered himself — and ultimately his life — in exchange for a hostage in the southern French town of Trèbes on March 24, 2018. The plaque read "For Arnaud Beltrame, victim of his heroism." His family protested and the wording was changed.

Persecution is among those "Christian virtues that have gone mad," to quote Chesterton. That the son of God came to Earth as a crucified slave to save humanity and elevate the poor and dispossessed was outrageous to men of antiquity, and also to Nietzsche, who was a big fan of strength and aristocracy. Jesus preached not for the rich and the mighty but for the meek and the fallen. With his characteristic blend of gentleness and aggression, he set in motion the ideal of rebellion against the powerful that would shape the entire Western world, including the great secular doctrines of modernity. What is Marx's working class if not the body of Christ formed into a revolutionary bloc to upend history and create the perfect society? What are minorities in "wokeism," if not so many Christ-like effigies for us to stop and revere? Their misfortune legitimizes them, especially when that misfortune is pluralized through "intersectionality," Kimberlé Crenshaw's concept of a crossroads where several forms of oppression meet. (The more, the better, for this mentality.) Hierarchies must be inverted and the vanquished elevated above the brutes. Where the victor says, "might makes right," conversely, the victim says, "my weakness is my weapon and my right."

This quasi-sacredness of the vulnerable is one of the great prerogatives of civilization. We are the beneficiaries of this revolution, for better and for worse. It is this revolution that, over the past two millennia, has promoted compassion and sympathy and solidarity into high ethical ideals, and made possible women's rights, children's rights, the rights of exploited and enslaved and oppressed and colonized people, and their emergence into the public arena a reality. But a perverse strategy has grafted itself onto this undisputed leap forward, with both countries and individuals enthusiastically identifying as victims. This trend seems more entrenched in rich countries, whose citizenry is devoted to material pleasures and structurally dissatisfied with its lot. On both sides of the Atlantic, our current pantheons are comprised only of the oppressed and the crushed. They alone are eligible for our sympathy, and new victims — and categories of victimhood — are identified each day. It has become our great democratic passion — even the privileged want to play the maligned. Freedom, the ability that each of us possesses to lead our lives as we see fit, has above all become the right to indulge in self-pity.

The word "victim" is polysemic. To be robbed or to be hurt in an accident is not the same thing as to be raped or to be tortured. But within the cult of victimhood there is no gray — only black and white. Everyone, especially since World War II, has aligned their own condition with that of the most afflicted. Traditionally, victim status has been accorded by historians or the courts: the former described the reality of a massacre, the latter confirmed that reality and drew conclusions from it. The road to recognition was long and often paved by countries or governments. But today, in a time of impatience distended by social media, people hurry the process along by crowning themselves martyrs. The French Revolution's lists of grievances set the precedent. But consider the phenomenon of what might be called grievance studies, these recriminatory departments in American universities that break down into a myriad of social groups who dub themselves martyrs from the outset. Armenians, Jews, enslaved people, colonized people, Harkis (the Algerian soldiers who enlisted in the French army during the Algerian War), and gays had to wait around impatiently for a long time before being recognized. We no longer have the courage to wait; we want to identify as pariahs now. What does it mean to be a victim? Is it a narrative identity we adopt and expect others to confirm? Is it a pathology of recognition, the desire to be identified without having to introduce oneself?

The intense hero-idealism of the nineteenth and twentieth centuries has been replaced by the intense victim-idealization of the twenty-first, at the risk of mass-producing false martyrs who crowd out the real ones. It has become the alibi of killers, such as Vladimir Putin, Recep Tayyip Erdoğan, and Hamas, who rely on some ancient wrong to drape themselves in the mantle of martyrdom as they commit their crimes. After 1945 and the Holocaust, the Jewish people were put atop a pedestal, and then toppled off it when they became Israelis, accused of every evil: colonialism, racism, imperialism. From blessed to cursed: from their model station the Jewish people have become the rival to eliminate if one is to take their place. We most clearly understand the entire Middle East conflict when we see it as a global fight to win the title of humanity's wicked stepchild. On a planetary scale, a competition is playing out for who can scream their distress the loudest. The brotherhood of the fallen is met by a cacophony of injured voices who hold the whipping boy in their highest esteem and feed the two great passions of revenge and resentment. White or black supremacists, radical Islamists, bitter male supremacists, wrathful neo-feminists, angry environmentalists, revanchist Slavophiles, vindictive neo-Ottomans — each claims a stolen glory or past disaster it can accuse its enemies of perpetrating. How many defeated empires, Russia, Turkey, Iran, China, don the raiment of the damned so they can indulge in the unbridled hubris of avenging ancient wrongs? How many independent countries point the finger at their former colonial powers only to continue to exploit their own peoples?

Once in power, the natural trajectory of any persecuted person is to become the persecutor. Painting oneself the victim is, in truth, a form of warmongering: the more you feel sorry for yourself, the more entitled you feel to punish those you call enemies, your tears fat with rage and animosity. Dispossessed status enables one to potentially enjoy every right, especially the right to accuse others in the name of one's trauma, even if the accusation is tantamount to a conviction with no other form of process or trial.

The final stage in victim identity formation is the crowding out of actual victims in favor of opportunist pariahs whose only distinction is having the networks and the reputation that enable them to stake their claims. In a dark comedy, the fortunate and the powerful also want to belong to the aristocracy of the margins and form new disadvantaged castes, brandishing their reduced fortunes like a weapon. How did the messages of the Enlightenment and of the French Revolution, messages of a better world rid of fatalism and zealotry, lead to a society of sniveling and fragility? But while victim status has become all the rage, what is really astounding is that suffering has become the new sacred. Formerly the fate endured by all of humanity, suffering is now a trophy one proudly displays to impress one's contemporaries. It provides you with a borrowed identity, transforms you into someone exceptional who can peacock in public on the cheap. Even Donald Trump has compared himself to Alexei Navalny. Trump's supporters have likened him to Jesus himself and elevated him, after his brushes with assassination, to secular sainthood — complete with stigmata! Silvio Berlusconi used to say that he was the Italian Jesus, prepared to endure any torment to save his people. (In fact he lived one of the least tormented lives on the planet.) The ultimate dream would be to achieve martyrdom without having to suffer anything worse than the misfortune of being born.

There are several explanations for this. Democracy's default setting is dissatisfaction; it perpetuates a thirst that it cannot slake and escalates rivalries. Its inputs are indignation, rebellion, and envy. It makes each of us citizens more worried about the things we don't have than about the things we do. The prosperity enjoyed by some fuels a permanent state of jealousy based on ceaseless social comparison, and the privileged are not spared. Collectively, as Odo Marquart has observed, we are struck with the syndrome of the Princess and the Pea, Hans Christian Andersen's heroine who tosses and turns all night because of a tiny pea stuck under her mattress. As modern medicine eases our living conditions, so does our sensitivity increase. Broadly speaking, the mythology of victimhood has been explained by the discrepancy between what the modern world promised and modern reality itself. But what if the opposite were true? If the unquestionable successes of science and industry instead have provoked our impatience? So many ills have been overcome, so many injustices righted, that we are astonished that they cannot all be resolved within the hour. The advanced state of our civilization creates, despite itself, as much suffering as it eases. By setting up well-being and health as a minimum standard, the lack thereof becomes all the more intolerable.

Today's prevailing hedonism accentuates what it would rather downplay: the omnipresent terror of pain, both physical and psychological. A society in which happiness is mandatory is also one that incessantly speaks the language of distress. In a warped shift of meaning, it calls anything that frustrates its ambition a "hardship." The Greco-Romans sought to limit suffering by applying logic to its causes; Christianity exalted suffering to redeem humankind; we, meanwhile, deny suffering's very existence in the crazy hope that it will disappear if we deprive it of any public expression, with the result that new categories of victims crop up every day and public or private grumbling has never been so common. Young people in rich Western countries have been called the "snowflake generation" as an expression of their extreme fragility. Hordes of "vulnerable groups" line up to share their despairs and fears.

When we compare previous centuries to our own, what has changed is not the number of scourges humanity is burdened with but the way we think about them. Europe's classical era could be pessimistic, merely confirming the dogma of original sin: crimes and atrocities ensued as proof of our wickedness, which will be redeemed by God. The tragedy starts in the Renaissance, with the hope for a better world, provided only that man account for his failures. This promise to build a reasonable Eden with the tools of the welfare state, education, and law remains, by definition, unfinished, and therefore perennially disappointing. Whatever we do to help ourselves, it is never enough. The more we try to make our lives easy, the more any residual difficulties seem to us insurmountable obstacles.

In France especially, where the welfare state is in equal measure bloated and ineffective, we live in a cycle of raised and dashed expectations. The government looks after us, takes its citizens under its wing and assures them their country will not forget them. In a society of thoughtful consideration, we are overprotected from cradle to grave, taken by the hand and set on the right track. Everyone's exposure to adversity must be lessened to the fullest possible extent. But as our protection is ever more provided for, so too do our fears loom larger. We are never sufficiently fulfilled, loved, or rewarded, and our structural disappointment grows.

Just one century ago, in a French secular republic emerging from a dehumanizing Great War, effort and endurance were the norm, the minimum discipline to which people had to submit in order to succeed. Now our comparatively enviable living conditions make us less tolerant of hardships. File "effort," "tenacity" and even "setback" under "unpopular." What is new is the indeterminacy of suffering and non-suffering. Every day new harms emerge to which we prove less than resilient. The difference is perceptible between generations, with older people better tolerating expectations deemed shocking by younger people. Every twenty years or so, our sensitivities recalibrate and what earlier generations deemed pain or pleasure is recategorized.

Consider our vision of work, particularly since the pandemic. For some, work is a "right-wing" value; for others, work has, since the Enlightenment, contributed to liberating the individual, raising people up from ignorance. To work is to transform oneself while transforming the world. People turn down traditional employment, such as physical labor, unless it is as play, in the form of sports or fitness. Jobs in building and road construction, the food-service and hospitality industries, but also nannies, security guards, delivery people, and house cleaners — these we leave to immigrants, in both France and the United States. Who are immigrants? Those who carry out the menial work we no longer willingly accept. When young generations in France and elsewhere say they want a job that has meaning, they forget, in their noble request, to consider caring and maintenance positions, the humble tasks that ensure that our streets are clean, our restaurants open, and our children supervised.

Citizens of modern democracies are both spoiled children raised rather permissively and exacting customers who are always right. My parents expected to have to wait, to delay gratification. Since 1968, we have only known multiple and instantaneous satisfactions, accelerated by developments in digital technologies. The individual in a democratic society no longer tolerates frustration and waiting, which is likened to an affront, almost an oppression. He remains until adulthood "His Majesty the baby," to borrow Freud's expression. Veruca Salt wants a Golden Goose *now*. The right to have rights has mutated into the right to have every right, with rights being confused with "whatever makes me happy." Any limitation or refusal makes me a victim and legitimizes my fury. Any duties, already reduced to a bare minimum, are experienced as new abuses. Whatever our age, we act like adolescent slackers irritated by the slightest restriction who confuse being subject to any confines with being clapped in irons. Hence, today's employees' preference for a maximum reduction of the workweek, if possible for the same salary. Hence, the reflexive aversion to any restrictive policy seeking, for example, to reduce the speed limit or establish low-emissions zones in cities, the latter being disadvantageous to owners of older cars. The memory of the Gilets Jaunes insurrection in 2019 is still too recent to regulate a means of transportation that remains essential for the majority. Prohibiting anything in a democracy without first embarking on a lengthy awareness-building campaign is still seen as political suicide.

Even higher education gets likened to serfdom. In seeking to spare our kids any vexation, after the 1970s, schools have often given up on educating. Grades became tantamount to violence and were swiftly replaced with letter grades that were then considered no less detrimental. We must help pupils blossom, not stuff their heads with useless knowledge! And when they *are* taught the classics, we must spare them any linguistic challenges, unacceptable anachronisms, and pompous wording, not to mention any negative representations of women or minorities, so as not to offend their fragile souls. As a result, standards fall and functional illiteracy rises.

Those private schools that still care about excellence and competition are thriving. Meanwhile, the new Internet professions (blogger, YouTuber, or Instagrammer) require no other skills than an appealing look, a glib speaking style, and an eye for novelty, while trivializing difficult work and underpaid advanced research. Discomfort has always been a code, across various societies, but one that has continuously changed over time. We no longer see misfortune in sharp focus, if indeed we ever did. The boundary between what is normal and what is pathological is in constant flux, at the risk of our losing all sense of proportion and mistaking temporary setbacks for unsurpassable disasters.

Instead of challenging each other to excel, people in the West too often race each other for a seat on the struggle bus and make it a point of honor to share how terribly they're doing. A good ego is now a suffering ego, never a conquering one. Hence, suffering now sells more than sex. Take, for example, the raft of crybaby "autofictions" vying each year to tug the hardest at readers' heartstrings with their tearful confessions. Authors both male and female describe the physical violence, sexual abuse, poverty, and nasty alcoholic parents at the root of their trauma. This genre is far from new, first appearing in Europe in the eighteenth century with British and French sentimental literature that the Marquis de Sade laughed at in his day. Child-abuse novels get vast print runs and influence court cases. In these highly coded works, you have to drip-feed the reader your pain, not tip from pity into grotesquerie. (Or, as the *Guardian* critic and journalist John Crace put it, "the art is to portray yourself as a victim while selling yourself as a survivor.") A terminal cancer diagnosis will have no chance of moving people unless you actually die, but then you won't be around to enjoy all your success. This trend salts the earth that literature grows in, reducing it from an imaginative creation to a mere laundry list of despondent moods. From their comfy beds, everyone breaks into their little formulaic laments. If all you had to do to have talent was suffer, people would know!

Misfortune is no longer obscene but takes up the whole stage, and as soon as it appears it silences doubters and demands respect. The rules of ordinary ethics no longer apply to those with a claim to victimhood, aglow with every virtue, part of the Holy Family of the outcast. This is why the market value of the dispossessed fluctuates over time. Landing the title of "victim" — and, above all, keeping it — is a tall order. Whatever one does, it will always be to the detriment of other oppressed people who are not in the public spotlight. Tell me who your preferred victim is and I will tell you who you are: for the Vatican, migrants; for environmentalists, the planet. For others, the victim animals, Claude Lévi-Strauss's "Other-of all the Others," hunted down with dogs, tortured in slaughterhouses, dealt the death blow in the corrida. For still others, it is the Ukrainians on the receiving end of Russian imperialism, the Uyghurs, the Yazidis, the Kurds. On the left now Palestinians are especially in favor since war broke out in Gaza in 2023. Through contagion by, proximity to, or solidarity with the one-hundred-percent-certified oppressed, you too can glom onto the great clan of the stigmatized. Generally speaking, *intersectionnalité oblige*. If both true and false martyrs abound, it is because of the vast crowd of candidates in the running.

To be acknowledged as a victim is to have every right, no strings attached. In France, where violence is a thousand-year-old tradition, riots still have a positive connotation in memory of the French Revolution, the July Revolution of 1830, the Revolution of 1848, and the Paris Commune of 1870. Global warming, the crises of rural and blue-collar communities, and the challenges faced by truckers, livestock farmers, and "excluded" housing projects, apparently warrant the damage caused by rebellious violence without anyone incurring the slightest punishment. Freud's idea of the crowd, that "collective soul independent of the individuals comprising it," is always innocent, the raging masses are an indomitable deity, and woe is he who would dare call them to account, especially in a court of law. These insurgent groups are not subject to basic law: drug dealers, armed robbers, even terrorists are exempt on the ground that they belong to the "racialized." Everywhere "excuse culture" is flourishing. In 2018 we watched the Gilets Jaunes destroy monuments, vandalize the Arc de Triomphe, threaten the French president's life, and brutally beat the security services (who also injured a number of Gilets Jaunes) without overmuch concern or having to pay for the damage caused, all in the name of "the People's" holy wrath. The right to demonstrate and express one's righteous fury is sacred, especially when the nobility of the cause (be it our burning planet or its downtrodden people) justifies the savagery of the means.

If we invert the opening line of *Anna Karenina*, we might say that the maligned are all alike, only happy people are happy in their own way. When it comes to miserabilism, extremists at either end of the political spectrum act identically, both in Europe and the United States. All adopt the defensive speech of the slave fighting for his survival: for example, the French racist journalist and politician Éric Zemmour's concept of "Francocide" in reference to the ghastly murder of a twelve-year-old girl by an Algerian woman. Why this need to transform an appalling news item into an instance of civilizational war? The trend is always to carry one's line of argument to the extreme, so as to move readers to anger or pity. Back in 1993, while an actual war of ethnic cleansing was underway in Bosnia, Jean-Marie Le Pen said the French were suffering from ethnic cleansing. Two years earlier he used the phrase "cultural genocide" (in reference to contemporary art) at a time when the left was in power, because the left "insisted upon compliant socialist art, worthy of Goebbels." You have to hold the voters' attention, and the more willing you are to exaggerate, the more persuasive you become. Now, as then, Nazi name-calling abounds, the vocabulary of the Second World War recycled *ad nauseam* and applied to every subject.

An identity built on victimhood is the democratic version of privilege. Like the aristocratic "de" of a noble surname, it is a distinction handed down from father to son, mother to daughter, the new blue blood that establishes you in one of the only two nobilities democracies recognize: merit and trauma. According to the French university professor Johann Michel, for example, one can "become a descendant of a slave" — his book is actually called *Becoming a Descendant of a Slave* — the way one becomes a woman according to Simone de Beauvoir, with a reconstructed ancestry, in this case focusing on the fight of the "Maroons," the formerly enslaved who rose up against their masters. Victimhood entrepreneurs begin as memory entrepreneurs, who revive painful chapters from history in order to claim them and unite. Theirs is a doleful aristocracy outlining a reverse caste system in which having suffered harm supersedes the advantages of high birth.

Our culture, as Robert Hughes presciently observed in 1993 in a book of the same name, is a "culture of complaint," of whiners upset by everything, even their successes. Affirmative action policies “send us the message that there is more power in our past suffering than our present achievements” as the African-American essayist Shelby Steele put it. Any attempt to flourish today would therefore be pointless; the traumas of the slave trade and segregation surely weigh too heavily to be overcome. Being the Wretched of the Earth is becoming a profession with hereditary transmission of victim and perpetrator status. Dynasties of despoiled people endure through the ages, armed with their prerogatives. At the risk of being labelled pretentious, or indeed a sham, as they take their places among the outraged, the cleverest have become masters in the dark art of trading on their underdog condition.

But any official victim will first encounter an enemy, not in the person of his torturer but in that of other sufferers, the sheer number of which repels him. This is why the Holocaust has become a symbolic treasure chest that must not be left to Jews alone. No, they must make way for all victims of torture, Native Americans, enslaved people, Africans, Palestinians from Gaza, the LGBTQ community, and so on. We are not trivializing genocide — on the contrary, we remain fascinated by this ultimate evil that should benefit other, more deserving, groups! In this respect, the Holocaust denialism of Robert Faurisson in France or of the Iranian or Turkish governments is a symbolic swap: some people deny that the gas chambers or the Armenian Genocide ever happened in order to better oppress those who claim to have been their victims. The Jews hide their crimes in the Middle East behind the screen of the Holocaust, the Armenians hide their complicity with Turkey’s enemies in 1915. The stakes are high. The great advantage that bad fortune has over good fortune is that it procures you a destiny. Only misfortune counts as admission to this new aristocracy. But there’s never much room on this mental pedestal, is there? It is an elite club and rough types, copycats, and pale imitations don't get past the velvet rope. The victim identity is a pitiless Darwinian one, which explains the sharp rise in antisemitism since October 7, 2023. The Holocaust is *ours*, not *yours*!

Oppressed peoples or groups have only one right, but it is sacred: the right to no longer be oppressed. And we owe them only one duty, that of coming to their aid if they are threatened with annihilation. But having been subjugated or discriminated against confers no metaphysical superiority on any category of human beings over others. The idea that such a category of people is always right, even when they resort to violence, is untenable. No minority gets a free pass for barbarity, nor does it enjoy some metaphysical grace that would exempt it from accountability in consideration for the suffering it has endured. So enough with these holier-than-thou groups, especially in the Global South, who brook no criticism and figure that they are forever owed whatever they want to make up for crimes perpetrated against them centuries ago.

Victims are our ambassadors in a land of darkness that they have surveyed with a courage that commands our admiration. As scars fade over time, so, too, can disaster be turned to our advantage. We are not merely the products of our history and backgrounds. We have this leeway called freedom and it enables us to escape determinism. We can switch tracks like a train, though it may require a long struggle, and see our afflictions end, with the old lines of hatred and anger falling into disuse, grown over with tall weeds. We are descendants but even more we are forebears, cutting the ribbon on an unwritten future. The miracle of childhood starts the human adventure all over again from a new starting point, and it need not perpetuate its elders' wrath. All we can wish for younger generations is that they cast off our old grudges.

To resist victimhood's self-righteous pull, you must step outside yourself, not surround yourself with self-proclaimed martyrs, so drunk on their own condition as to approach hypnosis. Building misfortune up into a sacred space makes any escape from one's wretched situation impossible. It is possible to recover from serious injury or disease or from a horrible experience and still continue to love, to hope, and to work. The greatness of a life well lived resides wholly in our recovery from disappointments and humiliations, our abandoning them to the black hole of the past to better step into a future full of unknown wonder. Cradled and coddled in the prosperous second half of the twentieth century, are we capable of facing the challenges of climate disruption, the return of war, and terrorist inhumanity? Who will instill the courage in future generations not only to face but also to overcome adversity with their heads held high, without faltering, without moaning, without failing? *That* is reality, and it alone will tear us from the narcissism of victim culture. We must learn to resist the seductive allure of panic, of admiring misery. We must learn to suffice with the heroism of being human.

Translated by Jennifer Gore

KARL KIRCHWEY

After Six Hundred Years, the City of Lausanne Appoints Its First Female Night Watch

for Cassandre Berdoz

Cassandra does not sing the fall of Troy,
where Little Ajax raped her in the sanctuary.
She does not sing her slaughter by Clytemnestra
while Agamemnon beat his fists on the ground.

From the tower of the Cathedral called Notre Dame,
what Cassandra sings is the passage of time.
She sings the hour, east toward Jerusalem,
then south across the lake to Évian,

through the cardinal points, following on
the great bell that is called *Mary Magdalen*,
that shakes you with the aftermath of its hum-tone.
And there is another bell than this hourly bell,

smaller, a bell called *Clemency*, whose do
sounds a warning to announce and follow
calamity, carved with a bas relief to show
a gowned woman kneeling on a scaffold,

and an angel stays the sword of the executioner.
But I swear to you by each cobble and rafter,
Cassandra, I swear by the narrow red door
  you opened for me in a wall of stone

melting like a sugar cube in the rain,
I tell you, long ago I knew someone
who heard the hours pass, felt the commotion,
  but could not rise to flee from where she lay,

in your city of staircases and Burgundian Gothic.
Cassandra, sing to the plume of crematory smoke
that drifted southwest out over the lake,
  sing to the killing hearth, *Cover your fire!*

Sing to the night that marriage is unmerciful.
With every breath, sing that there is no angel.
Cup your hands, when the growling bronze is still,
  and sing that the executioner's arm works in different ways.

Operation Pacific *(1951)*

It was just a B-grade submarine movie (or maybe all sub
movies are B-grade), a vehicle for John Wayne,
whose drawling virility I always resent,
while Patricia Neal plays his ex-wife, though off-screen
her lover Gary Cooper visited the set
to try to persuade her to abort their fetus.
And after all the khaki, depth charges and dud torpedoes,
while they're sitting together in a Honolulu nightclub,

at the very moment when her dazed come-hither look
was on my last nerve, somehow the writer-director
throws himself a life-ring, on this property
where the hero keeps returning like a commuter,
and borrows a few lines from the *The Odyssey*,
so Neal as Lieutenant (j.g.) Mary Stuart
reaches way back and, not missing a beat
while talking about a young pilot, says to Duke,

He wants to go someplace where they never heard of the Navy.
His idea is to fly back to Wichita, Kansas
and start walking inland carrying a pair of oars
and stop when he gets to a place where someone says,
"What is that anyway you've got on your shoulders?"
a place where they never season the food with salt,
and then he'll know that his wandering's done, that's it.
He'll die in his own bed surrounded by family.

And although the reference goes right over Duke's head,
it did feel somehow as if a black hull had surfaced nearby,
its teak decks sieving the creamy runnels of salt,
to watch a broken-backed freighter in its death agony:
and you could have knocked me flat for just a moment,
that prophecy of peace after so much war
definitely the last thing I would have looked for
amid all the routine lies of postwar Cold War Hollywood.

Anzeindaz

For years I lived on the mountain,
but I never drank from the high stream
where it flashes over gray scree

on its way down to the valley
after percolating through the glacier
that holds grains of carbon and pollen,

maize and grasses, smoke, plague and famine,
spores of fungus on the manure of cattle,
a thousand years legible in its core.

I wanted my words to be like that,
but I was too careful in my body.
Then one day I found I was dragging

a sled twice my weight through a plush tunnel
studded with fool's gold and inhabited
by pale eyeless creatures and mouths.

In one of a hundred gleaming caves,
I stopped to consider a hunger
that sickens before it is sated.

I found I starved down nicely.
I slept in a fetal curl and earned
some weeks of my own foul making.

When I woke, it was with the taste
of bitter coins in my mouth,
and the stream was nowhere in sight.

I was ready to drink anything I could read through.

The Woodcock

It was almost vulgar the way that it was just
so pronounced, how innocent they were.
—photojournalist Lynsey Addario, 3.15.22

On the front page of the newspaper this morning,
there was a photograph of a mother and her children
killed by a Russian mortar round

as they tried to flee across a ruined bridge.
They lay as if a strong wind had blown them down,
and I thought: They look like dead birds.

Later, on the ramp behind my office,
I found a dead woodcock, also known as
a timberdoodle, bogsucker, night partridge,

brush snipe, hokumpoke, or becasse,
and once thought to winter on the moon.
I studied its cryptic plumage,

the richest thing I had ever seen,
an earthworks, a stone tracery, a selvage,
with tuftings of the softest gray down,

like dawn coming up on the world
or the filling torn from an anorak,
and a row of dark eyes that did not blink,

rimmed with salt when some infinitely mild
touch lingered along its side
before leaving it to the viaticum

of its wounds and their copious blood
— since the woodcock is hunted as game,
"best cooked pink, and just a little bloody."

CELESTE MARCUS

America Giveth

The abstract principle that human beings are born with dignity is too difficult for a person to formulate on her own. It had to be formulated by many minds in concert over generations and then enshrined in philosophical texts which shape worldviews and governments. Though the idea of human dignity is at least as old as the Bible, it was not set down in a political philosophy until millennia later. Liberalism is the word we use to refer to the systems of belief and the politics which are buttressed by this principle. It instructs that human dignity endures even when it is abused. And as a political philosophy, liberalism constrains the power of government in service to this inalienable human dignity. Liberalism hectors, and long may it do so, that might does not make right. Might can ignore the truth, but it cannot annul it. In a liberal country — and America is the only country founded explicitly on that philosophy — our leaders serve at our behest. Power does not confer dignity: humanity does. We are blessed to be born late, after this tradition had been developed, and after the government formed upon it has grown fat and sophisticated.

Fat and sophisticated, but alas not always wise. In our country every four years the electorate grants power to a single executive, on the condition that that power be checked and bent to the citizens' will and rights and good. But it is possible for a liberal system to democratically grant power to an illiberal leader, a leader who has contempt for individual rights and who does not have faith in the liberal system. Insofar as they are only a poll, elections are value-neutral and can reward illiberal leaders and parties without being undemocratic. Such a leader, once elected, can corrupt the power of the presidency by governing as if power itself is constrained by nothing but other power, and that rights are a myth which the citizenry cannot insist upon. Such a leader, like a medieval king, mistakes rights for privileges, which he believes are his to give and his to take away.

There have been power-hungry American presidents before, but the power that they were hungry for derived from the mechanisms laid down in the Constitution. American identity has been perverted, misinterpreted, swollen, shrunk, and turned in on itself — but before Trump the many varieties of abuse dealt to the country by its elected leaders were all products of a particular president's perverted interpretation of what America was supposed to mean. Trump is different. For Trump, American power is in service to nothing but the personal interests of the man at its helm. Even more than he detests those who "poison the blood of our country," as he once put it, he adores himself. He is a misogynist but misogyny is not his worldview, and a racist but racism is not his worldview. Self -preservation and self-aggrandizement are his operating principles. Power for power's sake — fascism, in a word. Trump's prejudices are all handmaidens of his avarice.

Donald Trump's stranglehold on our power is premised on wringing out the liberalism which is the lifeblood of this country. He is a bloodhound, and he follows the scent of his own interests with a sub-intellectual zeal. The liberal system was designed to constrain precisely his variety of brute greed, and so he is hellbent on destroying the liberal system — our system, the system of government upon which American identity depends. The system that has made this country the most powerful source and defense of freedom in human history, and the philosophy which informs that system, is the price of his perpetual ascent.

On January 6, 2021, our current president goaded thousands of violent supporters to attack the U.S. Capitol because, he insisted, the election held that year had been stolen from him. He instructed the mobs to fetch for him what was rightfully his. This was a lie which he told in order to protect himself. That day was traumatic for the country because on it a former president sowed distrust in the democratic process throughout the population of a great democracy. But for Trump something else happened that day: for the first time, and irrevocably, he associated his interests with the obliteration of our democracy. When he returned to power — through the very system he now permanently associates with his own defenestration — he returned to destroy it.

It is often pointed out that, while Trump allies himself with various far-right groups (the Christian right, for example) he is not strictly speaking an adherent of any far-right ideology — of any belief system at all. This line of argument is sometimes trotted out to make the point that Trump is not as bad as the company he keeps. This is true: he is worse. His many allies have various discrete concerns, various uses for Trumpian contempt for the liberal system, but Trump's concern, his aggressive obsession, is with the system itself. And so every beneficiary of American liberalism — and American beneficiaries in particular — is duty-bound to consider Trump and his allies the gravest threat to our wellbeing and our future.

Powerful leaders of one minority group in particular, the American Jewish community, are already shirking that duty. I write as a member of that group, in the first-person plural, because I believe we have a duty to denounce the cowardice committed in our name.

On January 20, 2025 — the first day of Donald Trump's second and final term as president of the United States, the president issued about one thousand five hundred pardons and commuted the sentences of fourteen of the supporters of his who had, at his instruction, mounted that violent insurrection against the Capitol four years prior. Among those pardoned were members of the Proud Boys and the Oath Keepers, two violent white-supremacist groups. On that same day Rabbi Ari Berman, the current president of Yeshiva University, gave the benediction at Trump's inauguration.

Berman is not the only Jewish leader — in both America and Israel — to be displayed by this administration as proof that there are Jews, even important Jews, who give Trump their blessings, despite his flirtation with white supremacy and even Nazism. But it was a poetically significant moment — the Jew blessing the king on the same day that the king had pardoned and defended a man in a Camp Auschwitz sweatshirt. Berman's treachery is representative of a strategy that deserves analysis and condemnation. Black, Latino, and women leaders have also been called upon to sell their blessings in service to our Bigot-in-Chief, but this dishonor has peculiar relevance for the Jew.

Berman's pandering is a betrayal of his people because it gives support to the undermining of the liberal system by which Jews — for the first time in our history, including before both exiles and after the advent of the Jewish state — were acknowledged to have rights that are axiomatic, not an expression of a monarch's whim or economic need. Those rights, and the full citizenship that followed on them, were based on nothing other than our humanity. America was the first political power to insist that Jews have dignity because *all* human beings do. George Washington himself said as much in his sterling letter, written in 1790, to the Hebrew Congregation in Newport, Rhode Island:

> The citizens of the United States of America have a right to applaud themselves for having given to mankind examples of an enlarged and liberal policy — a policy worthy of imitation. All possess alike liberty of conscience and immunities of citizenship.
>
> It is now no more that toleration is spoken of as if it were the indulgence of one class of people that another enjoyed the exercise of their inherent natural rights, for, happily, the Government of the United States, which gives to bigotry no sanction, to persecution no assistance, requires only that they who live under its protection

> should demean themselves as good citizens in giving it on all occasions their effectual support.

For once, the Jews' sameness brings them security and even secures the legitimacy of their own institutions of power. America is special because, finally, Jews are not, because Jews here do not have to be. Separateness, cohesion, defenses against assimilation — all of these are choices Jews can decide to make or not. But America owes us the same rights as our fellow citizens, and for the same reason.

The Jewish American is a type of significance to both traditions. No minority which benefits from the largesse of American liberalism has spent more time than the Jew languishing in illiberal alien states. None has exerted more effort in developing mechanisms for securing privileges in societies which grant minorities no rights, of growing dependent on those privileges before, as inevitably happens, they are taken away and the process of dependence and gratitude and nervousness had to begin again somewhere else.

In the millennia that Jews have spent in the Diaspora, no country other than America has based its own right to exist on its duty to honor its citizens by making itself blind to those citizens' personal identities and group memberships. American liberalism was not an act of charity but of self-preservation. It is the only prudent way to guarantee social peace in a heterogeneous society. Equality is not a favor our elected leader does for us — it is his obligation, and the obstruction of our equality is a betrayal of the office with which he has been entrusted. Liberalism was the philosophical mechanism which granted America authority to separate from Great Britain and govern itself. No country is more indebted to and dependent on the liberal system — and more allergic to monarchy, or any kind of absolute and unquestioned authority, which was what liberalism sought to dissolve — than ours. And so Jewish success in America is a testament to the success of the American project, as is true of all minority groups. Insofar as the Jews are distinct from other vulnerable Americans, we are distinct because we have more empirical evidence, more lived experience, that no other system is as reliable and as ethical as the liberal system is. The alleviation of our vulnerability is proof of America's promise. America absorbed us — however incompletely, but then America does not demand complete absorption — and we are both, America and its Jewish inhabitants, stronger for it.

The Trumpian flirtation with monarchism titillates his followers. It winks at a bloody dispensation in which monarchs enjoyed absolute power — executive orders galore. Memory is strong, long, and alive in our bones: people respond automatically to Trump's invocation of monarchism by reverting to pre-modern genuflections. The tech bros trooping in and out of Mar-A-Lago, and then in and out of the White House, to kiss the ring distinguish themselves in this regard, but they are not alone in their atavistic behavior. Jews have also had to appease all-powerful leaders who had no respect for their rights or wellbeing. By the time liberal society had been invented, Jews had spent many centuries developing tools for securing protections. Trumpian illiberalism seems to have awakened in much of the American Jewish population a slumbering but deeply held faith, a kind of buried collective memory, that in an illiberal system a different relationship to power must hold. And so American Jewish leaders such as Rabbi Ari Berman of Yeshiva University morphed like clockwork into their medieval ancestors.

It is enlightening to situate Jewish hospitality to Trump in the political history of the Jews in the exile. Throughout the exile Jews used to develop formal alliances — and, where possible, informal relations — with the ruler of the country. These alliances with the supreme central power were preferred to the other option for establishing a measure of security for themselves — an alliance with the population among which they lived, or with local secular and ecclesiastical authorities whose antipathy to and fear of Jews was reliably more powerful than whatever benefit Jews could offer them. The sovereign, by contrast, could be tempted into a mutually beneficial relationship in which privileges — as opposed to "rights" — were granted in exchange for certain goods. The Jewish historian Yosef Hayim Yerushalmi called this strategy — by which Jews circumvented local communities and leaders and went straight to the highest authority in the land — "vertical alliances," and the rejected option of dependence on their neighbors "horizontal alliances."

Beginning with the Babylonian exile following the destruction of the first temple in 586 BCE, the Jews in exile replicated the governing structure held when they had sovereignty in the Holy Land. It was a sophisticated society. Jews were among the first nations in history to hold common property (the land of Israel belonged to the people, not to the king of Israel — a startling fact), to provide social safety nets, and to criminalize exacting interest from fellow Jews. This meticulously structured and tightly run society ensured that Jews were mutually dependent — that they could find political and economic security by depending on each other. The Jewish community in exile functioned, if not exactly like a state within a state, which became one of the classical canards of modern European anti-Semitism, then certainly as a corporate entity, with a greater degree of organizational independence and self-government than would ever be permitted in a modern European nation-state.

Under Persian, Macedonian, Ptolemaic, and Seleucid rulers, Jews were granted a great deal of autonomy by gentile leaders. The basic structure of the internal Jewish community, and its relationship to its rulers, was essentially fixed from the start of exile through the time of the French Revolution and the advent of the modern era. And throughout that time this independence was secured, often, by paying for it. Jews paid special taxes in exchange for the freedom to govern themselves, and this also spared the monarch responsibility for coercing compliance with the legal and the tax system. This system held the longest, and was the most comprehensive and mutually beneficial, in the exile in Spain. Even after Ferdinand and Isabella forced the Jews into exile in 1492, the Spanish Jewish exile Solomon ibn Verga wrote with pride and nostalgia about the halcyon days of his destroyed community, and of the vertical alliance system throughout Spain and France: "in general, the kings of Spain and France, the nobles, the men of knowledge, and all the distinguished men of the land used to love the Jews, and hatred obtained only among the masses who were jealous of the Jews."

During the Middle Ages, the relationships between Jewish communities and their political leaders were formalized in charters negotiated by prominent Jews on behalf of their communities and made directly with the highest authority in the land. The earliest extant examples of the medieval charters are Carolingian, issued by Louis the Pious (778–840 CE), and likely modeled on similar charters issued by Charlemagne himself. All of these charters share the same structure and differ only slightly in details and application (from individuals to communities and ultimately, in the thirteenth century, to the Jews of an entire country — Emperor Frederick II issued a charter for all German Jews in 1236). All have in common the basic commitment to protect the Jewish communities and to honor their right to practice their law, in exchange for a direct feudal relationship sworn on the part of the Jewish representative to the King. Jews were called *Juifs du Roi*, the king's Jews, or *servus regie camerie*, serfs of the royal chamber. Frederick Barbarossa wrote that the Jews "belong to our treasury," and the Jews appreciated this. It was the highest form of protection.

Similar dealings were conducted with the Papal authority, whose contempt for Jewish apostasy was tempered by Christianity's canonical dependence on the Jewish tradition. Popes could be by turns vicious and solicitous about their Jews. Thus Pope Innocent III — who presided over the Fourth Lateran Council, which in 1215 was the first to compel Jews (and Muslims) to wear badges — also issued the Edict in Favor of the Jews, which begins, "Although the Jewish perfidy is in every way worthy of condemnation, nevertheless, because through them the truth of our faith is proved, they are not to be severely oppressed by the faithful" and warns Christians to refrain from, among other indignities, desecrating Jewish cemeteries; killing, robbing, or wounding Jews; forcing Jews to convert; and disrupting Jewish holidays. At the same time the Crusades were viciously violating these papal prohibitions. Similarly, Gregory IX, the first Pope to order that the Talmud be burned, a cultural disaster that occurred in Paris in 1242, also urged Louis IX of France to stop the crusaders and their mobs from massacring Jewish communities. Jews learned to forge alliances with actors whom they knew harbored ill-will against them. They had no choice. Their neighbors and local leaders reviled them, too. Jews preferred an imperfectly reliable but powerful ally bound by utility to perfectly unreliable and weak allies sour with jealousy and fear (though there were quiet times and places in medieval Europe in which Jews and Christians lived in coexistence with each other).

Until the modern period, Jewish separateness was necessary for securing safety. Separateness — contained autonomy — is what the charters protected. Assimilation was both impossible and undesirable. Cohesion and insulation were protective mechanisms. Mixing with gentiles and weakening the bonds that delineated the Jews from gentiles would have confused the ruler from whom security had been so carefully extracted. In the seventeenth and eighteenth centuries, the Jewish bankers and businessmen who handled the finances of and lent money to the nobility, and who represented the Jewish communities in their dealings with the monarchy, became known as "Court Jews." These Jews enjoyed privileges withheld not only from their Jewish coreligionists, but often also from the gentiles. This political arrangement, the system of the Court Jews, was also premised on traditional Jewish separateness. The promise of equality, remember, was never on the horizon.

Until the eighteenth century. The French Revolution brusquely thrust France into the modern period, and the French Jews were the first to be fed the strange fruit of emancipation. Liberalism not only guaranteed rights to everyone, it also made demands of everyone. The possibility of full citizenship came at the cost of an unmixed loyalty to France and a significant degree of self-erasure. Insofar as the organized Jewish community was a quasi-political structure, it had to be dissolved, along with the special access enjoyed by the unelected wealthy Jewish leadership. As Mirabeau, one of the leaders of the revolution, put it, "*son pays deviendra sa patrie*" — his country must become his homeland. No dualities were allowed.

The old protectionist system of Jewish security vanished with the monarchy. Suddenly the French Jewish community was called to trust a new system which seemed discomfitingly dependent on the goodwill of their political and social leaders as well as the enlightenment of their neighbors — something Jews, like all minorities of liberal countries, recognized was too often honored in the breach. (Yerushalmi described "the royal alliance" as a "myth.") And so Jews for the first time had to ask ourselves the same question vulnerable minorities of liberal countries have been asking ever since: how big is the breach? How far from the ideal of itself was the reality of the liberal state?

In France, granting rights to Jewish citizens certainly marked something of a departure from the nativist identity of the state. But anti-Semitism burbled in the cauldron of French prejudice as a reminder that liberalism exists always in tension with the uglier impulses of every population which aspires towards it. The burble boiled over first with the Dreyfus Affair at the end of the nineteenth century, and then with the establishment of the Vichy government in the middle of the twentieth.

America was always different. For the American Jew, the distance between liberal promise and liberal fulfillment has always been smaller than anywhere else. Even before total enfranchisement, Jewish Americans recognized that when we were deprived of our rights we were deprived of something that belonged to us, something that the country owed us.

We could fight the abuse of our rights with the country's own principles.

Isaac Leeser was a Prussian Jew who joined his uncle in Richmond, Virginia, in 1824 at the age of seventeen, and became one of the most important leaders of early American Jewry. He published the first English language translation of the Jewish Bible in America (the twenty-two books arranged according to Jewish custom, as opposed to the thirty-nine books which make up the Christian Old Testament), and he was the founder and publisher of the *Occident*, the first general Jewish newspaper in the United States. In the pages of that paper Leeser published, in 1845, an article about the Maryland Bill, known as the "Jew Bill," which had been passed in the Maryland legislature nineteen years earlier, and which gave the Jews of that state the right to hold public office. Leeser pointed out that

> the few highly respectable Israelites who then lived in Maryland took a noble stand in defense of the good cause; they made no concession; they did not explain away the features of their faith, which might appear harsh and unpalatable to the Christians; but asked for their rights, and obtained them, as becomes freemen, unconditionally and without any trammels whatever. And at the present day, the Jews in Maryland are free, like all the other citizens. At the time when this act of justice was awarded, there was not even a Synagogue in all the state; hence it must be considered as the abstract triumph of liberality over bigotry and prejudice; and we therefore rejoiced the more at the passage of the bill in question, since it proved that Americans will be just whenever they are properly enlightened . . .

Leeser was contrasting the Jewish American strength with the self-conscious weakness of British Jewry's contemporary Reform movement, which, Leeser insisted, was a systematic attempt to alter Jewish practice in order to make the religion more palatable to British gentiles.

As Leeser makes plain, American citizenship granted the Jews something they had never had before and could never have anywhere else: a rights-based relationship that was not a deviation from the essential character of the country in which they lived, but was a full expression of the state's promise. In America, the possibility of Jewish success was and is proof of the health of American identity, because it is proof that a weak minority can prosper if treated as full and equal members of a pluralistic democratic society. There was anti-Semitism in America, of course, but it lacked political legitimacy: it was a contradiction of the country's founding values. In this way, America offered an epochal deviation, as a matter of principle and practice, from what Salo Wittmayer Baron famously called the "lachrymose pattern of Jewish history." And it accomplishes this in a way that not even the Jewish state does.

The Jewish state was founded as a democracy, but its democratic character has always been in tension with its Jewishness. This tension was inevitable, but the task of moderating between these two elements is a balancing act made nearly impossible by various elements. First, Israel has no constitution and no Bill of Rights — powerful tools with which Americans are immeasurably helped in safeguarding our democratic character. Israel does have a Declaration of Independence but, unlike America, Israel, which is similarly a multiethnic society, did not derive its right to exist from the equality of all its citizens, even though it guaranteed all its citizens the same rights. America grants Jews rights on the basis of equality. In practice, in 2025, Israel grants Jews rights on the basis of an increasingly popular theory of Jewish supremacy, which flies in the face of its Declaration of Independence. It did not have to be this way, but this is the way it is.

There are tragic reasons for this undemocratic devolution. Unlike America, Israel is straddled and partially populated by sworn enemies who have no state, no sovereignty, and no means of either distinguishing their own authority from Israel in a manner that Israel considers legitimate or assimilating as full members into the Jewish state. The Jewishness of Israel's majority is a bludgeon against the Palestinian members of Israeli society. In Israel, Jewish citizens enjoy full rights and Palestinian citizens do not. The Palestinian citizens of Israel account for twenty-one percent of the Israeli population, and they should enjoy the full rights which citizens of a democracy are owed; and this is true also, and more desperately, of the Palestinians in East Jerusalem, the West Bank, and Gaza, where the Israeli police, military, and other Israeli officials openly consider Palestinians their enemies.

Israel, under Netanyahu's leadership, makes the grotesque case on the global stage that non-Jews are not equal to Jews, and that Jews are entitled to rights in Israel because Israel is a Jewish State. This means by implication that in every other state — including America — Jews are not entitled to full rights. Israeli illiberalism undermines American Jewish equality, and it undermines the liberal project in general. This is more the case today than it ever has been since Israel's establishment.

Israel's example, Israel's brutality, compliments Donald Trump's, which is why Netanyahu settles so naturally into

Trump's menagerie. No Jew, in America or anywhere else, has dishonored his Jewishness by using it as a fig leaf for fascist and even neo-Nazi sympathies as visibly as Benjamin Netanyahu. Something unprecedented in Jewish history has happened: A Jewish state has determined that it is in its own interests to benefit from and accelerate the erosion of American democracy, thereby jeopardizing America's Jewish citizens in the name of its own tribal interests. Netanyahu's illiberalism, Netanyahu's nativism, gives Jews like Ari Berman and Stephen Miller a calling card for membership in Trump's thuggish troop.

It seems likely that the anti-Semitism that this administration tolerates and inflames will not be directly caused by the government, but the government will encourage, downplay, and forgive it. The bizarre prominence of Elon Musk and his raised right arm is evidence enough. Black, Latino, Native, and trans people were the first to bear the brunt of Trump's earliest executive orders, which were only the beginning. But Jews will pay a price for Trump's fascism, too.

And even if we don't, the policies Trump is already enforcing should be interpreted as a direct attack on the legitimacy of our membership in this country, since not too long ago it was our ancestors who were clambering at the gates to be let in. It was our grandparents — rather than Mexican or Arab migrants — who were slandered as burdens, job-stealers, spies, and thieves. Between 1820 and 1880, the American Jewish population ballooned from three thousand to three hundred thousand. In the half-century that followed, more than two and a half million Jews joined the slim community already here. This increase was despite the passage of the Johnson–Reed Act in 1924, which was intended to "protect" the country's "racial stock" by staunching the immigration of "undesirable" immigrants — Jews among them. The United States had no immigration policy, and the quotas set on Jews by the Johnson–Reed Act were not adjusted at all, between 1933 and 1941.

But perhaps more disturbing even than the quota system is the fact that immigration officials perceived that they would be rewarded for letting fewer people in and so they routinely failed to fill the quotas. The Johnson–Reed Act had capped the number of Germans permitted to enter the United States at 25,957, but in 1933 the State Department issued only 1,241 visas to German citizens, while 82,787 German citizens languished on the waiting list for visas that they could not afford. Through 1943, "Hebrew" was a racial category in American immigration law. Between 1939 and 1940, over half of all immigrants to America identified themselves as Jewish, and that number is likely incorrect, since many of the people fleeing the Nazis did not consider themselves Jewish even if the Nuremberg Laws did.

Two weeks after Kristallnacht, on November 24–25, 1938, a Gallup poll asked American citizens, "Should we allow a large number of Jewish exiles from Germany to come to the United States to live?" Seventy-two percent of the respondents said no. The following January, while Congress was considering the passage of the Wagner–Rogers Bill, which would allow special entry for twenty thousand refugee children, Gallup sent out another poll. This time the question read: "It has been proposed that the government permit ten thousand refugee children be brought into this country and taken into American homes. Do you approve of this plan?" And sixty-seven percent said no. Over the next few years, as war spread across Europe, Americans began to suspect that Germany and the Soviet Union were secreting spies into America in the hordes of

Jewish immigrants. Perhaps they thought the children were spies, too. This heartlessness was a failure of the American people to live up to the American promise. A hundred years ago, it was our ancestors who suffered for the American inability to rise to its own ideals.

One Jew's contribution to the Trump administration represents a betrayal of American Jewish history more than any other. Consider the case of Stephen Miller, the man responsible for shaping Trump's draconian immigration policies. Miller's radicalism began when he was in high school, a century after his mother's family arrived in America. Wolf Lieb Glosser and his wife Bessie were the first of Miller's ancestors to arrive in this country. The couple had fled vicious pogroms in Antopol, Belarus, and set sail on the German ship *S.S. Motke*, which docked in New York on January 7, 1903, twenty-one years before the Johnson-Reed Act instituted its quotas. Glosser spoke Yiddish, Russian, and Polish but not a word of English. As Miller's uncle, David Glosser, wrote in *Politico* in 2018,

> I have watched with dismay and increasing horror as my nephew, an educated man who is well aware of his heritage, has become the architect of immigration policies that repudiate the very foundations of our family's life in this country. I shudder at the thought of what would have become of the Glossers had the same policies Stephen so coolly espouses — the travel ban, the radical decreases in refugees, the separation of children from their parents, and even talk of limiting citizenships for legal immigrants — had been in effect when Wolf Liev made his desperate bid for freedom. The Glossers came to the U.S. just a few years before the fear and prejudice of the "America First"

nativists of the day closed U.S. borders to Jewish refugees. Had Wolf Lieb waited, his family likely would have been murdered by the Nazis along with all but seven of the 2,000 Jews who remained in Antopol. I would encourage Stephen to ask himself if the chanting, torch-bearing Nazis of Charlottesville, whose support his boss seems to court so cavalierly, do not envision a similar fate for him.

American Jews should take it personally when our president describes immigrants as criminals and poisons. It should scare and enrage us that the first bill which Trump signed into law in his second term was the Laken Riley Act, which will result in the deportation of migrants who are merely accused of a crime, and that at the ceremony for that occasion Trump remarked that "today's signing is bringing us one step closer to eradicating the scourge of migrant crime in our communities once and for all." Make no mistake, he was raising the specter of our grandparents, no matter the color of the people who will be turned away from our borders this time.

The ancestors of ours who made it here were not merely lucky. Luck was part of it but not all of it: America granted us what is by right our due *as human beings*. And as American citizens we have a right and a duty to insist upon that same dispensation for us and for others, which is why American Jews have also contributed significantly to the establishment of institutions in this country which work within the law to protect the vulnerable. It is true, we Jews have a tradition which teaches us to pacify brutes like Trump and to create and fetishize thugs like Netanyahu, but we have other traditions, too. Like every great nation we contain contradictions. We are not fated to emulate our ugliest examples. In Exodus, God told us, "You shall not wrong or oppress a stranger, for you were strangers in the land of Egypt." It is not moral and it is not wise to align ourselves with the merciless bigots who drew the blood that stains our history.

The first chapter of the Book of Job ends: "And Job said 'Naked did I leave the belly of my mother, and naked shall I return there, God gives and God takes away, may the name of God be blessed." Job's faith is freighted with lyrical resignation. He makes no demands. God's power is a force which acts over and through him. We have no right to repeat his concessions, not here, not in our country. America is ruled by no God and Donald Trump is no one's Lord, despite all his invocations of Jesus. America is an artifact, man-made, a product of human will and wisdom. It is not for us to bow and accept the caprice of its leaders. They work for us. America giveth because we designed her to give. When its goods are revoked out of turn it is because we have been poor stewards of our own inheritance. We must fight — not least in the name of our ancestors, the huddled masses yearning for the breath of freedom which is the only air that our spoiled lungs exchange — we must fight for what belongs to us.

LEON WIESELTIER

Impotent Musings

For Mario Vargas Llosa, a prince of our liberalism.

With one foot on the platform
and the other foot on the train

For many decades I have participated like a good soldier in the war of ideas, by which I mean the application of philosophical notions to public affairs for the purpose of persuading readers for or against certain political and cultural outcomes. It is a private-public activity: you cannot be a "public intellectual" unless you are also a private intellectual. Otherwise you are merely a polysyllabic sloganeer waiting for CNN to call, a college education looking for a buyer. Without philosophy, politics is just a contest for power, and without politics, philosophy is just a pastime for professors. Who in their right mind would abandon power to interests devoid of ideas? The search for justice inexorably leads back to concepts. *Don't be cruel!* But why should I not be cruel? *Because it is wrong!* But why is it wrong? *Because it hurts people!* But do you really believe in a hurtless world? *Well, how would you like it if they hurt you?* And just like that we are in the severe and magical kingdom of philosophy, because we are, even those of us who will not be reminded by that last question of the *Groundwork of the Metaphysics of Morals*, even the most obtuse among us, self-interpreting beings. Sooner or later everybody wants reasons.

One evening a group of Syrian friends, some of them refugees, all of them activists, asked if I could meet them for a conversation in the lobby of a local hotel. It was the Obama years, and we all despised him for his sanctimonious refusal to lift a finger against the savagery in Syria, but my friends did not want to discuss foreign policy. They wanted to talk about God — or more precisely, God and the chemical attack in Ghouta. A young man spoke first: "I was in Ghouta and I held dead babies and I resolved that I could never believe in Allah again." Then a young woman in a lavender hijab remarked: "I was also in Ghouta and I also held dead babies and I never needed Allah more." They asked me if I could help them make sense of the contradiction. The gravity of the request was not lost on me. I felt honored but mainly I felt humbled, since nothing like Ghouta had ever happened to me, though something was done to my mother in Nazi-occupied Poland that may have qualified me slightly to assist them in confronting their perplexity. (I did not mention it.) For almost three hours I discoursed on the multiplicity of God-concepts and the variety of theories of historical causality and the diversity of spiritual temperaments, and they responded with probing questions and more recollections of the horrors. The hotel might have exploded from the intensity. At one o'clock in the morning we embraced and said goodnight. They expressed their gratitude, but the gratitude was mine. I was drenched in sweat — the sweat of a non-recreational and non-journalistic exploration of ultimate meanings. As I walked out into the deserted street I was surprised by the wonderful thought that the entirety of my education, every single Penguin paperback I had ever read, was all for *this* night, so that I might be in some way helpful to *these* people, and leave them with some improvement in their understanding of the philosophical torment to which their brutal experience had sentenced them. The utility of the humanities!

The intellectual agitations that I made in all those decades, and those that I assisted, sufficed for a defensible, even a justified life, as a thinking individual and a dissatisfied citizen. I am one of the lucky ones who has had not a career but a calling. "A life of significant contention," as Diana Trilling famously described it. The significance to which she was referring was owed to the confidence that the disputations were not trivial, that the stakes for society were considerable. No doubt this led to a certain exaggeration of their — our — own importance (which for a while developed a small sub-genre of its own, the memoir of a visit to the White House); but the vanity is a small price to pay for the possibility that we really are clarifying our society and our culture to themselves. I recall many moments at my various desks when striking the keys felt like a form of national service. An open society seemed designed for precisely what I was doing, for how I was enthusiastically earning my living. It began to seem plausible that I might leave behind what a friend of mine called a scar on the map.

It was in my time of service, which is not yet over, that the war of ideas spread from the "little magazines" and the medium-sized ones to the editorial pages of newspapers, when Aristotle and Mill were suddenly staining your fingers with fresh ink. One momentous morning William Safire decided that a column of seven hundred words should be named "Essay." George Will helped to inaugurate what became a culture-wide addiction to quotation — a vernacular version of the old institution of proof-texts and the reverence for authorities that in the religious traditions frequently substitute for reflection. Now the editorial pages are replete with little middlebrow citation-ridden sermons on exceedingly profound themes: who knew that the form of the op-ed piece is adequate for the adjudication of the question of the existence of God, or the definition of a good life? Or that a column should be a regular report on the columnist's ostentatiously serious reading? (As I write, David French has discovered Carl Schmitt.) The shallowness is deep. The war of ideas has become the board-game of ideas, which has achieved its apotheosis in the festival of ideas, in which analysis and erudition are reduced to entertainment for the affluent and training for their dinner parties. Intellectual life should not be this affable.

And then, of course, the internet blew it all up. I speak not as a disgruntled gatekeeper, though I believe fervently in gatekeeping as an indispensable cultural position for which one must be qualified by more than merely landing the job. One should hardly be churlish about the digital democratization of intellectual activity: isn't this the dream of an open society? And so the tumbrils are filling with elites. (Never mind that there never before existed gatekeepers with the power of Zuckerberg and Bezos and Brin and Musk and Altman.) Unfortunately, the more intellectual activity has increased in volume, the more it has decreased in intellectuality. If only the speed and the scale had left the discourse alone! Instead the new bottles molested the old wine. On the internet Nietzsche and Moldbug are equals. Together they float in a contextless entropy as they compete for the attention of untold numbers of passive and gullible consumers who are eager to feel transgressive and to take them at their word. One of the strangest characteristics of mental life on the internet is that as it becomes more hysterical it feels less urgent. (I know, I know: there are praiseworthy islands of serious thought online, but I insist that they are noteworthy precisely for being the sites least affected by their marvelous medium.)

This has created the vexing problem of how to achieve intellectual impact on the internet. How fleeting can something be and still create something lasting? How evanescent and still leave a mark? Naturally the preferred measurement of influence became quantitative, because the technology generates nothing so abundantly as data, which is to say, numbers, and because this is how businesspeople think. Influence has been re-interpreted as virality. (In the old days we used to inflate our influence to deceive advertisers by including in our circulation reports the large quantities of issues that we would dump at airport terminals and the like.) I will tell a story. One day at my old magazine I ran into its owner — a young man pathetically ill-equipped for the stewardship of the great American institution with which his money had allowed him to play — in the corridors of our office, and he seemed glum. He said that he was actually on his way to see me because he wondered if we had made a terrible mistake. The mistake was that I had devoted too many of my pages — my colleagues had also devoted the cover of the issue — to a lengthy (and, in the view of its editor, unimpeachable) critique of Obama's foreign policy by Robert Kagan. "The numbers aren't great," lamented the boss, another metrics lad. His timing was impeccable: I told him that I had just gotten off the phone with Kagan, who had called to tell me that Obama had just invited him to lunch to discuss the essay. "Does the president of the United States count as one click?" I asked. He disliked the question. Quants do not know what to do with qualts. All I wanted him to understand is that influence — which is, after all, the objective of serious journals of thought — works in many and diffuse ways, even when there are iPhones in our pockets. If we had disturbed the Oval Office, surely it was worth every penny. (Kagan's analysis has been dismally vindicated in the intervening years.)

I imagined us in the late eighteenth century having just published "Common Sense" as a special issue of the magazine, and the billionaire in stockings and sticker shock mumbling, "You know, the Paine piece isn't doing well." Never mind that it was doing good. Like almost all the owners of "legacy" publications, he had mistaken a sterling act of citizenship and patronage for an investment. (It came as no surprise when he destroyed the institution almost completely.) "This is not a charity!" another of the owners of the magazine, who has in recent years established himself as one of America's most renowned bullies, once barked at me. I barked back at his disrespect, and at his odd assumption that the writers and the editors were somehow responsible for what he and the business staff failed to achieve. But frankly I can think of many worse charities. Making one's society less stupid is a noble cause. If I had the money, I would pay for it.

But who do we toil for now? We must have intellectuals, I mean genuine ones, learned ones, honest ones, inconvenient ones, because we are a polity that was founded on ideas, and because the search for human purposes is not an elite pursuit, and because we are too deeply wounded to carry on thoughtlessly. The work of intellectuals, however underappreciated (and underpaid) by society, can have a strong cumulative effect, which is why I construe it as an enterprise in climate change, the sedulous creation of a better moral and cultural weather, without inflection points or tipping points, without media sensations, just the diligent and careful refinement and promulgation of what one believes is right and true, as clearly and as persistently as one can do it, in the hope, and even the expectation, that it will eventually enlighten an individual and a society. Whatever the intrinsic satisfactions of argument, it is essentially extrinsic. Contrary to the pervasive sentimentality, ideas are not at all the antithesis of power. Without power no idea can be tested, no idea can succeed or fail. When it fails, the blame, and in some instances the shame, will properly be laid at its author's doorstep. If what matters to you most is that your hands always be clean, you should write poems.

But who do we write for now? If, as the economists teach, value is to be found in scarcity, then our work has never been more valuable; and yet I am uneasy. My unease about the condition of intellectual life, and about its prospects, is of a piece with what I feel every day about everything public: a sickening powerlessness. Every morning I wake up nauseous and brace myself for the nausea that the afternoon will bring. My deepest convictions about the sanctity of struggle, about the unsinkable force of hope, about the incontrovertible reality of truth, about the resilience of the human heart (and of the miracle that Madison wrought) — all this now sounds too often like happy talk, like Jon Meacham–style uplift. The transports of eloquence are not cutting it. Forgive me, but we are rotting. Solidarity has collapsed and I do not see how we will get it back. The ignorant and the malevolent are winning, here and abroad, and all I can do about it is vote and watch and grieve. I am not the sort who attacks the Capitol.

What I am experiencing, in this regular sensation of impotence, is not the melancholy of the loser. Sometimes you lose. I like losers; they know more. And there is dignity in losing if you are prepared to continue the fight. A political defeat is not an intellectual defeat, not at all. I will tell another story. In 2017, not long after Trump began his first term, I attended one of those ludicrous high-level international conferences that bring out the Robespierre even in me. (Even at this stratospheric event there were VIP tables! The thirst for hierarchy is never quenched. I was reminded of what an Indian friend once told me about his country's greatest contribution to the vocabulary of status anxiety: the concept of the VVIP.) Trump had just retaliated militarily against Bashar al-Assad's chemical attack on the village of Khan Sheikhoun: it was, therefore, for me at least, an exhilarating evening, but at dinner I angered H. R. McMaster, the National Security Advisor, by asking whether this was the blessed beginning of a new policy or a tweet in fifty-four cruise missiles. I had been invited to the gathering to present my thoughts on populism, a subject that was much in demand after Trump's victory but hilariously ironic in that setting. Tell us, Mr. Wieseltier, who are all those real people whom we hear about? After I finished my talk, in which I discussed the populist myth of the people and the populist myth of the leader, an elegant French woman, a renowned international civil servant, raised her hand with a question. "Now that Trump has won," she asked, "how should we revise our views?" I was a bit shocked by the question and its unembarrassed expedience about beliefs.

I explained to her that a defeat at the polls did not require any revision of what we believe, which in this case was trans-Atlantic liberalism, though it certainly demands a withering look at our empirical assessment of the electorate. Trump's victory did not prove that our views are wrong. It proved that our views are unpopular. The popularity of a view has no bearing upon its truth. And, intellectually speaking, success proves nothing. Who would want to win as what they are not?

Who would want to win as what they are not? Quite a few people, apparently. Authoritarian governments would be nothing without accommodationists. The toadies are the grease.

I am a man rich in loyalties. I love two countries. I love them for the good that they have done and for the values that they have proclaimed. I have known all my life that they are far from perfect, and that they have committed crimes and abuses, but a state that has not committed crimes and abuses has never existed, and the political systems that my countries established for themselves made them corrigible. I have also known that, official declarations and founding documents notwithstanding, no society is morally and philosophically uniform, so that both my countries have always been characterized by bitter debates about their first principles — debates that were possible because of the freedom of speech to which they were committed, and often took the form of political parties and movements. Yet one must love not blindly, but with eyes wide open, so that one is not afraid of the full truth about the object of one's love and can therefore participate in ameliorations and reforms. I have always admired dissent, not because one must always "speak truth to power" — sometimes power has a point — or because it requires valor — in my two countries it usually requires no valor at all — but because it is evidence of the rarest human attribute in the world, independence of mind. Neither of my countries tremble at the prospect of exigent citizens, even if the success of such citizens in holding their country to a high standard has often been thwarted by the baser regions of its society and its culture.

Even where courage is not necessary, cowardice flourishes.

Is it treasonous to love a country conditionally? We know from personal life that it is possible to love a flawed or culpable person. (What other kind of person is there?) Unconditional love, which is the signature of parental love, has been broadened to encompass many bonds in which we would like to avoid the discomfort of judgement. But judgement is one of the obligations of membership and citizenship, so the question of the limits of love in the event of evil recurs. What would my country have to do to forfeit my love? There is honor in not rushing to the exits, in staying to fight; and there is little substance to a love that is renounced at the first sign of disappointment and even disgrace. Such a devotion was never reliable in the first place. But neither is absolute love, because it will go along with anything, which is not how one properly serves a country or a friend.

I will do everything I can to never take back my love. Such a pledge is an obligation of my Americanism and my Zionism. It is also selfish; a life without these memberships and their treasures would be desolate. And so, I am embarrassed to admit, I have sometimes averted my gaze and looked away. There is nothing shameful about the impulse to defend what one loves, but there are times, such as now, when we should emphatically prefer the full unedifying truth.

Lincoln held that even the perpetration of human bondage, even the mass genocidal murders that attended it over the centuries, did not justify the destruction of his country. The proposition that slavery did not make the country worthless is morally jarring. But he adamantly did not support the erasure of his own country, even though he was a Biblical man who studied the ancient accounts of national destruction as a divine punishment for sin. This saving complexity of purpose was his retort to John Brown, the absolutist and the terrorist. (And our contemporary.) I do not recall that in the post-Auschwitz period anybody called for the erasure of Germany. Decent societies are not built by absolutists. And indecent societies always contain decent people.

But now my loyalties have been distressed and darkened. Both my countries, the United States and Israel, have chosen to confront the crises that beset them by means of cruelty. They are pursuing solutions to their problems that inflict misery on the already miserable, that proudly elevate heartlessness into state policy, that make a despicable farce of the humanist values about which their leaders used to boast. They despise the weak and they scorn the unfamiliar. These countries should have been havens from the poisons of ethnonationalism, which anyway flies in the face of their multiethnic realities. They should have pointed away from the retrograde direction of the world. Instead they have joined the malevolent herd in the post-liberal stampede. They are complicit in the creation of the lowest and most debased era in a hundred years.

The second Trump administration could not be more candid about its appetite for destruction, and about its indifference to the human costs of its policies. Its controlling values are retribution and profit. Consider a few examples. While there are precincts of American life in which DEI has become a protection racket and an exercise in thought-policing, it is impossible to avoid the impression that the government's frenzied campaign against it is animated mainly by racism. They are against DEI because they are against diversity, equity, and inclusion — the values themselves, regardless of the manner of their implementation. And while there is no doubt that the American immigration system is a shambles with bipartisan origins, and that the deportation of criminals who are in the country illegally is not an abuse of power but a valid exercise in law-enforcement, the virulence with which the government speaks about all immigrants leaves no doubt that what really lies behind its panic about the border is a rank nativism and a fear of the ethnically mottled society that we are. We have for too long flattered ourselves with the legend about our hospitality to immigrants — that uplift again; the truth is that we have struggled against our own callousness toward the refugee and the stranger since our origins. Immigration should be legal, of course, and a country should control its own borders, but if the government really intends to fulfill the spirit and the substance of its immigration program, we are about to witness a nightmare of federally authorized brutality. The bastards are even talking about reviving family separation.

And while it is undeniable that the size of the federal government is unimaginably large, the administration's approach in its own bizarre experiment in "downsizing government" seems to relish the human damage, at home and abroad, that its bureaucratic "reform" can accomplish. Yet the MAGA mandarins despise government at their peril. The despised technocrats serve society. One of the reasons that the American government is so huge is that American life is so complex: specialized and arcane knowledge is a condition of effective and humane government in an era when fiscal policy and health care policy and climate policy and regulatory policy and military policy are byzantine in their details. And anti-elitism does not qualify as the knowledge of anything. Quite the opposite. It is usually a prejudice against knowledge. (One of the worst episodes in the history of American nativism was called Know-Nothingism.) The age of Trump will be known for the sudden respectability of the animus against higher education, as if a democracy can function without a knowledgeable citizenry, as if it is an insult against populism and "the people" to want them to study the world and strain their minds. (Among the most comic figures of our unfunny time is the Ivy League–educated skeptic about higher education. It's Yale or nothing, I guess.)

The Trump administration will immiserate the people who elected him and bow and scrape before the people who paid for his election. The main product of this government purportedly consecrated to American security will be the relentless expansion of American insecurity. It will preside over a new age of social Darwinism and uncontrolled oligarchy. The most obscene sight in America now is the smile on Elon Musk's face. In sum, we are entering a new age of American pain.

Israel, too, has become renowned for its pitilessness. This is Benjamin Netanyahu's contribution to Israel's reputation, and to the education of young Jews everywhere. I understand that it has its strategic uses ("the restoration of deterrence," though never for long). But the scale of what was done to Gaza cannot be explained or scanted in strategic terms, as the acceptable price of a national security policy. There are many ways of establishing national security, of diminishing — because eliminating it by military means is simply impossible — the danger in which Israelis live. But first a few heresies must be defended. The Hamas attack of October 7 was one of the worst atrocities of our time. It was motivated by a bloodthirsty anti-Semitic hatred and by a fanatical interpretation of the Islamic faith. Israel, which will one day wrestle with the astonishing failures of its political and military establishments on that hideous day, was perfectly justified in retaliating, and ferociously, to the slaughter. No self-respecting state would have done otherwise.

Moreover, the moral and strategic outcome of the Hezbollah-Israeli war in the north have been decidedly positive. Innocent civilians were killed, but why are Israel's wars the only wars that are measured against the fantastical standard of no non-combatant deaths? The destruction of Hezbollah's leadership and of most of Hezbollah's arsenal was an incontrovertible victory over an evil enemy, and also a historic opportunity for Lebanon to regain its sovereignty. It represented also a dramatic weakening of Iran, the mastermind and the operational enabler of all this jihadi violence, which had been already humbled by the haplessness of its missile attacks against the Zionist Satan; and this in turn resulted in the spectacular overthrow of Bashar al-Assad, the highly accomplished butcher of his own people who somehow failed to provoke the ire of Hamasniks and progressives and undergraduates in the West. (These same justice warriors are not to be found on streets or in encampments to protest the murder of a hundred and fifty thousand Sudanese civilians and the use of chemical weapons against them.)

Yet forty-seven thousand Palestinians were killed in Gaza. Forty-seven thousand! Even if a third of them were Hamas soldiers, that amounts to a wanton slaughter of innocents on a scale that must torment every Jewish conscience. I should immediately note, since the contrary notion is being bruited about, that this requisite outrage has nothing to do with Judaism. Israel is still a secular state and the bombings of Gaza were not carried out by the Netanyahu regime for religious purposes. (The same cannot be said of the anti-Palestinian violence perpetrated in the West Bank by the settlers and Itamar Ben-Gvir's malicious vigilantes, in which almost a thousand Palestinians — not Hamas, not Islamic Jihad, just men and women and children living on their land — have so far perished. During this period twenty-five Israeli residents of the West Bank were killed by Palestinians.) There are many sources in the Jewish tradition that warn against bigotry and cruelty, but there are many more that endorse bigotry and cruelty, as is the case with every religion that has ever tasted power or embraced exclusiveness, especially in its beginnings. Classical Judaism contains no concept of equality, and along with its Scriptural insistence upon human dignity it is riddled with contempt for the other, as the religious Israeli right will be happy to show you. My advice to Jewish progressives is not to play the prooftexts game, because it is not a game that they will win. And how is their appeal to midrashim any different from Smotrich's and Ben-Gvir's appeal to midrashim? I advise them also to search their hearts to verify that the politics that they claim to draw from their religion is not really the religion that they draw from their politics. Whether or not Israel is guilty of war crimes, and I think it is, the Torah is the Torah.

The attacks of October 7 traumatized every Israeli. Anybody who does not recognize this psychological convulsion holds an imprecise and indecent analysis of what subsequently happened. This collective trauma had, to put it mildly, a basis in reality. It is a commonplace in the literature on trauma that it is experienced as a sudden descent into helplessness and vulnerability — in Freud's words, as "a breach in an otherwise efficacious barrier." In the anguished weeks after the attacks, I became possessed by the question of whether post-traumatic rationality is possible. No giant leap of empathy was required for me to grasp the temptation of revenge, but I feared the consequences of a military campaign undertaken in a spirit of angry abandon. It would result in a war fought with moral sloppiness. (Aren't all wars fought with moral sloppiness?) October 7 inaugurated the most perilous period for Israel in fifty years, and I worried that the catastrophe that had made it essential for Israelis to keep a level head was the same catastrophe that would make a level head impossible.

To this worry I added my concern, now decades old, about the suppression of the Palestinian question in Israeli life — the cowardly refusal of liberal politicians, most recently Benny Gantz and Yair Lapid, to discuss the matter, so that the subject has become a centrist taboo. (It is not a taboo on the right!) At one of the anti-government demonstrations on behalf of the hostages, a representative of the families' lobby remarked that it "appealed to Israelis' hearts instead of their reason, which would dictate that we should occupy Gaza and expel its residents." Perhaps that is post-traumatic rationality.

It is certainly consistent with the growing respectability in Netanyahu's Israel of the foul dream of population transfer. Will the expelled now expel? Such an eventuality is almost too odious to imagine — but it may take the intervention of the Sunni states, who are on the brink of a grand bargain that will bring the Arab-Israeli conflict to an end, to save Israel from its most inglorious impulses. Not long after October 7, I visited the Israeli ambassador, an acquaintance from shul, and after we discussed various strategic and diplomatic matters I asked him about the Palestinians, and he responded with a dismissive wave of the hand, as if to say that they are not worth talking about. That was all. This dogmatic silence about the Palestinians, which the Palestinians have certainly done their share to inflame, is a prudential blunder and an ethical delinquency.

For all the differences between the demons of contemporary America and the demons of contemporary Israel, there is another failing that they share: the absence of a vital opposition. A democracy cannot work without the resistances of an opposition. The system is designed for regular challenges of principle and policy, and in the absence of such friction it can degenerate into a kind of *de facto* one-party state. The point is not that the opposition has to win, though political power is finally the only effective way to reverse a deplorable course; the point is that the opposition must meaningfully exist. The collapse of the Democratic Party in the United States, its damaged sense of reality, its inarticulable identity, its self-immolation in sectarian commotions — all this had the grotesque effect of making Trump increasingly attractive. Kamala Harris' giddiness now looks vaguely psychotic. Unless there is an about-face in the midterm elections, the unbound authoritarian will proceed unchecked with his chaotic cruelty. Never in our history did a man so deserving of impediments face so few.

In America, however, the wreckage of the Democratic Party is at least clear about its adversarial stance, even if it cannot settle on a shared sense of its grounds and its methods. There is a healthy disgust at what is happening. And there are sound statistical refutations of despair: in a country of 334.9 million people, 156,202,318 people voted in the last election, in which Trump won 77,284,118 votes, or 49.8 percent, and Harris won 74,999,166 votes, or 48.3 percent. Those are not apocalyptic numbers. Indeed, of all the crises that may afflict a democracy, we may be experiencing the most intractable one of all: a more or less evenly divided society. The same state of affairs is also hobbling my other country. The most recent election in Israel was, in the popular vote, a tie: the Netanyahu bloc received 2,361,739 votes, or 49.57 percent, and the Gantz-Lapid bloc received 2,331,788 votes, or 48.94 percent. It was only his enormous and unscrupulous skill at forming coalitions that returned Netanyahu to power. Israeli society is bitterly divided against itself. It turns out that a house divided can stand, at least long enough to do lasting harm.

In the beginning of Netanyahu's new term, it became apparent that he is no longer a traditional conservative who believes in law and equality and the hallowed institutions of democratic governance — a political worldview that he imbibed not only from Israeli conservatism and the example of Menachem Begin, but also from his many years in the United States. But Netanyahu is not, alas, the reincarnation of Begin, who, when he recognized the costs and the deceptions of his war in Lebanon, had the decency to have a nervous breakdown. No,

Netanyahu is a repulsive innovation in Israeli politics. After hanging out with Trump and Putin and Modi and Bolsonaro and Orban, he decided that their way — the populist trickery, the, um, unitary executive, the politics of contempt, the cult of the personality — was the better way. He set out, immediately and brazenly, to destroy the Supreme Court, which was the most formidable obstacle to the expansion of his power and the implementation of his policies, especially his Palestinian policies. The months and months of mass demonstrations against his "judicial reform" saw the finest hours of Israeli democracy — the streets were a heaven of peaceful political participation, and the lawyerly coup was defeated. (Still, the anti-Netanyahu protests also illustrated the limitations of Israeli liberal discourse: I noticed at the demonstrations in Jerusalem that placards with the word "Palestinian" displayed on them were shunted to the side.)

The problem with Russian ethnonationalism and Hungarian ethnonationalism and Indian ethnonationalism is not that it is Russian or Hungarian or Indian, but that it is ethnonationalism. An ethnonationalism is not virtuous because it is ours.

Then came the disaster of October 7, over which Netanyahu, the self-styled invincible shield of the Jewish people, presided, and then came the war, and suddenly the streets were silent. There were understandable reasons for the disappearance of dissent: the country was collectively plunged into mourning, and everybody's sons and daughters were in uniform in Gaza. As it became clear — this was another of the many shocks that he has administered to his society — that Netanyahu felt no urgency about the Israeli hostages in Gaza, even if the ransoming of captives had always been the most immediate priority for Jewish communities throughout Jewish history — when this became clear, the families of the prisoners lost their wartime inhibition about criticizing the government and the streets began to fill again. But the hostages were the only socially permissible subject for protest. Which is to say, there was no significant Israeli opposition to the conduct of the war, not even when its drastic nature became plentifully clear. The solidarity, again, was natural, but even when the numbers of the Palestinian dead in Gaza attained terrifying proportions, and the IDF's tactics obviously made massacres inevitable, all the targeting technologies and ethics manuals notwithstanding, the leaders of the opposition had nothing to say. I do not know of a single political speech that would have outraged the consensus, even if it would have secured a place in the moral history of the Jewish state. (There were a few military resignations, but they had to do with the professional failures of October 7.)

Is the Israeli public in agreement and at peace about the human costs of the Gaza war? Is it generally believed in Israel that the lives of Palestinians and the rights of Palestinians are worthless? (The other day I came across this in a Talmudic passage: "What do you think, that your blood is redder than his? Maybe his blood is redder." But never mind the Talmud!) Does the scruple about means and ends vanish when it is we — I am not an Israeli but I am a Jew — who are threatened? All those decades of indifference and apathy and complacence and illusion about the seven million people with whom the Israelis live have done their work. Yet even Israelis who cling to their own callousness about the Palestinians and are weary of the moralism of the left (if they can find the left) must eventually acknowledge that reconciliation with the Palestinians, some kind of political and diplomatic settlement, is a condition of Israeli security. The Zionist idea was that the Jews be not only free but also safe.

And the American Jews: how long will we applaud our brothers and sisters in their short-sightedness? I would have thought that the telling of truth, however unpleasant, is also an expression of solidarity. Surely the American Jewish community can rouse itself from its all-too-comfortable posture of endless mourning to attend to the actual needs of Israeli security, which include more than the very latest iteration of AI. Kaddish is not a strategy. But the American Jewish community prefers commemoration to candor. Does the magnitude of the destruction in Gaza really not trouble the sleep of the majority of American Jews? I think I know the answer. And so I wish to reassure my brethren that humaneness is not a surrender to Hamas. After all the fortifying sermons about the justness of Israel's cause, a rattling sermon about moral culpability in a just cause would seem incumbent upon an ethically wakeful community. Disturb only a single Shabbat, but disturb it. We need to know more than our own righteousness. We have many obligations to the Jewish state, and one of them is to keep our consciences intact.

It is one of the characteristics of an atrocious time that Yeats' poem about the best and the worst is ubiquitous, but in this instance we really are slouching toward Bethlehem.

After the depredations of Trump and the depredations of Netanyahu, I live with the bitter feeling that as an American and as a Jew I will never be young again. (At my age, it is probably just as well.)

A few weeks ago a dear friend, an Iranian dissident, a happy warrior, sent me a wish: "May we always smile in the pursuit of justice!" This put me in mind of a conversation long ago with a brilliant friend who had just written a devastating essay about Judith Butler (God's work!) for my pages. She concluded her long and meticulous analysis with a remark about "the joy of justice." I called her to say that the phrase seemed not quite right to me. The achievement of justice, I suggested, cannot be attended only by joy, because justice is always preceded by injustice, it never comes first and it always comes too late. The joy of justice is a fantasy of light without shadow. I have never seen such an unalloyed sight. A just outcome deserves to be celebrated, but when you dance with justice you dance with ghosts. I do not mean to recommend morbidity, which is sorrow as kitsch, sorrow become mechanical, sorrow performed for others. But I recall that conversation now because of the almost stupefying sobriety into which these harsh days have cast me.

In Nicholas Jenkyns' magnificent study of Auden in the 1920s and 1930s, I learned that decades later the poet wrote: "Ah! Those twenties before I was twenty / When the news never gave one the glooms." Now the news gives nothing else. Impotently one lives in the glooms.

Sorrow does not cease when suffering ceases: what it knows can never be unlearned.

The problem is that a grieving spirit is not a fighting spirit. The line between wise acceptance and unwise resignation is difficult to draw. The exhaustion of the opposition in both my countries frightens me, because it suggests a wide diminution of liberal energy. How can the heirs of Milton and Jefferson and Mendelssohn and Mill and Constant and Lincoln and Douglass and Mazzini and Herzen and Weber and Roosevelt and Brandeis and Niebuhr and Camus and Popper and King and Berlin and Havel and Sakharov be so wan, so lifeless, so unexcited by their own patrimony? The path out of our predicament must include a vigorous refreshment of liberalism. What was once the most encouraging transformation in the history of political belief, the one with the likeliest chance of advancing justice, has become a cliché, a banality, without sufficient strength to respond effectively to the slanders against it upon which a new order is being built. For too long liberals have received trouble without making trouble. The old pieties are true, but they need to be made strong, and lustrous, and perhaps less pious.

Consider the question of patience in politics. Patience is often lauded as the quintessential liberal virtue, which has effectively protected liberals from the ruinous fictions of revolution for centuries. We have been taught to restrain ourselves and to contain ourselves, with the aim of preventing rash mistakes and hasty excesses, so that respect may be established in political society and deliberation may become a meaningful political activity. But sometimes patience has the lamentable effect of turning a player into an umpire, and umpires have no sides. It is easy to confuse the patient man with the man who has risen above the fray. (This was the case with Obama, except when he was running. Then the arc of history had to bend *fast*.)

Sometimes patience signifies that your threshold for political and philosophical pain is too high.

Don't just defend the rights of others. Use your own.

Impatience may be dangerous, but human suffering must not be regarded under the aspect of eternity, at least if one is to view it as a problem in need of a solution — that is, politically. Nothing could be more anti-political than the cosmic view of human suffering, which is a justification for quietism.

John Lewis, then twenty-three years old, was chosen to be one of the speakers at the March on Washington in the summer of 1963. When he completed a draft of his speech, he showed it to Bayard Rustin, a man who was uncannily able to combine the most uncompromising idealism with the most uncompromising practicality. After Rustin read Lewis's text, he phoned his hotel room. "We have a problem," he told the young activist. What follows is taken from David Greenberg's superb biography of Lewis.

> "A problem? What problem?" Lewis asked.
>
> "It's your speech. Some people are very concerned about some of the things you're going to say in your speech. You need to get down here. We need to talk."
>
> Lewis went to Rustin's room. Several others were there. They explained to Lewis that an associate of Archbishop Patrick O'Boyle, who was to deliver the invocation the next day, had shown the clergyman the speech. O'Boyle was refusing to participate if Lewis delivered the speech as written.

As Rustin and Lewis spoke, Rustin said he thought O'Boyle might be appeased with one fix. A line in Lewis' speech spurned counsels of "patience," calling it "a dirty and nasty word."

"This is offensive to the Catholic Church," Rustin said.

"Why?" Lewis asked.

"Payyy . . . tience." Rustin dramatically articulated the word. "Catholics believe in the word 'patience'." It was a theological tenet, cited throughout the Bible and by thinkers like St. Augustine.

Lewis relented.

But not completely. In his address from the Lincoln Memorial, Lewis declared, to enormous applause: "To those who have said, 'Be patient and wait, we have long said that we cannot be patient. We do not want our freedom gradually, we want it now." And he concluded: "For we cannot stop, and we will not and cannot be patient."

I wonder if the archbishop recognized that before a quarter of a million people Lewis had repudiated a quietist conception of time in favor of an activist conception of time. The impatience of the liberal! This conception was in keeping with Dr. King's thinking. A year later he published *Why We Can't Wait*, the most complete statement of his philosophy of political action. He began the book by explaining the historical origin of the alleged long-sufferingness of American blacks. The civil rights revolution, he wrote, "is not indicative of a sudden loss of patience within the Negro. The Negro had never really been patient in the pure sense of the word. The posture of silent waiting was forced upon him psychologically because he was shackled physically." Later, in the "Letter from a Birmingham Jail," which was included in the volume, King declared that "for years now I have heard the word 'Wait!' It rings in the ear of every Negro with piercing familiarity. This 'Wait" has almost always meant 'Never.' We must come to see, with one of our distinguished jurists, that 'justice too long delayed is justice denied'." (It was actually William Gladstone who coined the adage, but it now belongs to King.) This was followed by one of the most eloquent pages that King ever wrote, a rending inventory of concrete acts of oppression perpetrated against individual blacks, with its grim peroration: "There comes a time when the cup of endurance runs over."

Liberal cups sometimes fill too slowly. All the sage lessons about moderation notwithstanding, dare one suggest that this is a time when liberals should grow a little impatient with patience?

Patience should not make us fools, or pawns. The enemies of liberalism have been spoiled by our high-minded forbearance, by the liberalism of old men. And the illiberals, the party of Trump and the party of Netanyahu, have also made good use of patience. (The repeal of *Roe v. Wade* was a triumph of conservative patience.) "How poor are they that have not patience? What wound did ever heal but by degrees?" Those fine meliorist words were spoken by . . . Iago! He was praising the utility of "dilatory time" for plots and conspiracies.

A suspicion of impatience can disguise an allergy to alacrity. What are Netanyahu's adversaries waiting for? Or can the snail's pace of political outrage be explained by the deeply demoralizing fact that 72 percent of Israelis immediately supported the American plan to expel two million Palestinians from Gaza?

Alienation can drive one toward the fight or away from the fight. It is not only an emotion, it is also a decision.

Patience is a friend of impotence.

And yet there is one thing for which, alas, we must always be patient. It is courage.

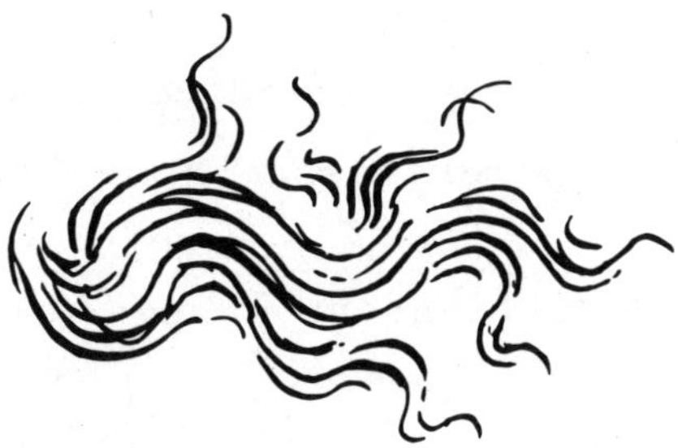

CONTRIBUTORS

YAROSLAV HRYTSAK is a professor of history at Ukrainian Catholic University and the author of *Ukraine: The Forging of a Nation*.

DAVID A. BELL is the Sidney and Ruth Lapidus Professor in the Era of North Atlantic Revolutions and Director of the Shelby Cullom Davis Center at Princeton University.

DURS GRÜNBEIN is a German poet and essayist. His most recent collection of poems in English is *Porcelain: Poem on the Downfall of my City*. His work here was translated by **KAREN LEEDER**.

CLIFFORD THOMPSON's memoir *Twin of Blackness* appeared in 2015.

DAVID GROSSMAN is the author, among many books, of *To the End of the Land*.

ALFRED BRENDEL, the pianist, is the author most recently of *The Lady from Arezzo: My Musical Life and Other Matters*.

AGNES CALLARD is a professor of philosophy at the University of Chicago. Her book *Open Socrates: The Case for a Philosophical Life* was recently published.

PAULA BOHINCE's most recent poetry collection, *Swallows and Waves*, appeared in 2016.

ENRIQUE KRAUZE is a Mexican essayist, producer, and publisher. He is the author of many books and the founder of the magazine *Letras Libres*.

JAMES TRAUB's book on civic education, *Teaching America*, will be published next year.

JAROSLAW ANDERS is the author of *Between Fire and Sleep: Essays on Modern Polish Poetry and Prose*.

GARY SAUL MORSON is Lawrence B. Dumas Professor of the Arts and Humanities at Northwestern University and the author most recently of *Wonder Confronts Certainty: Russian Writers on the Timeless Questions and Why Their Answers Matter*.

KENDA MUTONGI is the Ford International Professor of History at Massachusetts Institute of Technology.

PASCAL BRUCKNER is a French writer and the author, among other books, of *A Brief Eternity: The Philosophy of Longevity*. This essay was translated by **JENNIFER GORE**.

KARL KIRCHWEY is a professor of English and Creative Writing at Boston University.

CELESTE MARCUS is the managing editor of *Liberties*.

LEON WIESELTIER is the editor of *Liberties*.

Liberties — A Journal of Culture and Politics is available by annual subscription and by individual purchase from bookstores and online booksellers.

Annual subscriptions provide a discount from the individual cover price and include complete digital access to current and previous issues along with the printed version. Subscriptions can be ordered from libertiesjournal.com. Professional discounts for active military; faculty, students, and education administrators; government employees; those working in the not-for-profit sector. Gift subscriptions are also available at libertiesjournal.com.

As a matter of principle, *Liberties Journal* does not accept advertising or other funding sources that might influence our independence.

We look to our readers and those individuals and institutions that believe in our mission for contributions — large and small — to support this not-for-profit publication.

If you are interested in making a donation to *Liberties*, please contact Bill Reichblum, publisher, by email at bill@libertiesjournal.com or by phone: 202-891-7159.

Liberties — A Journal of Culture and Politics is distributed to booksellers in the United States by Publishers Group West; in Canada by Publishers Group Canada; and internationally by Ingram Publisher Services International.

LIBERTIES, LIBERTIES: A JOURNAL OF CULTURE AND POLITICS, is published quarterly in Fall, Winter, Spring, and Summer by Liberties Journal Foundation.

ISBN ISBN 979-8-9854302-8-8
ISSN 2692-3904

Printed in Canada.

The insignia that appears throughout *Liberties* is derived from details in Botticelli's drawings for Dante's *Divine Comedy*, which were executed between 1480 and 1495.